PETiquette

Solving Behavior Problems in Multipet Households

Also by Amy D. Shojai

Complete Kitten Care

Complete Care for Your Aging Dog

Complete Care for Your Aging Cat

The First-Aid Companion for Dogs & Cats

New Choices in Natural Healing for Dogs & Cats

PETiquette

Solving Behavior Problems in Multipet Households

Amy D. Shojai

M. Evans and Company, Inc.
New York

M.Evans and Company, Inc.
216 East 49th Street
New York, NY 10017

Library of Congress Cataloging-in-Publication Data

Shojai, Amy, 1956-
 Petiquette : solving behavior problems in multipet households / by Amy
D. Shojai.
   p. cm.
 Includes bibliographical references and index.
 ISBN 1-59077-076-5
 1. Dogs--Behavior. 2. Cats--Behavior. 3. Dogs--Training. 4.
Cats--Training. I. Title.
 SF433.S465 2005
 636.7'0887--dc22

                        2004027549

Typeset and Designed by Chrissy Kwasnik

Printed in the United States of America

9 8 7 6 5 4 3 2 1

Dedication

To the cats and dogs who wander lost and alone,
To the caring professionals who map their way,
And to loving owners who guide pets safely home.

Others see, care, and honor your steadfast love.

This book is for you.

Contents

PART ONE
Understanding Com*pet*ability

The Joys Of Multiples

The Pet Generation • Nobody's Perfect • Risky Business

How Dogs Think

Educating Rex • Understanding Dog-Speak • The Physical Dog •
The Canine Pack

How Cats Think

Learning to Be a Cat • Speaking Felinese • The Physical Cat •
The Cat Clowder

PART THREE
The Multicat Household
Common Problems and Practical Solutions

PART FOUR
The Dog-Cat Household
Common Problems and Practical Solutions

PART FIVE
Common Multipet Frustrations

Pet Peeves
Chewing • Clawing • Digging • Jumping • Talking

PART SIX
Appendixes

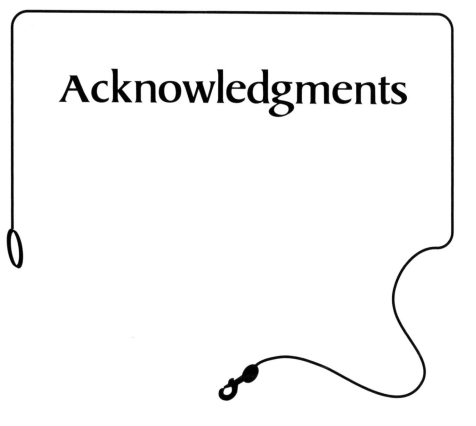

Acknowledgments

Many individuals helped make this book a reality by sharing expertise, help, and unwavering support during the birthing process of *PETiquette*. My husband, Mahmoud, and my caring and supportive family never fail to inspire. Dear friends from the Cuchara gang, the Warped crew, Trinity Lutheran, my "second-act" family, and especially Frank, who juggles eggs better than anyone I know—you remind me daily of what's truly important, and I can't thank you enough.

My colleagues from the Dog Writers Association of America and Cat Writers' Association Inc. never fail to impress me with their professionalism. I'd especially like to thank Maggie Bonham, Steve Dale, and Deb Wood for sharing some of their tips, and the staff and members at CatsForum and DogsForum and new friends at ivillage.com, who always inspire me with their unwavering dedication to helping pets.

Sincere appreciation goes to Dr. Stephen W. Crane, executive director for the 2004 Western Veterinary Conference, for arranging press privileges for me to attend the conference and interview the top behaviorists and lecturers in the field. This book would not have been possible without you. I also must thank David Frei of the Westminster Kennel Club for press privileges that made it possible for me to talk with top dog breeders, handlers, and caring owners. My dear friend and colleague, Michael Brim, offered comparable courtesies for me to contact top cat breeders and exhibitors at the Cat Fanciers' Association International Cat Show—I am in your debt. In addition, my editors Enrica Gadler and Matt Harper helped bring the book to life. Grateful thanks yet again to my tireless agent, Meredith Bernstein, who does all the really hard stuff so I can live my pet-writing dream.

Finally, this book wouldn't be possible without all the special dogs and cats that share our hearts and the loving owners dedicated to providing the best care possible for their furry family members. Without you, this book would never have been written.

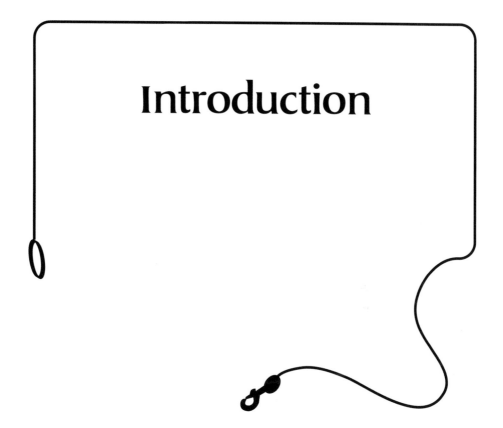

Introduction

Many years ago, more than I care to admit, I became an accidental pet writer. I grew up rescuing orphaned bunnies and baby birds that had fallen from nests, turned turtles and snakes into pets, and lured squirrels and raccoons to eat from my hand. I loved feeding Grandma's chickens, horseback riding, and milking the cows (or trying to).

But my deepest affection was for dogs and cats.

It seemed fated when I found a job as a veterinary technician and met countless caring owners. But many felt frustrated by their relationships, and all too often, heartbreak resulted. I never set out to be a writer, and my career as a pet journalist would never have happened without the countless veterinarians, behaviorists, trainers, researchers, and pet lovers who put up with my endless questions. Thank you!

If you're reading this, you belong to the "pet generation," part of the 60-plus percent of U.S. households that keep cats and dogs. The audience of pet lovers increases each year. The National Pet Demographics (NPD) Group "Pet Ownership Forecast, 2006" projects that the cat population in U.S. households will swell to 82 million, while the dog population is expected to increase to 64 million by 2006. That's a lot of furry love!

PETiquette is written for owners like you who share homes with multiple pets. According to the 2003/2004 American Pet Product Manufacturers Association National Pet Owners Survey, 23 percent of those surveyed own two dogs, while 12 percent own more than three dogs. Similarly, 28 percent of all cat owners own two cats, and 21 percent own more than three cats. Of these, over 40 percent of owners live with both a cat and a dog.

The more time we spend with our cats and dogs, the stronger our bond becomes. The medical profession has legitimized these attachments through multiple research studies that prove the positive impact pets have on human health. So, while in the past we may not have admitted these affections, today our love affair with pets has become a very public one. The 2004 National Survey of People and Pet Relationships by the American Animal Hospital Association states that 94 percent think their pet has human-like personality traits, such as being emotional or sensitive. Deep affection toward and a new awareness of our enhanced relationship with pets—and the way cats and dogs relate to each other—drives today's owner to seek the most current, highest-quality behavior care to preserve this loving bond. Pet spending doubled from $17 billion in 1994 to a projected $34.3 billion for 2004, a trend that will certainly continue for the foreseeable future.

This dedication toward pets isn't surprising. Economic

conditions that prompt young professionals to delay marriage and/or having children can result in them lavishing affection and attention on their pets. But emotional attachment to pets continues when owners marry and start families. Pet love only begins there—older people relish the interaction and unconditional love offered by dogs and cats.

This book offers prescriptive solutions for the owners of multiple pets, to help you better understand how cats and dogs think, relate to each other, and can best be taught to follow your rules and get along. It provides quick answers to common, everyday concerns, helps improve pet behavior, and provides information that allows pets to live longer and healthier lives. I've presented information in an easy-to-use format with step-by-step tips to help you build your very own peaceful kingdom.

HOW TO USE THIS BOOK

You're reading this book because you already know how much fun multiples can be, but you anticipate or are already challenged with behavior issues inherent to loving more than one pet. *PETiquette* provides expert behavior and care information for cohabiting cats and dogs and offers the tools needed to make educated pet-matchmaking choices, prevent potential problems, and handle any troubles that occur.

You won't find the answer to every behavior question here, though. While much of the information in this book translates to single-pet homes and you'll sometimes be asked to train pets one at a time, the focus is on behavior problems and solutions of *multiples*. I've included the most common behavior challenges that directly impact the other animals living in the house.

For example, you won't find direct advice about *what* to feed your cats and dogs; instead, I've provided tips on *how* to manage dinnertime so all the pets munch from the correct bowl and don't cat from eating from the dog's bowl and how to prevent a dog from guarding its food from other pets. Rather than a section on housetraining your new puppy or kitten, you'll discover practical tips for fixing bathroom problems that are prompted by the presence of other dogs and cats.

The majority of the book deals exclusively with how pets interact and impact each other and ways to manage this to fix or prevent behavior problems. Expanded information is included on aggression (see Chapter 5, Aggression Dogma; Chapter 10, Cat-egorical Aggression; and Chapter 15, Fighting Like Cats and Dogs) since this dangerous behavior not only affects the other animals but also the owners who must manage the problem. The stress of living in a multiple-pet home can increase aggression toward humans in the house or even strangers who visit. Helping your cats and dogs accept *human* family members and friends is a vital part of a happy, blended-pet family.

PETiquette offers three sections of information. Part One, Understanding Competability, consists of four chapters that cover dog-specific information, cat-specific details, and background on behavior modification and training techniques applicable to both cats and dogs. These chapters also discuss how pets learn, dog and cat communication, and each animal's social structure. It will be very helpful for readers of multiple dog homes to read Chapter 2 and cat households to read Chapter 3, while those introducing cats and dogs will benefit from both.

Parts Two, Three, and Four address the specifics of aggression, bathroom challenges, emotional issues, feeding concerns, and introductions in multidog, multicat, and dog-cat households, respectively. Each section discusses the most common behavior problems you'll face with each situation and includes practical solutions. Suggestions from a variety of expert sources offer choices so you can decide which tips work best for your individual situation. Choose the sections and individual chapters that best address your multipet challenges.

Part Five, Pet Peeves, addresses the top behavior complaints of pet owners. You'll learn tips for dealing with barking, scratching, and chewing, for example. Throughout the book, several running sidebars point out information of special interest: Calming Signals offers the best-bet tip from experts; Comfort Zone suggests helpful pet products; and Vet Alert! warns you about situations that need expert help.

Appendixes make up Part Six and include a list of the expert sources who provided information in this book. I've also added a Further Reading list of behavior or training books by these experts and other resources that you may find helpful.

THE P.E.T. TEST

Throughout the book you'll find references to the P.E.T. test, which stands for **P**hysical Health, **E**motional Well-Being, and **T**raits of Instinct. The P.E.T. test helps you figure out the "why" behind a problem behavior. By knowing what triggers a "bad" behavior, you can devise a plan to address the situation.

PHYSICAL HEALTH

Sick cats and dogs tell you they feel awful by behaving badly. When dogs suffer from skin allergies, they often act out with aggression because sore ears and tender skin make them reluctant to be touched. Pain of any kind can make cats lash out, and those suffering from hyperthyroidism typically display aggression or hyperactivity. Older pets can develop kidney failure that prompts indoor accidents. Any sudden change in behavior should be a wake-up call to get your pet checked by the veterinarian to rule out a physical cause. A complete evaluation with blood tests and metabolic screening may be necessary to find subtle problems causing a change in personality or behavior. When you can identify and treat these illnesses, the behavior problem usually goes away.

EMOTIONAL WELL-BEING

It's impossible to separate emotions from the physical realm. The stress of a new dog coming into Sheba's home can make her scratch-mark the sofa to feel more secure. Your old dog's fear of the new, rambunctious puppy may make him bark more and be aggressive toward you around his food bowl. Upset feelings can prompt overeating or snubbing dinner. Negative emotions not only make pets unhappy, but they also make cats and dogs succumb to illness more easily and take longer to recover. Unhappiness makes them more reactive to the other animals in the home, which can cause a cascade effect that sends your whole furry family into a meltdown. When your veterinarian has ruled out a physical problem, an emotional issue may have prompted the bad behavior.

TRAITS OF INSTINCT

Pets are born with certain inherent tendencies that make them behave in proscribed ways. The natural instinct to herd shines through when shepherds chase bicycles or the new puppy, and terriers bred to "go to ground" instinctively excavate lawns or stalk the cat. Cats scratch furniture to mark territory and avoid a litter box that's not up to cleanliness standards. They don't act out to be "bad" or get back at you for some imagined slight—they simply can't help themselves and are doing what comes naturally. You can't change instinct, but you can help your cats and dogs learn to redirect these behaviors into more acceptable actions—scratching a post instead of the sofa or chasing a Frisbee instead of the cat.

THE L.E.A.S.H. TECHNIQUE

An important part of living with more than one pet is understanding the dynamics of interactions to increase the odds for success. Proper introductions are the single most important step you can take to ensure your pets will get along or even become fast friends. Depending on their age, breed, and history, cats and dogs want different things from companion animals, and the chapters on dog-to-dog, cat-to-cat, and cat-to-dog introductions detail step-by-step tips for various scenarios.

Before those nose-to-nose meetings, though, take some time to consider what your resident pets would like. After all, Rex and Sheba are already an important part of your family; just because *you* have fallen in love with a furry waif at the shelter doesn't mean they'll welcome him with open paws.

If you want to adopt a particular dog or cat breed, invest in a canine or feline encyclopedia for an overview of their care needs and personalities. Then visit at least one (more is better!) cat or dog shows. Speak frankly with the breeders and exhibitors and ask for guidance choosing the best fit for your furry family.

The better the match, the smoother the introductions will go and the sooner you'll build a peaceable kingdom between all the pets in your home. Use the L.E.A.S.H. technique to help make informed decisions about matchmaking the new pet to your existing pack or clowder. The acronym, which stands for **L**ineage, **E**nvironment, **A**ge, **S**exual Status, and **H**ealth, incorporates five considerations when choosing your new pet friend and can also be used to evaluate current resident pets.

LINEAGE

Lineage has great impact and variation among dogs; some breeds are known for specific temperaments and behaviors. Choosing a mixed-heritage dog offers more variation and less predictability, so guesstimate size and personality based on visits with the parent dogs.

Personality figures prominently in the mix. Choose a very friendly and/or submissive new dog to avoid the worst problems. Well-socialized resident dogs more easily accept new ones, but if the resident dog lived alone for years without canine contact, it may be a tough sell. Selective breeding created herding specialists such as the Corgi while Dachshunds dig after varmints. If your

Parson Russell Terrier or Greyhound loves to chase small furry critters, a tiny puppy or kitten could be in danger without precautions. Also consider the size, which can range from the small Chihuahua to a large Mastiff, which may tip the scales at nearly 200 pounds. A gentle giant may hurt a tiny dog or cat without meaning to, simply by sitting on him.

Cat breeds have less variation in size, looks, and personality than do dogs, but some are known to be more vocal (Siamese), sedate (Persian), or active (Somali). An acrobatic cat may pester your resident pet half to death, while a 20-pound Maine Coon could injure a tiny puppy. A larger, mature cat may be better able to hold her own against a canine household; it's not unusual for a feline to rule in a doggy home. At least one study documented that kittens sired by "friendly" fathers would be more likely to inherit a "friendly" gene. When a kitten's father willingly interacts with you, chances are his offspring will also be more confident.

ENVIRONMENT

Environment influences both the way introductions should be made and how well the pets get along once in the home. How would you feel if a stranger moved into your one-bedroom apartment and demanded to share your bed, food, and time with loved ones? Why are we surprised when dogs and cats object?

A good rule of "paw" is to have no more pets than you have bedrooms. You can fudge this rule if the cats have extra vertical space (cat trees, window perches, hiding places) and dogs also have access to a safe, fenced outdoor territory. Dogs seem more flexible when sharing space and are very interested in meeting the "new guy." But cats prefer the status quo and must be persuaded to put up with more pets. Not enough space in the house raises stress levels for both cats and dogs. A "house of plenty" in terms of food, toys, bed, and space offers fewer opportunities to argue over who owns what.

AGE

Age of the pets involved is vital. A puppy threatens a resident dog's social status less than a dog of the same age. Older dogs allow a puppy many liberties; as he grows up, the pup learns from the top dog what's allowed and all the social skills that he needs. Be aware that adult dogs naturally pick on adolescent canines to keep them in their place. A puppy won't threaten the resident cat's social status, either; if you decide to adopt a Labrador, Sheba won't be as shocked by the smaller, puppy-version as by an adult. She can "train" the pup before he grows too big to manage.

Although kittens look like a midnight snack to dogs, they are fearless compared to adult cats and tend to adjust more quickly into an existing pet household. Adult cats feel challenged by cats their own age, so pick a feline younger than your resident cats. Choose older (six- to-nine-month-old) confident kittens to introduce to your dog family. That age allows them to stay out of the way of the curious poking dog nose.

SEXUAL STATUS

Sexual status and gender greatly impact how well pets get along— or won't. Spaying and neutering all the pets in the household goes a long way toward leveling the playing field. The worst aggressions occur between same-sex pairings, so pick a new pet of the opposite gender.

Dog society consists of a linear hierarchy, often with both a male hierarchy and a female hierarchy. Males tend to be more dominant around territory (the yard and house), while females are more likely to be territorial about toys, food, and other belongings. Therefore it may be helpful to match a cat with a female dog because the girl canine won't care if the cat "owns" the house as long as the dog controls the nifty toys. When you have more than one resident pet, figure out which one rules and choose a younger animal of the opposite sex.

HEALTH

Health issues make everything else unimportant. A medical problem automatically lowers the social standing of a given dog or cat. That means a newcomer canine brimming with health may immediately outrank your beloved geriatric dog. Similarly, an ill or elderly resident feline likely will loose top-cat status to the healthy newcomer. Healthy dogs and cats commonly pick on a health-challenged pet, and the stress, change in routine, and shift in status may make these pets feel even worse. So when Rex and Sheba aren't healthy, delay introducing a new pet until they feel better or take steps to ensure the safety and quality of life for all the pets involved.

I'm confident *PETiquette* will help you and your multipet family. Pets have certainly changed my life for the better, and I hope this book will make a positive difference in the lives of cats, dogs, and those who love them.

PART ONE

UNDERSTANDING
COMPETABILITY

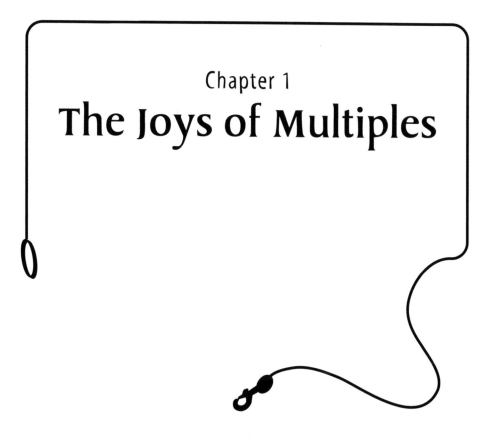

Chapter 1
The Joys of Multiples

People love dogs and cats, and they love us back. This treasured relationship has developed over many thousands of years and continues to evolve today. We cherish dogs because, at their best, they represent what humans aspire to be: devoted, honest, faithful, forgiving, and ever ready for joyous fun. Felines also reflect the best parts of human nature: honest and confident, with loving personalities and an unbridled passion for life.

For many of us, pets are furry family members, surrogate children, purring confidants, barking buddies, and a non-judgmental support system that buoys our spirits. What a gift, that they also return our love!

If one dog or a single cat provides these benefits, two or more multiplies the pleasure. Sharing your home with more than one fur-kid offers the best of all possible worlds, allowing you and your family to experience the myriad personalities dogs and cats represent. Having more than a single cat or dog can mean more work, but the benefits are worth it.

Young pets clown and play, prompting our forgiving laughter even when they make mistakes. Who can resist a kitten or puppy snoozing amidst the unrolled flourish of toilet paper? Adult dogs and cats know when we've had a hard day at work and silently commiserate with a welcome lap-snuggle, lick away tears, or transform frustration into fun with a spontaneous game of fetch. Aged pets represent milestones in human lives because they stood by your side through the good, the bad, and the challenging; they are a constant reminder of love and support. When you have more than one dog, a couple of cats, or some of each, you increase the potential to have a "purrfect" pet partnership for every situation.

Cats and dogs come in an amazing array of looks, sizes, and personalities, so you can always find the right match when adding a new kid to your family. Many pets develop strong, loving relationships with each other. A confident pet can help bring a shy one out of her shell, while high-energy youngsters give stuck-in-the-mud older animals a fun kick in the tail.

Sharing your home with a pack of dogs or a clowder of cats means all the humans in the house have a good chance of finding their "heart dog/cat" able to share not only love, but even special interests. For instance, human athletes enjoy a morning jog with a like-minded canine, while artistic owners relish the introspection and inspiration of a furry muse. A variety of people-pet activities are available, such as dancing with dogs or feline agility, to increase the pleasure for both you and your pets. Refer to the Appendixes for a list of some of these resources.

THE PET GENERATION

There are several reasons for the current surge in multiple-pet families. You may be "adopted" by a stray mother dog or cat with a litter on the way and end up keeping some or all of the offspring. But, most likely, the makeup of your human family evolves, prompting change in the pet count.

Blended families combine pets from both households when couples remarry—his dogs and her cats. A newly divorced adult child may return home and bring her dog to join your existing pet family. Situations in which a single adult family member or friend becomes ill or dies may leave you to care for the pets. More and more, owners unexpectedly find themselves unprepared to face these situations since they never anticipated having to deal with interspecies or multiple-pet relationships.

Today, equal-opportunity pet lovers don't want to settle for one or the other—they enjoy the unique qualities of cats and dogs and share their homes with both. Dogs encourage social contact and interaction. Walking a dog guarantees meeting the neighbors and other dog lovers, and you get exercise along the way. Interacting with dogs is a pleasant and painless way to increase human exercise and promote our own health.

Cats seem to fulfill a more spiritual need and appeal to our introspective side. Because they do not require outdoor exercise or bathroom breaks, cats may be more convenient for less active people or those who must spend long periods of time away from home. Felines may not be able to jog with an owner, but they promote emotional health benefits as well as dogs do.

Modern pet owners recognize that cats and dogs have social and emotional needs and try to satisfy them. People facing career demands that keep them apart from their pet for long work hours may try to balance the animal's increased alone time by matchmaking him with a furry companion. In one American

Animal Hospital Association survey, 44 percent of pet owners acquired a pet simply to keep another pet company.

NOBODY'S PERFECT

Today more pets double the fun but also increase the potential for problems. Historically owners living in rural communities enjoyed feline and canine companionship with few conflicts, since both cats and dogs spent a large percentage of their time in the backyard, the barn, or the field. That dynamic changed when pets moved into the family room and were asked to coexist.

It would be ideal if all our cats and dogs loved each other at first sight, played nicely together, and read our minds so they never made behavior mistakes. The truth is, all owners of multiple pets will be faced with minor-to-major behavior problems. If you're experiencing problems, you are not alone!

When we welcome a cat and dog into our lives and homes, we must accept that they are individuals with very different needs and desires. Just as human siblings don't always agree, a few squabbles are inevitable. But that does not mean owners or pets must accept rude behavior, irritating or dangerous antics, or constant warfare.

The right pet-matchmaking choices must be considered to keep the fur from flying. While we love having more than one pet, the potential for conflict increases when multiple animals share the same house or apartment, the same rooms, and sometimes even the same bed as human family members. Dog-dog, cat-cat, or dog-cat conflicts upset the pets' physical and emotional health, create stressful or dangerous behavior problems, and damage the loving bond with owners.

If you're like me, it offends you to have a pet referred to as "it," yet it can be awkward to say he/she over and over. For convenience's sake, the book refers to dogs as "he" and cats as "she" (but advice applies to both genders unless otherwise stated), and uses the generic pet names "Rex" for dogs and "Sheba" for cats.

RISKY BUSINESS

While behavior problems in dogs and cats prove challenging and annoying to owners, they become life-threatening to the pets themselves. Shelters overflow with animals relinquished by those unable or unwilling to deal with often fixable problems. Most of these fur-kids never get a second chance and end up losing their lives. *PETiquette* can help you resolve a large percentage of behavior problems so you can preserve the loving bond you share with your pets. Advice must be interpreted correctly, though. For instance, it can be difficult to figure out which dog rules the roost so you can apply recommendations to the right canine.

Certain kinds of aggression have far-reaching consequences and can prove challenging to even the most savvy professional. Aggression not only puts Rex's life on the line, but also risks other cats, dogs, and people and becomes a liability issue for you. Dogs bite an estimated 4.7 million people each year; 800,000 of these individuals require medical treatment. Approximately half of all children in the United States will be bitten before their twelfth birthday, but most of these injuries can be prevented with appropriate training of both the dogs and the children. Any time your pet has caused wounds in another pet or person that require medical care, you will need help beyond the scope of this book. Refer to the Appendixes for contact information regarding animal behavior consultants and trainers.

If you diligently follow the tips outlined in *PETiquette* but see no progress—or you feel so frustrated that you want to scream at your pet—yell for a professional instead. Individual people and pets absorb information in different ways and speeds, and a demonstration by a veterinary behaviorist or the use of a behavior modification program under the direction of an expert trainer may help you better understand the tips in this book, save your sanity, and preserve the love you share with your special cats and dogs.

THE TOOLS OF PETIQUETTE

You'll find a host of helpful commercial and homemade products recommended throughout the book. The best ones engage one or more of your pets' senses to persuade them to do the right thing, naturally. Some work better for cats, others for dogs, and a few prove helpful for both. An overview of the most useful products follows, including how, when, and why to use them, what they do for your cats and dogs, and where to find them.

THAT GENTLE TOUCH

Touch can be pleasant and used to reward or humanely guide pets into an acceptable behavior. Painful or uncomfortable touch can also be something Sheba and Rex dislike, and so avoid.

FOR DOGS:

 Halti and Gentle Leader head halters fit over the dog's face and are available from many veterinarians, pet product stores, and Internet sites. With gentle guidance even giant-size dogs will go where directed. These tools help owners communicate humanely with Rex to retrain him and control his movements without neck jerks or electric shocks, which can cause more problem behaviors.

 SENSE-ation Harness (www.softouchconcepts.com) is a specialized body harness that has earned raves from behaviorists and trainers. It uses gentle pressure similar to the body language dogs naturally use to "herd" each other.

 Drag line is a two and one-half foot rope or line, shorter than a leash. Step on the drag line to stop Rex in his tracks anytime he makes an illegal move toward another pet. Allow six to eight inches to trail on the ground. The drag line can be homemade or you can use a leash for this purpose.

FOR BOTH:

 Sticky Paws (www.stickypaws.com) double-sided tape products keep cats and small dogs away from forbidden locations such as furniture, countertops, and plants, as well as prevent scratching illegal targets. The unpleasant sticky surface pulls tender toe fur and keeps pets at bay.

 The Scarecrow (www.yardiac.com) motion-activated sprinkler keeps unwanted critters out of your yard (other dogs and cats, strays, or wildlife).

 The Garden Ghost (www.premier.com) works on the same principle as the motion-activated sprinkler, but uses a safe, nontoxic spray technology to keep unwanted animals away.

SOUND ADVICE

Their acute sense of hearing not only benefits cats and dogs, it also gets them in trouble. The noise of outdoor critters or other scary sounds often throw pets into a tizzy. You can use sound to cover up problem noises and soothe upset feelings. Music affects emotions in a positive way and can help sedate or energize your pets. Other sounds work well to humanely interrupt a bad behavior.

FOR DOGS:

 Tone Trainers employ a sound or tone to persuade dogs to behave and often are used to stop excessive barking. Some training collars also have remote activators to engage the tone from across the yard or from indoors when the dog is outside. They must be set appropriately to ensure inadvertent noises (other dogs or sounds) don't set off the collar and "punish" Rex when he did nothing wrong. The best tone trainers and collars provide thorough instruction and sometimes a video that demonstrates proper use. The PetSafe Remote Trainer (www.petsafe.net) is a good option for about $50.

FOR BOTH:

- *Harp music* has a natural sedative effect; in people it has been shown to relieve pain. Harp music lowers the heart rate and blood pressure, slows respiration, increases endorphins (natural pain relievers), and has a naturally calming influence for dogs and cats.

- *Pet Melodies* (www.petmelodies.com), *Canine Lullabies* (www. caninelullabies.com), and the *Pet Music* collection CD (www. naturespet.com/petmusic.html) are particularly helpful. Music affects the emotions because the heart rate and brain waves tend to mimic (entrain) the rhythms and patterns. That's why slow, soft music soothes and calms while peppy music with a driving rhythm energizes. Any slow, calm instrumental arrangement can help soothe anxious pets.

- *Noise machines,* available on the Internet and other specialty stores, create white noise that covers up distracting or unpleasant sounds that disturb your pets. You can make your own noise machine simply by tuning the radio to static.

- *The SSSCAT* (www.ssscat.com) cat-repellent device sprays a hiss of air when the cat or dog triggers the built-in motion detector. The sound startles and shoos pets—especially cats—away from illegal areas; owners don't have to be present for it to work.

- *Air horns,* available in sports supply stores, work great for breaking up fights.

SMELL PERSUASION

Pets live life through their nose. You can use scent to reward good behavior, prevent bad habits, and teach new skills.

FOR DOGS:

- *Scent collars* primarily use citronella, a very strong but pleasant odor, to signal dogs to stop barking. Most of these collars can be set to allow one or two barks, perhaps with a warning tone, before squirting the scent in front of Rex's face. A variety of commercial citronella collars are available on the Internet and from pet product stores, including the *Gentle Spray Anti-Bark Collar* (www.premier.com)

FOR CATS:

- *Catnip* is a great kitty reward and incentive. This harmless herb, a member of the mint family, contains a volatile oil that acts like a feline hallucinogen to reduce cat inhibitions and shyness. About one-third of cats react strongly, another one-third react mildly, and the last one-third don't react to catnip at all. You can spike new claw objects with catnip to lure and train cats into scratching the "right" object. Catnip also helps cats calm down and better accept new felines. Purchase at pet product stores or grow your own. Use only once a week or the effect can wear off.

- *Vanilla extract* or other pleasant scents, such as your perfume or cologne, can be applied to all the pets to make them smell alike. Since cats identify friendly family members by a shared scent, dabbing vanilla extract under the chin, back of the neck, and base of the tail of all pets helps Sheba more quickly accept interlopers of any species.

- *Citrus* odors help keep cats at bay. Spray orange or lemon scents on forbidden furniture to help keep cats off. Scattering citrus peels in the garden helps shoo stray cats away.

FOR BOTH:

- *Vicks VapoRub* repels many pets and can be applied to illegal chew or scratch targets. Paint onto the object or apply to a cloth and drape over the area.

- *Enzymatic odor neutralizers* virtually "eat" the smell associated with pet waste. The scent of urine and feces entices dogs and cats to return to the scene of the crime, and cleaning away the mess—and the smell—is paramount. Avoid ammonia-based products, which mimic the urine scent and can tempt pets to reuse the area. Several good products are available from pet product stores, your veterinarian, or online sources. My top picks include:

    - *Anti-Icky-Poo* (www.antiickypoo.com) earns raves from animal behaviorists.

- *Petastic*, formerly Nature's Miracle (www.petastic.com), is a stain and odor remover.

- *Petrotech Odor Eliminator* (www.sea-yu.com) also works well.

- *Simple Solution* stain and odor remover is available at many pet stores.

- *Tuff-Oxy* (email them at info@tuffcleaningproducts.com).

THE EYES HAVE IT

Cats enjoy watching the world go by and can be entertained—and stay out of trouble—if you provide something for their viewing pleasure.

FOR CATS:

- *Bird feeders* or *bird baths* positioned directly outside windows keep cats' attention for hours and decrease boredom and emotional upset.

- *Video Catnip* (www.videocatnip.com) and other video products provide views of birds, fish, chipmunks, and other critter antics that cats treasure. Indoor cats are most likely to enjoy watching kitty TV, while those who have experienced the real thing may not be interested.

SAFE SEPARATION

During introductions, training, and general day-to-day living, cats and dogs need their own space. You don't need to have a ten-room home to accommodate their yen for separate territory, though.

FOR CATS:

- *Purr...fect Fence* (www.purrfectfence.com), a complete backyard fence enclosure specifically for cats, creates a safe outdoor and escape-proof environment. The do-it-yourself kits are easy to install and virtually invisible, needing no existing structure. *Cat Fence-In* (www.catfencein.com), cat-containment system, another good option, attaches to existing structures.

- *Cat tunnels* provide hidden pathways for shy cats to navigate. Tunnels are particularly helpful when introducing new cats into your feline home or mixing dogs and cats together.

- *Second story properties* such as window perches and cat trees, tickle every cat's fancy and keep Sheba out of Rex's nose-sniffing range. They also give the cat a legal perch so she'll avoid your countertops and have permissible places to scratch. Visit pet product stores or online sources such as www.drsfostersmith.com or www.angelicat. com for a range of feline furniture, window perches, and scratch objects. Choose products with a variety of scratch surfaces, levels, and hide-holes to satisfy multiple cats. Offer *at least* one scratch object per cat—more is better.

  - *Homemade furniture* makes cats purr, too. A plain wooden log on which to scratch thrills many cats and is available from firewood supply outlets. For perching places, clear a bookcase shelf, the mantel, or offer your cats a wooden ladder. Hang cat toys from the rungs, wrap rope around a leg for scratching, and situate a bed on the ladder's fold-out paint rack.

FOR BOTH:

- *Baby gates* segregate pets during introductions, help retraining, or provide boundaries (such as keeping dogs out of the litter box). A variety of styles abound (www.babygates.com) and can be used to shut off single rooms or stairs, divide hallways, or allow some pets access over or through while restraining larger dogs. Some baby gates can be stacked in a doorway to confine leaping felines while allowing visual and scenting opportunities through the barrier.

- *Pet doors* (www.petdoors.com) provide access to an outside yard or interior room of the house and can allow access for selected pets. For example, a small cat door installed in the laundry room door will allow Sheba access while preventing Rex's intrusion. Electronic pet doors employ a "key" collar worn only by the pet that's allowed to use the door. The magnetic collar opens the door when the pet approaches; pets not wearing the collar can't pass through.

FUN AND GAMES

Toys entertain cats and dogs, and interactive play teaches them confidence, reduces shyness, and helps them associate positive things with you and other pets. Toys also reduce boredom, one of the major causes of canine destructive behavior, and give pets legal outlets for using teeth and claws.

FOR BOTH:

- *Fishing pole toys* for cats and small dogs (especially terriers) build on the predatory instinct to chase. You'll find many commercial versions, but cat favorites include *Kitty Tease* (www.kittytease. com) and *Da Bird* (www.go-cat.com). Make a similar product for your terriers by tying a stuffed toy to the end of a piece of heavy twine or rope.

- *Flashlight beams* and *laser pointers* entice many dogs and cats to chase that elusive flicker. Light chasing allows owners to sit in one place while pets run and exercise. Some pets become obsessed with chasing this lure, though, so teach Sheba and Rex that the light always appears and disappears in the same place (the toe of your shoe, for instance). That way, they know when the game is over and won't continue to pester you. Also, avoid shining the light directly into your pets' eyes to avoid injury.

- *Puzzle toys* keep pets occupied when owners aren't home. They can be stuffed with peanut butter, aerosol cheese, Kong Stuff'N, or with a portion of the pet's regular food. Pets must manipulate the toy to be self-rewarded with the treat. Puzzle toys work well for bored pets and those suffering from separation anxiety. They can also be used to offer separate meals to different pets. *Treatballs* for cats, the *Goody Ship* and *Buster Cube* for dogs, the *Groovy Stick* (www.ourpets.com), and any of the *Kong* dog products (www.kongcompany.com) work well and can be found at pet product stores.

PETiquette offers a simple message: You can do more for your cats' and dogs' happiness and health—and your own peace of mind—than you think. Pet love is a lifelong adventure, filled with chills, spills, and more than a few thrills. So, if you're ready to double, triple, and even quadruple your fun, enjoy the ride! You won't be sorry.

Chapter 2
How Dogs Think

Owners often become disappointed when Rex acts like a dog instead of the perfect fur kid they want him to be. We tend to interpret doggy actions in terms of human motivations and blame pets when they fall short of these expectations.

In a similar fashion, Rex filters what you say to him through a distinctively canine point of view. Chewing up the television remote, leaving fragrant deposits on the new carpet, and squabbling with other dogs makes perfect sense to Rex. Problem behaviors result from two-way miscommunication between people and their dogs. Since dogs can't read, the human component of the partnership must learn how to understand and communicate more effectively with the canine mind.

While we all aspire to have a perfect pack, owners of multiple dogs must learn to compromise and understand what constitutes reasonable expectations. The ideal dog-people partnership takes work to create, but together you can each learn how to improve your relationship. It's also a whole lot of fun.

EDUCATING REX

Much of what dogs are, aspire to be, and will become depends on three educational components. One of these we can influence. The best we can do with others is to recognize them and deal with the consequences.

The first component, genetics, influences everything else. Puppies can't pick their parents, and you can't change a dog's inherited looks, instincts, or temperament. But by understanding genetic influences, you can choose puppies or adult dogs that have the best potential for being positive fits for your pack.

Dogs learn how to be dogs very early, as puppies. The people and other dogs that puppies first encounter teach them the positive and negative lessons that will follow them the rest of their lives. Think of yourself and your other dogs as kindly uncles who are guiding the inexperienced youngsters' development. That's a huge responsibility!

The final component is serendipity. Neither owners nor dogs can control all aspects of their environment, and we all learn lessons from each experience. Understanding the impact of such "accidental" education can help you take advantage of good opportunities, and avoid or deal with problematic ones.

FAMILY TIES

Dog genetics have been manipulated to produce specific kinds of dogs. Those bred to perform specialized jobs do better with tasks that pertain to their genetic function. One might expect a terrier to be more adept at ferreting out cookies hidden in nooks and crannies, while sight hounds run down a jackrabbit in an eyeblink; it never occurs to a Bloodhound to lift his nose from the pavement and look for moving prey.

Dogs are as smart as they need to be. Each breed has strengths and challenges that go beyond intelligence or lack thereof, and every puppy inherits a combination of looks, temperament, and smarts from his doggy parents. The genetic roll of the dice means some puppies become canine Einsteins while their littermates are dim bulbs. The very smartest dogs often are challenging to train because they question everything and think too much. Highly "biddable" dogs may not be as intelligent but excel at training because they thrive on owner approval.

PUPPY PRESCHOOL

Socialization refers to how baby dogs learn to interact with the world around them—you, other dogs and animals, and other people. Canine learning involves both nature (genetics) and nurture (environment). Puppies that inherit the potential for aggression and shyness, for example, may never exhibit these problems if properly socialized.

Dogs can be trained at any age and continue to learn throughout their lives. But the prime socialization period falls into a narrow window during babyhood when learning the wrong lessons can emotionally cripple the pet. Puppies that are not exposed to positive experiences with humans during this period will never accept people. During the prime socialization period, from six to eight weeks of age, puppies develop canine social and communication skills and learn to identify acceptable and unacceptable members of the canine clan. Mother dogs teach many lessons by example. If Mom-Dog becomes hysterical around men, her pups will pay attention and copy her behavior.

People who are raising litters must begin positive lessons

before the babies go to new homes. Socialization continues through sixteen weeks of age and through the juvenile period (eighteen months) in some cases, says Patricia Pryor, DVM, who is an assistant professor of behavior at Washington State University. It's vital that the babies be exposed to positive experiences with other pets and people if they are to accept them as part of their "family" and become loving, well-adjusted pets.

Gary Landsberg, DVM, a behaviorist practicing in Ontario, says some animals experience a "fearful" period anywhere from age six to twelve months. It's important to strive for a positive outcome for the dog in all new situations and to continue to provide exposure to a variety of people (wearing hats, uniforms, and of different ages), of places (home, grandma's, the mall), and of novel situations and objects to explore.

Many training schools or veterinary hospitals provide puppy classes that can help your new baby learn the ropes, particularly around other dogs. Encourage the pup to walk and eliminate on novel surfaces, as dogs only used to kennels or cement floors may refuse to potty on grass.

CALMING SIGNALS: PASS THE PUPPY

Too often, aggression later in life arises from shyness and fear born at an early age. Snapping and squealing are signs of a lack of confidence and should be addressed in puppies at an early age as a part of socialization exercises.

"A puppy is a huggable unit," says Ian Dunbar, Ph.D., MRCVS, a veterinarian, animal behaviorist, dog trainer, and creator of the Sirius Puppy Training series. "Teach it to enjoy being hugged." He suggests playing "pass the puppy" during puppy classes to help the baby become used to handling by as many people as possible. Every five minutes, the pup gets passed on to a new person who handles his paws (then gives a treat), handles his ears (then gives a treat), rubs his tummy (then gives a treat), and so on. When the pup seems very frightened, the process is slowed and the puppy spends more time with each person before passing him on.

Confidence-building exercises are also recommended. The puppy is praised every time he plays, for example. "For shy dogs, the most important feedback is to praise and reinforce the absence of snaps, squeaks, growls, and lunges," says Dr. Dunbar. Don't take your dog's good behavior for granted. "Always praise your dog for good behavior, even if it's the absence of a bad behavior," he says.

For a good puppy class, look for puppies who are off-leash all the time and have interruptions of their play at fifteen-second intervals. This allows them to learn bite inhibition from each other while they are socialized to other dogs.

Create a puppy kindergarten for your new dog. While human kids are taught the three Rs in school, puppies can be socialized based on the three Ts—touching, talking, and timing.

Touching the youngster not only feels good to you and your puppy, but also teaches him that contact with people is pleasant, not scary, and self-rewarding. Petting also places your scent on him, so he associates your smell with feelings of well-being. Petting is one of the first sensations newborns feel when Mom licks and grooms them, and petting harkens back to this wonderful safe experience.

Pleasant touching also prompts a reduction in blood pressure and heart rate and can change brain wave activity. Studies have shown that handling furry babies for five minutes a day during their first three weeks increases the pet's ability to learn later in life.

Talking is equally important and teaches the youngster to listen and pay attention to your voice. They may not understand all the words, but will recognize if you're happy with them, aggravated, amused, or affectionate. The more you speak to your dogs, the better they will learn to understand and react to what you want, which enhances and improves your relationship.

"Teach the phrase, 'Say hi,' so dogs learn that means they get to meet somebody," suggests Deborah Wood, a dog trainer and pet columnist in Oregon. "That's especially helpful for fearful dogs, who then know that person is safe and nothing to fear." She also suggests teaching "Look" or "Check it out" while pointing to various objects, to show dogs they're safe to investigate. You can increase healthy curiosity and confidence in your puppy by hiding tasty treats beneath a towel or cushion, toy, or other object, so when the dog investigates, there's a reward waiting.

Timing is the third T in the equation. Puppies won't know what's right and what's wrong unless you tell them *at the right time* exactly what you like or dislike. If he leaves a deposit under the piano, for example, and you find it twenty minutes later, he won't have a clue why you're angry. Only by catching him in the act (or within thirty seconds) will the youngster be able to connect your displeasure with the incident. It's more powerful to use timing to catch him doing something *right*. Offer a treat when he greets the mailman with a wag. Celebrate with a favorite game when the puppy and adult pets play together nicely—they've graduated pet kindergarten with flying colors.

THE ACCIDENTAL EDUCATION

Puppies and dogs learn an incredible amount simply by observation. Lessons continue long after the prime socialization period ends, with young dogs receiving lessons from you, other dogs, and new situations. When your current dogs know good manners, they can serve as wonderful role models to the newcomer pets. Resident dogs help teach newbies the ropes. By observing your interaction with old Rex, young Rex learns he must sit at the door to make it open. If he notices that old Rex gets treats for certain things, before long he'll be mimicking the old guy in order to get his share of the booty.

The new dog can also learn bad habits from resident dogs, and vice versa. If you allow young Rex to break the rules, old Rex may also test limits. Dogs manipulate owners to do doggy bidding. Rex trained you to open the door, for instance, when he barks and wakes you at 4 A.M. Pets pay particular attention to consequences and put these equations together very quickly. If a particular behavior (growling) gets him what he wants (you stop grooming), he'll remember to use the behavior over and over again.

When dealing with dogs and behavior issues, pay attention to the pet's actions as well as your own. Corporeal punishment— hitting, yelling, using force—almost always makes the behavior worse. Any strong emotional state of arousal (happiness, aggression, fear, etc.) means the pet can't learn, says Dr. Landsberg.

High arousal prompts an immediate response to the situation because the dog is reactive and not thinking. When arousal level remains low, options are reviewed and learning can occur.

UNDERSTANDING DOG-SPEAK

Canine language is a complex system of sign language, vocalization, and scent cues people can't detect. Many of these signals define and reinforce the dog's social position within the family group, be that other dogs, humans, or other animals. Dogs seem to be much better at understanding languages of the other species than people are.

Signals that ask for attention seek to *decrease* the distance between individuals while warning signs are designed to *increase* this distance. Dogs don't just "talk" from one end of their body, but use a whole repertoire of signals that must be read together to understand their true intent. In multiple-dog homes, understanding what your dogs tell you (and each other) means the difference between a happy home and chaos. Learn the basics to translate doggy dialect into people-speak.

WOOFS, WHINES, AND WHIMPERS

Dog vocalizations have nearly as much range as human vocalizations, with inflection, tone, and context able to change the meaning. There is also variation between dogs, sort of a "dialect" that your own pack employs that other dogs don't typically use.

Behaviorists consider barking to be the ultimate in "conflicted" behavior. It can mean, "I like you, but I'm not sure," or "I want to play . . . but I shouldn't." Barking also can be a canine fire alarm to tell the rest of the family that something needs attention. Barking that develops into habit out of boredom becomes a nuisance issue. (See also "Yapping Maniacs" in Chapter 20.)

Howls express emotion and plead for missing family members

to join the lonely dog. Northern breeds such as Siberians seem more likely to howl and use a signature "woo-woo" in happy conversation. Dogs respond with more sustained howls in response to sirens or groups of coyote or wolves announcing they "own" a particular territory. A joyful variation includes baying, performed by hound breeds during a hunt. Whining, whimpering, and yelping communicate submission, fear, pain, and sometimes frustration. Such vocalizations also solicit attention or food from humans.

Distance-increasing signals indicate unease, fear, or aggression, and often are used as a threat. But growls also can solicit play. Some dog breeds, such as Chesapeake Bay Retrievers, tend to "talk" about everything, so be sure to ask your breeder about your dog's heritage so you won't be taken by surprise.

Growly dogs typically are middle-ranking insecure males that have limited experience. A true top dog rarely resorts to obvious threats—he doesn't need to. Instead, the dog in charge uses subtle signals and, if they're ignored, he follows up immediately with direct short consequences (bites), which hopefully are inhibited and do no damage.

CANINE CHARADES

Silent communication makes use of the dog's body, from nose to tail. Some signals seem ambiguous. Showing teeth can be an offensive, defensive, or submissive gesture, says Dr. Pryor. Dogs pull their lips back in defensive displays. With the mouth wide open, dogs "grin" and show their teeth by pulling their lips back horizontally. By licking their lips and assuming a low body posture at the same time, they indicate they mean no harm. In contrast, during an offensive tooth display the dog's lips push forward but retract vertically.

Similarly, canine ear position can tell you he feels neutral (ears back) or alert (ears forward). Dr. Pryor says that just as people perceive crop-eared dogs differently than those with natural ears, so do other dogs. A Doberman Pinscher with cropped ears (erect) looks quite different than with natural ears (dropped), and this can signal different things to the rest of the pack. Eye contact is a universal sign of confidence, dominance, and sometimes challenge. This signal can be confused or misread in dogs with fur over their eyes.

Even fur position indicates the emotional state of the dog. Piloerection—fur standing off the body—signals strong arousal, such as fear or aggression. Raised hackles (fur along the top line of the neck and shoulders) shout "Warning!" to other dogs. Owners of a Rhodesian Ridgeback, though, need to understand that the unique backward-growing "ridge" of fur along his back that gives him a distinctive look can be off-putting to other dogs. They think he's aroused (hackles raised) even when he's perfectly calm, potentially leading to a miscommunication.

The wagging tail has many meanings, depending on how fast it moves and the carriage. The higher the tail is set, the more alert and offensive the dog is, while the lower the tail is, the more fearful and defensive the dog is. A tucked tail is the canine equivalent of hiding his face because it covers the genitals and interferes with the sniffing behavior that identifies him to other dogs. A dog shows his low standing, relative to you (or another animal), with loose, wide low-arcing wags that often include hip wags.

When a dog feels confident and acts in a dominant fashion, he holds his tail high and wags rapidly in tight, sharp arcs. But aggressive dogs also hold their tails high, often tightly arched over their back with just the end jerking very quickly back and forth. A high-held stiff tail signals imminent attack. Dr. Pryor suggests sighting between the dog's ears—if you can see the tail tip, beware!

Watch for piloerection and movement to "read" the message in a docked tail. Breeds with naturally curled tails may not be able to lower their tails to show submission or fear; and to other dogs, this may appear offensive even when the dogs are neutral.

PLAYING AROUND

Dogs of all ages enjoy playing. Behaviors for fighting and fun are similar, but you must know how to tell the difference between aggression and play-acting. Watch for "meta signals," which tell participants that whatever comes after is meant in a play context. Dogs commonly drop toys on your feet or lap to solicit a game and offer toys to other dogs in the same way. A play bow, where the dog sticks his butt and tail into the air and bows forward on lowered forelegs that dance from side to side, is the classic signal and invitation for the games to begin. Often, "fighting" behaviors seen during such games will be exaggerated to indicate play, or the "fight" behavior sequences may be jumbled.

Play includes inhibited mouth-open bites often aimed at the legs and paws of other dogs. Dogs also paw and bat each other without force to hurt. In appropriate play, all the dogs willingly participate. If you suspect one of the dogs doesn't like the activity (one dog repeatedly tries to escape or hide), gently separate the pair to see if they go back for more. If the play session was too rough, one will sneak away.

CALMING SIGNALS: BODY BLOCKS

Patricia McConnell, Ph.D., a certified applied animal behaviorist, owner of Dog's Best Friend, Ltd., and an adjunct associate professor in zoology at the University of Wisconsin-Madison, explains that in order for dogs to understand what we want, people should speak "dog" the way canines do.

Dogs don't have hands to control the movement of other canines, so they use their bodies to manage space by blocking other dogs' access to the areas around them. Sidling up to you may mean he wants company or that he's maneuvering for spatial control or dominance. Think of the way herding dogs manage sheep or cattle, by positioning themselves to influence the other animals' movements in the desired direction, often without nipping or contact at all.

Therefore, Dr. McConnell recommends that people use their torso to control a dog's movements. Tuck your hands at your chest and lean toward the dog to keep him off your lap or leaping up at you. Occupy the space before the dog does, and you'll rule the interaction. Blocking the space he was about to occupy stops the movement. Very sensitive dogs give way if you simply lean toward them, while others may test a bit and bump you. Be ready to turn into a herding creature, able to move right or left as needed.

Inappropriate play results when one (or more) dog is frightened, hurt, or overwhelmed. Bully dogs always end up on top, while in appropriate play you'll see dogs take turns chasing and pinning each other during wrestling. Mouthing aimed primarily at the head or neck or uninhibited bites means play has gotten out of hand. You'll hear yelps from the bitten dog. Consistent play up on hind legs may indicate problems. Ongoing mounting, clasping, and thrusting also can lead to problems, as can the resting of paws, heads, or whole bodies across another dog's shoulders to intimidate or achieve social status.

Growls don't usually indicate problems, but play can be so exciting that the action escalates into aggression. Listen for louder, lower-pitched growls, and be prepared to break up the session before they get too aroused.

BOSSY DOGS

It can help you to understand your dog's attitude by recognizing what constitutes a pushy, controlling, or dominant attitude. Dogs use the following in any combination to get their way. You'll notice that biting, barking, and fighting are not typical of the dominant dog's repertoire—he's more subtle and manipulative than that! He knows he's top dog and doesn't need outrageous displays to prove it.

- Maintains eye contact.

- Rotates ears forward.

- Retracts lips vertically.

- Holds his head high, with erect, tense, and rigid posture (standing on tiptoes).

- Stands or "looms" over the dominated individual.

- Holds his tail above horizontal.

- Fluffs his fur, especially along the hackles (piloerection).

- Rests his head/chin/paws over neck/body of the subordinate.

- Indulges in body slamming, pushing, or bowling over.

- Grabs the muzzle or neck of the subordinate (inhibited bite).

- Engages in mounting or clasping behavior.

THE PEACEKEEPER POOCH

Dogs use body language to calm each other down, appease perceived or real aggression in others, and signal that they are not a threat. Dominant dogs use these gestures to tell frightened dogs they mean no harm, while subordinate dogs signal to appease the top dog so he won't mistakenly attack.

Your dog may misunderstand your displays of affection. In dog language, leaning over him, patting the top of his head, and hugging means, "I am dominant over you" and makes Rex uncomfortable. Subordinate dogs lick a more dominant dog's face or side of the mouth as an appeasement gesture—Rex may do the same thing to you. If you "kiss" him on the mouth and declare submission to Rex, that could cause problems.

Displacement behaviors help dogs maintain a healthy social hierarchy and resolve conflict without bloodshed. You can also use the signals effectively. For instance, you can yawn several times to calm down your nervous dog during a vet visit. Approach timid dogs in an indirect, curving direction rather than head-on. Understand that "splitting" behavior (the dog jumping between you and your spouse when you hug) simply means Rex fears a fight might break out and tries to stop it. Internationally known Norwegian dog trainer, Turid Rugaas, calls these "calming signals." All dogs use calming signals, which also include:

- Averting the eyes and/or turning the head away.

- Licking the lips.

- Freezing, or moving very slowly.

- Play-bowing (with front legs motionless).

- 🐾 Sitting with his back to another dog or you.
- 🐾 Lying down, belly to the ground.
- 🐾 Yawning.
- 🐾 Pawing.
- 🐾 Sniffing.
- 🐾 Curving—approaching not in a direct line, but in an oblique path.
- 🐾 Crawling while wagging tail wildly.

THE PHYSICAL DOG

"A behavior change is the first indication that a pet is unwell," says Kersti Seksel, a veterinary behaviorist practicing at Seaforth Veterinary Hospital in Sydney, Australia. Sometimes a pet retains the new behavior, such as growling, even after the physical problem (pain) has resolved. Pay attention to your dog's "normal" behavior. That way, you'll more easily recognize something different and be alert to a potential problem.

FIDO FORM AND FUNCTION

Although dogs come in all shapes, sizes, weights, and temperaments, a seven-pound mixed pooch that spends hours on a lap each day and the seventy-pound German Shepherd that works cattle from dawn to dusk have more similarities than differences. Canine function suits doggy design, and vice versa.

For the most part, dogs are endurance specialists who love to run. They are designed with pursuit of prey in mind. Of course, modern dogs more typically target balls rather than sheep or rats.

In lieu of hands, dogs use their mouths to pick up and carry objects. The function of capturing prey results in jaws capable of crushing bone, yet in breeds such as retrievers, this has been modified so they can carry raw eggs without cracking the shell. When they mean business, though, dogs grasp prey by the neck and shake the critter (or towel or other toy) to break its neck. Dogs also use mouthing to communicate.

Whatever their size or lifestyle, every dog requires regular exercise to keep muscles toned, the body healthy, and the mind active. A fifteen-minute exercise period twice a day suffices for most dogs, but working dogs need more. A tired dog is a well-behaved dog.

MAKING SENSE OF SENSES

Sense of touch offers both pleasure and discomfort and has a great impact on dog behavior. Each dog has different thresholds or sensitivities to extremes of touch. Fur offers protection, but every hair on the dog's body acts like an antenna, buried in the skin adjacent to nerve receptors. Brushing the tips of the hair coat transmits information to Rex about air movement, barometric pressure, petting, or punishment. A matted coat, for instance, can cause severe bruising and pain when snarled fur interferes with movement.

Canine eyes see about as well as we do. Recent studies reveal that various breeds see the world quite differently. The eyes of longer-nosed dogs include a visual streak—a high-density line of vision cells across the retina that allows them to see 320 degrees, while the vision is blurred above and below the line. This gives sight hounds (and other chasing breeds) the ability to see movement out of the corners of their eyes. Short-faced dogs, instead, have a centrally located area of vision cells on the retina, with three times the density of nerve endings as the visual streak. Short-faced dogs see in much higher definition than long-nosed dogs; some even watch TV. This may give them an advantage in reading an owner's facial expression. Regardless of nose conformation, dogs that lose their vision due to cataracts, glaucoma, or age often develop temporary behavior problems until they are able to adjust.

Although dogs and humans hear approximately the same low-pitched sounds, dogs hear much better than people at higher frequencies. People hear sound waves up to 20,000 cycles per second; dogs hear up to 100,000 cycles per second. This hearing range is constant for dogs despite size and breed. As age increases, the risk of deafness goes up as well. Hearing loss can severely interfere with communication between dogs or with their owners.

Preferred taste can be quite individual between dogs. They share similar tastes to people, including a sweet tooth. Strongly flavored or scented treats often are an ideal tool to communicate with dogs during training. However, many dogs eat indiscriminately or become possessive about food.

The sense of smell defines the dog's existence. Scent serves as a nametag to identify friend from foe, to gather and send information, and to interact socially. Humans have about five to twenty million scent-analyzing cells, compared to the dog's range of over twelve million to 300 million. The longer the dog's nose, the more details he can sniff, which is why the German Shepherd can out-sniff the Pug.

In addition to scent particles, dogs have the ability to detect and react to pheromones, or species-specific chemicals that animals naturally produce. Patrick Pageat, DVM, PhD, a behaviorist, says smells and odors are very different from pheromones. "Odors need to go to the cortex [area of the brain], the very highest way to analyze information," he says. Experience teaches dogs what a scent means. For example, the dog associates the aroma of a cooking steak with the memory of what it tastes like.

But pheromones have nothing to do with memory. "Pheromones go to the lower part of the brain, the limbic system," says Dr. Pageat. Pheromones are part of the chemical communication between animals. "During evolution, you have selected receptors to this component and the brain directly recognizes it. It's hardwired; you're born with it," he says. Puppies react from birth, even before their eyes or ears open. Dogs rely on this specialized pheromone communication all their lives.

PUPPIES, JUVENILES, ADULTS, AND OLD FOGIES

Dogs behave differently as they mature, just as humans evolve from playing and cooing infants to juveniles who test limits, responsible adults, and set-in-their-ways old-timers. When you have dogs of different ages, you'll need to adjust your thinking to accommodate their maturity (or lack thereof). The dogs themselves make accommodations as well.

The hormone testosterone makes the dog's urine smell "male" and influences how he is perceived by other dogs. This urine odor labels the age of juvenile male dogs; the smell of puppy urine is distinct. Coupled with the size, shape, sound, and other behaviors, the baby might as well scream, "I'm a pup, don't hurt me, I don't know any better." Most well-socialized adult dogs recognize this puppy license to misbehave and act with tolerance toward them, oftentimes allowing the baby to get away with murder.

In most mammals, adult males have a higher level of testosterone than youngsters. But in dogs, Dr. Dunbar says the testosterone levels rise at four to five months of age; by ten months, juvenile testosterone levels can be up to five times greater than that of an adult male dog. From the scent, adult dogs recognize these adolescent pups need to be schooled in the proper ways of respecting adult dogs and begin picking on the youngsters. It's common for bitches to offer toys or bones to youngsters as a dare to touch or take the object, which prompts the bitch to give a lesson in manners to the youngster.

Dr. Dunbar says it's a dog rule that older dogs (three years and up) get stiff and growly, especially with juvenile male dogs. They discipline and harass them to keep the pup in his place before he tries to challenge the established authority. By supporting the older canine in this effort, you'll have a much more peaceful household. A pup's testosterone level falls to adult levels by eighteen months; then, the harassment should fade.

Dogs become "old" at different ages, depending mostly on the size and breed of the dog. Very generally, the smallest dogs age more gracefully than larger ones. When age-related changes take place, such as sensory or mobility challenges and other health issues, tired old fogies often go through a personality change as a result. The confident, vital attitude gives way to the mild-mannered, weary, or uncertain senior citizen dog. Some of these old fogies become crotchety and short-tempered with younger canines, while others mellow and put up with more. Care must be taken that vital, energetic youngsters don't browbeat the golden oldies of your pack.

YOU SEXY DOG!

Behavior and sexuality cannot be separated. Mounting, clasping, and thrusting behavior appears first during puppy play and is performed by both males and females. Adolescent male dogs continue to experiment and often mount anything that doesn't move faster than they do—chairs, other pets, your leg, the family cat.

Female dogs come into season as early as six months of age, and most can breed twice a year. Males also can father puppies as early as six months. Hormone-related behaviors include leg-lifting to mark with urine, roaming far from home seeking true love, and dominance displays that can evolve into aggression.

Spaying removes the ovaries and uterus of female dogs, while castration removes the testes of male dogs. Both surgeries are referred to as neutering and eliminate the chance of accidental procreation. When performed prior to sexual maturity, neutering prevents or reduces hormone-related behavior problems.

Many animal welfare organizations advocate neutering pet dogs as puppies once they reach two pounds or more in weight. Delaying the surgery increases the potential for hormone-related behavior problems. "Castration during development decreases the dog's fervor of sexual interest," says Dr. Dunbar, but even castrated dogs often continue mounting behavior.

Neutering has no effect on the dog's maleness, sexual orientation, urination postures, or scent preferences. "That's all predetermined during fetal development by testosterone from the fetal testes," says Dr. Dunbar. Castrated males still prefer to interact both socially and sexually with females, continuing both leg-lifting and mating behaviors.

Castrating a dog weeks after birth, before puberty or during adulthood, won't directly reduce a dog's aggressiveness or ranking in the social hierarchy either, says Dr. Dunbar. However, because the testosterone level drops to make castrated males smell more female, neutered dogs won't be viewed as a threat; therefore, other dogs won't challenge him as vigorously. Neutering all the dogs, male and female, in the household greatly reduces the potential for sexual competition and resulting behavior problems.

THE CANINE PACK

To be efficient and harmonious, the doggy social structure depends on a hierarchy of dominant and subordinate individuals. Social ranking decides which dogs get the preferred or prime access to valued resources: resting spots, food pans, water, toys, bones, your attention, and so on. However, dominance has nothing to do with bullying or aggression, nor does submission necessarily correlate with fear or shyness. In the past, much was made of the "canine alpha" dominance hierarchy of dogs; today, behaviorists describe it as a subordinance hierarchy.

"It is the relentless, active appeasement and deference of subordinate animals that allows for harmony in social groups," says Dr. Dunbar. The canine communication often described as submissive behavior could more accurately be translated as signaling *noncontest*, or *let me be your friend*, says Dr. Dunbar.

Studies on the behavior of domestic dogs make it clear that

dog social ranking follows a pretty rigid linear hierarchy. This happens from puppyhood on, with a "top dog" and "bottom dog" usually established in a litter by eight weeks of age. Boys are usually bigger than girls, so the male often is the top dog. The top and bottom pups (and adult dogs) have the easiest time dealing with canine society; since everyone is either above or below them, they know how to act and react.

Middle pups have a harder time establishing rank and won't have a firm sense of social position until about three months or so, when rank usually correlates pretty strongly with sex and weight. But in nonrelated pups of different ages, once they all socialize to each other, the most important determinant of rank is age and sex. Pups that grow up with other dogs quickly learn that exaggerated appeasement gestures can cut short the harassment with a preemptive apology characterized by a low-slung, wriggly approach with ears back, a submissive grin, and tail and hindquarters wagging.

Older males usually rank higher; size and strength help determine ranking as pups grow. Once they've grown up, though, and take their places within an already established adult hierarchy, there may be no correlation between rank and weight. Among adult male dogs, an individual's relative rank decides nearly everything in advance, such as who gets the toy, who sleeps where, and which one gets to greet the owner first. Relationship between males and females can vary from day to day.

Girl dogs have a linear but less rigid hierarchy, with day-to-day success depending on the individual circumstances. The top bitch always gets the preferred toy or treat first; if she's not there, the second-ranking bitch likely will score the trophy. However, the girls seem to respect ownership a bit more than the boys. While the highest-ranking male might challenge a subordinate and take away his bone, the highest-ranking female often allows a lower-ranking girl to enjoy the treat when it's already in her possession—signaled by keeping a paw or two on the toy or just looking at it. While a subordinate boy dog typically gives up the bone if a higher-ranking male tells him to, a lower-ranking girl may defend her ownership of the goodies. Think of this as a sort of "finders, keepers" mentality. Once a dog relinquishes possession, though, any lower-ranking dog of either gender can have at it with impunity.

Maintaining the existing social structure relies on the lowest-ranking dogs to express respect for the dogs of higher rank. The major function of the hierarchical structure is to lessen the need for fighting. For example, if two dogs see one toy but the "owner" is predetermined by rank, there's no need to fight. Fights or noisy disputes are rare because top dogs have no reason to fight and low-ranking dogs know they'd be foolish to try. "Excess growling and repeat fighting are symptoms of insecurity and uncertainty about social rank compared to other dogs, and are the hallmark of middle-ranking males," says Dr. Dunbar.

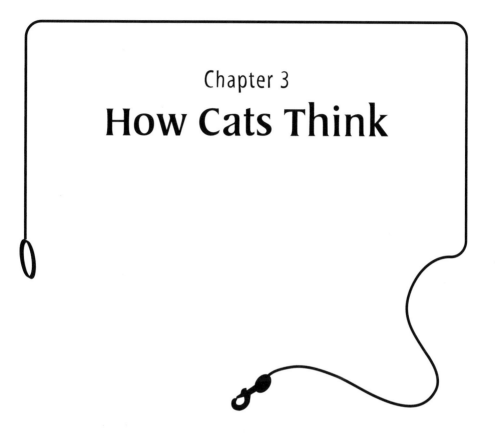

Chapter 3
How Cats Think

Humans have shared their laps with cats since the days of ancient Egypt. While they command our respect and we cherish their grace, devotion to loved ones, and wild-child perspective, we still fall short in understanding how Sheba thinks. Feline behavior problems typically reflect a human misunderstanding of normal cat needs; adding to your kitty quotient increases the potential for problems.

Cats challenge our patience when they claw the sofa, "water" the potted palm, and throw hissy fits with other cats. People unfamiliar with felines perpetuate the myth that cats are untrainable, independent creatures that "walk alone" and prefer solitary lifestyles. While cats are territorial, they are also social animals that enjoy contact with the special people and pets in their lives. But Sheba picks her friends carefully, so owners and other cats and dogs must meet her on her terms to earn full affection and cooperation. Once you learn how to communicate with and understand the feline mind, your relationship will improve by leaps and pounces. Your purrfect pet partnership awaits!

LEARNING TO BE A CAT

Kittens aren't born knowing the rules of feline behavior; instead, they must learn the proper "cat-titudes" by both observation and experience. Earliest cat lessons are taught by Sheba's mom-cat, and she won't understand human expectations without proper instructions from you. Kittens with the worst genetic roll of the dice can develop a wonderful personality with the proper teachers. Conversely, the kitten with an ideal personality can turn hissy if she learns the wrong thing. Everything that Sheba experiences influences her behavior, even accidental lessons you never intended to teach. Understanding how kittens and cats learn helps you be the best feline teacher possible so they play by your rules and you understand theirs.

THE FELINE FAMILY

Kittens inherit a lot from cat parents, including looks, instincts, and even personality tendencies. Both parent personality and health play a crucial role in determining a cat's future behavior. Kittens born of "friendly" fathers tend to inherit "boldness," a positive response to unfamiliar or novel objects. The bold kitty meets life head-on and has less overall stress-related health issues as compared to shy or fearful cats. Studies also show that kittens from undernourished mothers have less ability to learn and display more antisocial behavior toward other cats. Even if these kittens are fed enough later in life, some of these deficits will be passed on to the next generation.

While there are more similarities among cats, researchers speculate that some differences in behavior may correlate to looks inherited from parents. Coat coloring pigments (melanin) are produced by the same biochemical pathway in the brain as dopamine, a substance that plays an important role in brain activity; hence, coat color may influence behavior. One study suggests that cats carrying the nonagouti allele—a type of gene that produces solid coat colors (usually black cats)—may be more tolerant of crowding and the conditions of urban life as well as have greater amicability. In other words, black cats may adjust more readily to living in groups of felines.

In the early days of experimental psychology, adult cats often were used as subjects in learning studies. Felines quickly discovered how to escape from puzzle boxes with novel kinds of fasteners, but they couldn't learn by trial and error the concept of pressing a lever to receive food—something pigeons quickly mastered! In modern experiments, researchers found that kittens who watched mom press a lever to get food quickly learned to perform the trick when they had a role model. Too, kittens who watched their mom learned more quickly than if they watched a strange female cat; thus, learning improves if the "mentor" is familiar. This illustrates that cats aren't well-suited to learning monotonous tasks, but like a challenge and model behavior by example. Sheba evolved to out-think smart prey that hides in ever-changing locations.

Cats exhibit two major personality types: sociable/confident/trusting, and timid/nervous/shy. While you can't control what your cat inherited, you can help promote positive nurturing with training. The very smartest cats know they are smarter than you are and are challenging to train, yet they may feign being "slow" simply to get away with murder. Understanding the basics of feline learning better prepares you to stay a step ahead of your cats and enhance your relationship.

KITTEN KINDERGARTEN

Cats learn all their lives but are virtual sponges from two to seven weeks of age, during the prime socialization period. This narrow window during babyhood prepares kittens for the rest of their lives; however, learning the wrong lessons can emotionally cripple the pet. If they are not exposed to positive experiences with humans during this socialization period, kittens will act like wild animals for the rest of their lives and never accept people.

During this time, kittens develop feline social and communication skills while learning to identify acceptable and unacceptable members of their family. Mother cats teach these skills through example. Babies learn to use a litter box by following mom-cat to the facilities. If the mother gets hissy around dogs, her kittens will copy the behavior. Similarly, mom-cats that like people teach kittens to accept human attention. This helps socialize the baby so that the kittens will later "generalize" this response and react positively to other people, too.

Kittens separated too early from maternal and sibling interactions develop poor social bonds later in life, but when they are accompanied by their mom-cat and siblings, their anxiety level goes down. Hand-raised kittens tend to become overly rambunctious and less inhibited with their teeth and claws. Ideally, kittens should stay with mom and littermates at least until twelve to sixteen weeks of age. People raising kittens must socialize them before they go to new homes. Once the baby arrives in her new home, the owner(s) should strive for a positive outcome in new situations and continue to provide exposure to a variety of people (men, women, children), places (home, grandma's, the vet), and novel situations and objects to explore.

To promote a trusting relationship and a confident cat, begin by creating a kitten kindergarten, teaching the three Ts—touching, talking, and timing. The more you touch a kitten, the friendlier she will be toward humans. Studies have shown that handling furry babies for five minutes a day during their first three weeks increases the pet's ability to learn later in life, but about an hour a day during the sensitive period is ideal. Touching the youngster not only feels good to you both, but it also teaches her that contact with people is pleasant, not scary, and self-rewarding. Touch also places your scent on her, so she associates your smell with good feelings. Petting comforts kittens because it harkens back to one of the first sensations newborns feel when mom licks and grooms them. In addition, your pleasant touch prompts a reduction in blood pressure and heart rate, causing a positive change in brain wave activity.

Talking to the youngster teaches her to listen and pay attention to your voice. Kittens may not understand all the words, but will recognize if you're happy, aggravated, amused, or affectionate. Make a point of using your cats' names as you speak to them in a positive way: "What a lovely, smart Sheba! Scratching the right object—good Sheba!" This teaches a cat to associate her name with good things related to you. The more you speak to your cats, the better they will learn to understand and react to what you want.

Timing is the third T and extremely important when you understand that kittens have the attention span of a four-year-old child. If you find claw marks on the Persian rug and drag Sheba to the scene of the crime, she won't have a clue why you're angry. You must catch her in the act—or within thirty seconds of the behavior—for her to associate your displeasure with what she's done. When training, praise always works better than punishment, and you'll get better results by catching her in the act of scratching the *right* object. Reward good behaviors immediately, with praise, a treat, or favorite toy. Use timing to your advantage, and your cats will look for ways to please you.

THE "WHOOPS" EFFECT

A "whoops" experience can be a happy accident or create future behavior problems. Kittens and cats continue to learn an incredible amount through observation, even after the prime socialization period ends. A friendly, trusting cat needs only a few positive interactions with a strange person to show positive behavior toward them, and it takes significant negative experiences to override this initial response. On the contrary, a shy cat needs *lots* of positive experiences with a stranger to overcome the lack of socialization during the sensitive phase, and she will react adversely toward even minor negative encounters.

In other words, the socialized cat generalizes positive experiences quickly, but the unsocialized cat must learn gradually to trust the individual person or family and does *not* generalize later positive experiences. Instead, she expects that one negative experience will apply to all new situations.

When your current cats know good manners, they serve as wonderful role models to new pets. By observing your interaction with a resident cat that meows at a certain time each day to get fed, Sheba more quickly makes that connection. New cats also learn bad habits from a resident feline, and vice versa. If you allow Sheba to get away with wild antics, the older cat also may start pushing your buttons. Adult cats learn by watching you, too. After seeing you open a door, they learn to jump up and hang on the door latch to open it.

Cats are experts at getting their way. They are so good at training their owners that we often don't recognize we are being manipulated. Sheba easily trains you to fill the food bowl when she paw-pats you awake you at 5:30 A.M. It only takes one or two repetitions of this cause-and-effect for cats to remember what works in each situation. If rattling the wooden window blinds makes you let her out the door, she'll remember and use that ploy again and again. Therefore, pay attention to not only what Sheba does but also your own resulting behavior to get a clue about how she's training you.

There are times when our patience runs out, and owners may be tempted to react with anger. To be blunt, corporeal punishment doesn't work. Hitting, yelling, or using force not only is inhumane, it almost always makes the bad behavior worse. Dr. Landsberg explains that any strong arousal interferes with Sheba's ability to learn because that portion of the brain must deal with the emotional fallout instead. Instead of thinking, these cats react out of instinct (the fight-or-flight response) and typically either attack or hide. You'll teach a lesson you don't want Sheba to learn—to fear or dislike you.

SPEAKING FELINESE

Cat communication consists of a complicated system of vocalization, scent signals, and body postures that define and reinforce the cat's social position within the family group. While we can't "read" the odiferous messages, cats give us clear postures and vocal signals about their intentions; ignoring these warnings can get you in trouble.

Signals can be divided into those that seek to *decrease* the distance between individuals or that warn you to *increase* the distance. Cats use their ears, tail, fur, eyes, and every part of their body to "talk." To understand felinese, pay attention not only to the individual body parts, but to the entire repertoire, or you'll risk misunderstanding Sheba's message. In multiple-cat homes, understanding what your pets tell you—and what your own body language and vocal tone tells them—means the difference between a happy home and chaos. Learn the basics to translate cat language into people-speak.

CAT CALLS

Cats are one of the most vocal of the carnivore species, says Sharon L. Crowell-Davis, DVM, director of the behavioral service at the University of Georgia Veterinary Teaching Hospital. Behaviorists describe sixteen distinct feline vocal patterns that fall under four general categories: *murmur patterns,* including purrs and trills; *vowel patterns,* or meows in all their variations (cats can produce several diphthongs, too); *articulated patterns,* or chirps and chattering that express frustration; and *strained intensity patterns,* which are warnings such as hisses and growls, or shrieks of pain. Both males and females use strained intensity patterns in sexual communication. The abruptness or volume of the pain shriek may also be designed to shock or startle the attacker into loosening a grip. Experts also speculate that some cat vocalizations may be so subtle or pitched at such a frequency that only cats can hear these "silent" meows.

Cat language begins early in life. Kittens less than three weeks old vocalize a defensive spit, contented purr, and distress call (similar to an adult meow) if the baby becomes isolated, cold, or trapped. Interestingly, the call for "I'm cold" sounds much higher pitched and disappears from the repertoire once the kitten can self-regulate body temperature at about four weeks of age. Cats rarely meow at each other. They learn to direct meows at humans because we reward them with attention. Each cat learns by association that meowing prompts feeding, access to locations, and other resources provided by humans. Some cats learn to produce unique meows for each circumstance.

The purr, on the other hand, is more complex and something that we still don't completely understand. Kittens purr almost from birth, causing some experts to speculate that the infant's purr tells the mother all is well with the baby or solicits contact or care; adult cats retain this infantile trait once they grow up.

Purrs arise on both the inhale and exhale of breath, in a continuous unbroken sound. The sudden buildup and release of pressure creates the sound as the glottis alternately opens and closes, causing a sudden separation of the vocal folds. The laryngeal muscles move the glottis to generate this cycle every thirty to forty milliseconds. Purring almost always takes place in the presence of another person or cat, and another theory suggests that purring acts as a calming signal to declare to others, "I am no threat." While we usually associate purring with contentment, cats also purr when in pain or frightened, and some purr as they die. The vibrations associated with purring have been shown to help speed healing and may function as a unique self-healing benefit.

KITTY POST-IT NOTES

The ancestral cat hunted and lived alone, and like other animals that don't routinely meet face-to-face, modern cats still communicate with scent. Scent messages allow a delay of hours to days between a cat's deposit of the scent and another feline's sniffing of it, so encounters with rivals can be avoided based on scent signals. "The cat's sense of smell is a thousand times stronger than ours," says Bruce D. Elsey, DVM, owner of the All Cat Clinic in Englewood, Colorado. Because today pet cats don't live the same lifestyle as their wild cousins, feline scent communication may have modified through domestication. Evidence of this lies in the theory that cats living in groups produce colony, or group-specific odors. These group odors develop when cats groom each other, cheek-body-rub one another (called allorubbing), and sleep together, says Dr. Crowell-Davis. Skin glands located on the chin, lips, cheeks, forehead, tail, and paws produce the "nametag" scent that identifies one cat from another. Friendly cats rub their tails against each other's bodies and twine them together. Face rubbing (bunting) not only marks the target as "owned" by the kitty, it may be a subtle sign of deference with the subordinate feline approaching and bunting the more dominant pet or person.

Grooming each other (allogrooming) not only spreads communal scent, but also serves as a clue about which cat rules the roost and how your cats prefer to be petted by you. Mutual grooming targets the head and neck, and the recipient usually cooperates with head tilts and purring. Dominant cats tend to groom less dominant ones more often, and this can sometimes be a form of redirected aggression or dominance behavior.

Other kitty Post-it Notes arise from the scent glands located between the pads of the paws. Sheba deposits scent when she scratches, and this doubles as a visual marker that communicates to other felines that the property is owned. Notice where your cat prefers to scratch to figure out the best position for cat trees and other legal scratch objects you provide. Cats target scratch sites distributed along regularly used routes—the path between the front window and the food bowl—rather than at the periphery of the territory or home range. That's why Sheba ignores the post hidden away in a back room.

In addition to smells, cats detect and react to pheromones, species-specific chemicals that animals naturally produce. "Pheromones are a type of chemical communication between animals," says Marie-Laure Loubiere, DVM, a veterinarian involved in pheromone research with CEVA Santé Animale in France.

Daniel Mills, BVSc, PhD, a professor of veterinary behavioral medicine, at the University of Lincoln, United Kingdom, says scent detection is very different from pheromone communications. Odors must be analyzed in the cortex, or the "thinking" portion of the brain. "That's what we call cognition," he says. The cat learns what an individual scent means and associates, for example, the tuna odor with a memory of its taste.

Pheromones have nothing to do with learned memory. The limbic system of the brain perceives pheromone information directly, and no thinking takes place; the brain automatically processes the message which prompts the reaction. "Pheromones change the behavior without having to involve the cortex," says Dr. Mills. Kittens react to pheromones from birth, even before their eyes or ears open. Cats rely on this specialized natural pheromone communication all their lives, using the pheromones produced in skin glands and urine to react appropriately to what other kitties mean. Urine contains pheromones used in marking and territorial communication (sort of a "pee-mail" message) and also announces the sexual status of the cat who sprays. Spraying of an intact male cat helps suppress the sexual behavior of less-dominant cats that venture in that territory, while intact female cats spray to announce their breeding receptivity.

BODY TALK

Cats have a wide range of body postures used as visual signals primarily to regulate aggressive behavior. Determining the meaning of a signal or group of signals depends on context and what the rest of the body says. Rolling, for example, is a component of female sexual behavior, usually accompanied by purring, stretching, and kneading, interspersed with object-rubbing bouts. But when an immature male cat rolls in the presence of a dominant male, the behavior signals appeasement, and says, "I'm no threat, treat me nice." Neutered cats (both male and female) use rolling behavior toward humans as an appeasement gesture and sometimes as an invitation to interact or play.

Similarly, the tail can be an important indicator of a cat's mood. Kittens greet mom-cat with tail-up posture, and adult cats use tail-up directed at humans or other cats to say, "I come in friendship." One cat may signal from across the room and then approach when the other kitty returns the friendly gesture. Conversely, the tail wrapped around the body is a distance-increasing gesture that tells others to stay away.

In any situation (offensive, defensive, or relaxed), cats control space from a distance with stares. During the preliminary stages of tense encounters, they may avoid looking at each other, but eventually the dominant cats will use long-distance stares to keep other cats away from owned property (such as a litter box).

As aggression increases, more overt signs develop. An aggressive cat fluffs his fur (piloerects) and stands at full height. Ears are barometers of kitty mood. Erect, forward-facing ears indicate interest, but the more of the backs of the ears he shows, the greater his agitation and threat to attack. Lashing of the tail from side to side also indicates arousal. "Cats don't do submission," says

Dr. Pryor. They communicate fear or noncontest by crouching on the ground, flattening their ears, and withdrawing their head into the shoulders. You can gauge kitty fearfulness by the degree to which the ears flatten.

LET THE GAMES BEGIN

Play reaches its peak by age nine to sixteen weeks and declines thereafter. While adult cats tend to fall into the playful or lapsitter categories, all felines continue to play to a certain extent. Play behavior in cats can be described as locomotory, social, and object-oriented. Running, jumping, rolling, and climbing (locomotory) can be done individually or with others. Object play involves the cat targeting anything from a bug to a feather and turning it into a toy. Social play means cats interact with each other or owners and can include wrestling, biting, pouncing, play-fighting, and chase-tag games.

Because behaviors for fighting and fun are similar, you need to recognize the difference; play-fighting can escalate to aggression and require a human referee. Cats exaggerate fighting postures to indicate play, or the sequences may be jumbled. They may roll on the ground to invite play, "hop," or tiptoe sideways with fluffed fur, or bring a toy and drop it nearby. On occasion cats will race past another cat and slap him with a paw as a drive-by invitation to play tag. During wrestling games, cats use inhibited bites and retracted claws. In these instances of appropriate play, all the cats willingly participate and take turns chasing each other.

Inappropriate play results in one or more cats frightened, hurt, or overwhelmed. Mouthing aimed primarily at the back of the neck or uninhibited bites means play has gotten out of hand. You'll hear hisses or screams from the bitten cat. Vocalizations are rare during cat play, so if one or both cats get noisy or repeatedly try to get away, separate them to see if they go back for more.

FELINE POKER

Cats use a variety of dominant postures and avoidance behaviors to either bluff their way into positions of authority or to cry uncle and fold their cards without losing face. They interact in such subtle ways that it can be easy to miss these feline "conversations." Pay attention to the following body signals to understand if one cat seeks to rule the roost or to just "get along" by appeasing feline housemates. Keep in mind, though, that while Sheba may be dominant in the TV room, another cat often "rules" other locations. A dominant cat:

- Maintains eye contact and stares to control space.
- Rotates ears forward.
- Holds head high, with erect, tense, and rigid posture (standing on tiptoes).
- Fluffs fur all over her body (piloerection).
- Grasps the other cat by the nape of the neck (inhibited bite).
- "Power grooms" the other cat (aggression may follow).

Once you understand what Sheba says, it improves your relationship. Use the signals yourself—averting your eyes or turning your head away—to calm a fearful kitty. Offer your fist for the cat to sniff because some cats may react to this as though to another cat's round head that "bunts" to signal no threat. Other common feline appeasement gestures include:

- Play bowing (with front legs motionless).
- Sitting with her back to the other cat or you.
- Crouching.
- Repeated rolling.
- Yawning.
- Nose touching.

Approaching with tail up.

THE PHYSICAL CAT

Feline behavior and health directly impact each other. A behavior change commonly indicates a health problem, but cats may continue the misbehavior (for example, miss the litter box) long after the physical problem (constipation) has resolved. Cats hide discomfort extremely well, but may bite or claw in response to petting that inadvertently hurts them.

FELINE FORM AND FUNCTION

All felines remain amazingly similar in size, function, and personality, but many can be categorized into two very broad body and behavior types that are based on how they evolved. The oldest breeds arose spontaneously as a result of their environment, and major differences are coat length and body conformation. The *warm weather* body type (Oriental), such as the Siamese, arose in the temperate climates of Asia and is characterized by lithe, muscular cats with long, lean legs, whiplike tails, large ears, slanting eyes, a longish muzzle, and a thin single coat. These cats tend to be vocal, active, swing-from-the-drapes type of cats. The *cold weather* body type (cobby), typified by the Persian, appeared in the colder climates of Europe. They have short, square, compact bodies with a broad head, small ears, short muzzle, round eyes, and a thick, weather-resistant double coat. These cats often are sedate, quiet lap-snugglers.

Feline design ideally suits the cats' ultimate purpose as predators of small game, whether she weighs four to six pounds (as in the Singapura) or is a heavyweight like the twenty-plus pound Maine Coon. Cats hunt by stalk-and-pounce, using bursts of energy to explode upon unsuspecting prey. They use paws like hands and paw-pat everything before trusting it in their mouths.

Adult cats kill quickly and efficiently with a bite to the back of the neck that severs the spinal cord. For pet cats, of course, the "victim" is usually a catnip mouse and stuffed feather toy. Give Sheba a legal outlet for her energy by providing regular exercise to keep her muscles toned, her body healthy, and her mind active.

CAT SENSES EXPLAINED

Feline senses are much more acute than our own, and cats rely on eyesight much more than dogs do. They expertly detect movement from peripheral vision, need only one-sixth the amount of light that people do, and use twice as much of the available light, enabling them to function in low-light conditions. If human eyes were proportionally the same size as the cats,' our eyes would be eight inches across. When cats lose their vision due to cataracts, glaucoma, or age, oftentimes they develop temporary behavior problems until they can adjust.

Scent communication between cats serves to identify family from stranger and aids with social interactions. Besides their noses, the vomeronasal organ (located between the soft palate and nasal passages) reacts to pheromones, specialized chemicals that communicate directly with the cat's brain. Because cats rely so much on scent to determine food safety and stimulate appetite, a stuffy nose has dire health consequences.

More than scent or sight, cats rely on their ears and hear sounds in a 10.5 octave range, a wider span of frequencies than almost any other mammal. This range allows her to detect extremely high frequencies and even ultrasonic squeals of mice. Since cats need this sense above all others, age, which increases the risk of deafness, can severely interfere with communication between cats or with their owners.

The feline sense of touch is most sensitive in the area surrounding the muzzle and on the paw pads. Each hair on kitty's body originates deep in the skin, next to a nerve receptor sensitive to vibration, touch, heat, cold, and/or pain. Just brushing the tips of the whiskers, for instance, telegraphs information to Sheba about air movement, barometric pressure, petting, or punishment. Overstimulation, such as from excessive petting, can prompt aggression in some cats.

Specific tastes vary between cats. Though they often share similar tastes as people, they don't detect the same sugar and sweet flavors; instead, they are most attracted to meaty tastes. Strong-smelling treats can be a great training tool for food-motivated cats. That's one reason cats react so favorably to the pungent aroma of fishy canned foods.

KITTENS, JUVENILES, ADULTS, AND OLD FOGIES

As kittens grow up and mature, their behavior evolves during each life stage. From five to seven weeks of age, the drive to copy mom-cat becomes consuming. Babies learn to eat solid food, use the litter box, and play "nice" with peers. While adult cats may not care for them and avoid contact with furry infants, most recognize them as babies and rarely harm the youngsters.

Juvenile delinquent behavior develops during months three to six and can be aggravating for even the most laid-back adults. More confrontations between adults and delinquent kittens take place either because the adults want to teach manners or the kittens haven't a clue and continue brainless behavior. While some adult cats of either gender (intact or neutered) take these teenage kittens under their paws and have great patience, more often than not the older feline avoids the miscreant or whips her furry tail into polite behavior.

According to Bonnie Beaver, DVM, a professor of behavior at Texas A&M University, kittens are very social until they reach six to ten months of age, then they experience a dramatic change in personality. Interactive play becomes rougher and tends to end with aggression. Over time the length of play bouts decreases, while aggression increases and becomes more intense. In a feral setting, this serves to disperse the littermates, but in a household, owners bear the brunt of rough interaction. The personality can't be changed back, but you can redirect aggressive play toward legal toys.

Conventional wisdom suggests cats reach adulthood by twelve months of age. However, bodies and coats continue to develop up to twenty-four months in certain breeds. Social maturity takes place between two and a half and four years of age, at which time these maturing cats may challenge older ones for a higher ranking in the social hierarchy. Cats age quite gracefully and may not show age-related changes until they reach eight to ten years or older. Sensory or mobility challenges and other health issues often result in crotchety older cats' behavior changes.

ACTING ROMANTIC

For all cats, behavior is inseparable from sexuality. Kittens practice mounting, neck biting, clasping, and thrusting during play, and adolescents continue to experiment as they mature. Male kittens often mount a variety of objects including pillows, blankets, other cats, or even your arm. Mounting behavior between adult spayed or neutered cats often is a dominance display; masturbation can be a way for a stressed kitty to calm himself down.

Oriental-type cats, such as Siamese, mature quite early, with girls sometimes able to become pregnant as early as four months of age. Females go in and out of season every twenty-one days, from about February through October, and theoretically could have up to three litters a year. Males mate as early as six to nine months. Hormone-related behaviors include female rolling, crying, and screaming during heat, spraying urine in marking behavior, roaming to find willing mates, and dominance displays that can evolve into aggression and fights.

Spaying removes the ovaries and uterus of female cats, while castration removes the testes of male cats. Both surgeries are referred to as neutering and eliminate the chance of accidental babies. When performed prior to sexual maturity, neutering prevents or reduces many hormone-related behavior problems.

Today, animal welfare societies often perform the surgery once pets reach two pounds, during kittenhood.

THE CAT CLOWDER

Cat society defines how cats deal with each other. No longer thought of as antisocial loners, today we know felines relate and interact with each other in dynamic and very fluid hierarchies. When enough food and other resources are present, adult females associate in lineages, which are the building blocks of cat society. Similar to lions, domestic kitties in colony settings may suckle each other's babies, sever umbilical cords, move kittens to new locations, and otherwise communally raise the infants.

Large cat colonies may have several such lineages. Each usually consists of related adult females and successive generations of their offspring. Females relate within their lineage and, to a lesser extent, outside of it. These tend to be friendly, well-integrated groups of cats, with the eldest female holding the highest status. Juveniles and kittens automatically become socially integrated to their birth lineage, and these ties usually last a lifetime if the cats remain in each other's company. Ties of adult females to their sons and daughters are stronger than to nephews and nieces.

Most observation of free-living cats suggests that adult males rarely are affiliated with any one lineage, usually only temporarily during mating. However, cats in feral situations often choose to sit together and establish feline friendships; each individual favors company of some over others. The age, sex, social status, and blood ties of the individuals involved govern these associations.

Toms also are said not to be involved in kitten rearing, but Dr. Crowell-Davis says that's not always true. Intact toms have been seen helping queens defend kittens from invading toms, groom the babies, share food with juveniles, and curl up around abandoned kittens. Males also sometimes disrupt intense wrestling play between juveniles, using a forelimb to separate them without using aggression against either.

Felines in any given family group—composed mostly of females with some immature males and the occasional tom— offer a united front and show hostility toward strange cats that attempt to join the society. Nongroup members are not allowed to casually approach and enter the group. If the unknown cat or kitten persists, they may eventually be integrated into the group, but only over time and many interactions. Therefore, introducing a new cat into a resident cat's territory almost always proves challenging for owners. Introducing very young cats of the opposite sex into a resident adult's social group works best, as it offers the fewest social challenges to the dominant feline.

The feline social structure depends on a hierarchy of dominant and subordinate individuals. Rank of the individual cat decides which one gets the preferred access to valued resources: resting spots, food pans, water, toys, your attention, and so on.

Cats don't follow a clear linear hierarchy, though. There is usually an obvious top-cat and one or two bottom cats (called pariahs), but no number two, three, or four cats ranking below the dominant feline. Instead, most cats share an equal "middle space." This more fluid social standing requires a decision about who eats first, crosses a path first, gets the best sleeping spot time after time, on a case-by-case basis, says Dr. Beaver. Sometimes the calico wins one day while the tabby gets her choice another time.

This timeshare mentality allows every cat (even middle management) to feel like a king. Timeshare means the cats don't need to fight over property. It may appear that one cat owns the second floor of your home while another cat owns the family room. This makes perfect sense if you consider that people also bow to the whims of a boss while at work, but call the shots in our own homes.

Subordinate cats signal deference by looking away, lowering their ears slightly, turning their head away, and leaning back when they encounter a dominant cat. Often close encounters are simply avoided by giving way spatially—the subordinate cat gets off the path, jumps off the chair, or otherwise acknowledges the other cat's right. Cat #1 may own the second floor, but when she's not around, Cat #2 lounges there with impunity—timeshares the area because the first cat isn't using it. When the owner returns, the subordinate cat pretends not to care, looks the other way (so he doesn't have his nose rubbed in it!), and relinquishes the territory when Cat #1 returns.

Dominant cats show their status with a direct stare, stiffening of the limbs, holding their ears erect while turning them sideways, and elevating the base of the tail while the rest of it droops. The display usually prompts the subordinate cat to defer.

Fights occur most often during introductions of new cats into an existing feline society, or when a change in social status due to infirmity or maturing adolescent cats takes place. Ownership of property rates very highly among cats. When rare, valued resources must be shared, the potential for arguments escalates. It's important for owners to acknowledge the dominant status of the highest-ranking cat (by feeding first), while providing enough resources for lower-ranking cats (multiple litter boxes and feeding stations).

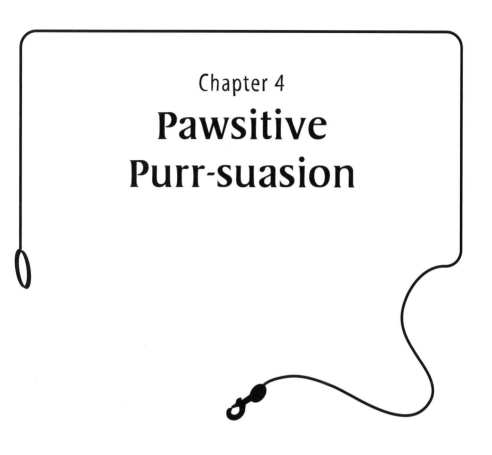

Chapter 4
Pawsitive
Purr-suasion

Owners have long turned to dog trainers to teach Rex better manners, but until relatively recently, cats have gotten shortchanged. In recent years this way of thinking has changed, and savvy cat owners now recognize that Sheba can also be trained. Professional trainers and animal behaviorists toss around complicated terms and concepts. While the rest of this book speaks to these issues in plain English, an overview of the terms and science of training and behavior modification will help you to better understand the concept behind treatment recommendations.

Classical conditioning, introduced by Pavlov and his bell-ringing, dog-drooling experiments, is one tool. He showed that an unconditioned trigger (such as food) prompts an unconditioned or unlearned response (salivation). More importantly, Pavlov showed that neural stimuli, such as a bell, once associated with the uncontrolled stimuli (food) prompts a conditioned reflex. This technique teaches dogs and cats to learn, or become conditioned to, a sound, smell, or behavior associated with a particular response.

Operant conditioning, introduced by B. F. Skinner's box experiments, prompted rats to learn how to press a lever to get food pellets. Operant conditioning deals with relationships between stimuli, responses, and consequences. The pet learns that what he does (sit on command) is critical to what happens next (get a food reward).

"Behavior modification seeks to get the desirable versus punish the undesirable," says Dr. Lansberg. You do that through the use of various types of reinforcement and *punishment.* Punishment can either be "positive" or "negative," with varying results.

- Positive punishment: The word "positive" means you *add* something the pet doesn't like to get the desired results; it usually causes some degree of fear in the pet. For example, the electric collar adds a shock to prevent Rex from leaving the yard, while hitting Sheba makes her stop climbing the drapes. Positive punishment that causes pain or fear has little to no place in modern training.

- Negative punishment: The word "negative" means you *remove* something that the pet likes, so a "good thing" goes away when the pet performs the undesirable behavior. For example, if the puppy or kitten bites during play, the game stops. Negative punishment can be used humanely and effectively.

Reinforcement refers to some sort of incentive that prompts the pet to want to perform a particular behavior. Different dogs and cats respond better to various reinforcers, but a special treat or toy—whatever floats the pet's boat—works best, particularly if you reserve it only for training. For example, the dog only gets his favorite liver treat during training sessions.

- Positive reinforcement means the desired behavior results in *adding* something pleasant or positive. For example, a treat lures the dog to sit or the cat to wave. To be effective, positive reinforcement must be contingent upon the desired behavior taking place, must be associated with the behavior, and must be used consistently.

- Negative reinforcement means the desired behavior results in the *removal* of something unpleasant or negative. For example, a frightened dog barks at the mailman; the mailman's departure negatively reinforces the dog—thus, he'll bark in the future because it worked to make the scary thing go away. Negative reinforcement often builds on the pet's avoidance or escape response. It may take only one or two experiences for Sheba or Rex to learn this response.

- Intermittent reinforcement means the positive treat or negative (the mailman's departure) doesn't happen every time, only intermittently. This teaches the pet that since it happens sometimes, it's worth a try. Intermittent reinforcement increases the likelihood of repetition of the good or bad behavior.

TRAINING STYLES

The old-style coercion methods popularized after World War II that often relied on positive punishment are less popular today. *Physical training* uses pushing or pulling the dog into position with your hands on his rump to force a sit, or jerking on a slip or choke collar to prompt him to follow. Electronic collars that deliver a remote-controlled, low-impulse shock (positive punishment) to correct poor behavior are even more controversial. With this method, dogs learn the meaning of the physical prompt so well that they sometimes ignore verbal communication. Such dogs often work well while under leash or E-collar control or when they're near you, where they can be moved into the proper position. Too often, though, training goes out the window if the collar or leash isn't used.

Punishment training teaches pets to dislike training and the owner. Yes, pets often obey out of fear of reprisals, but the method also teaches *avoidance* behaviors. Yelling or hitting the dog for running away from you when you call him teaches him to avoid coming—he knows he's going to get it! Slapping or shaming the kitten for going potty in the house teaches him either to hide it better or to poop only when you aren't around. Punishment training in shy and aggressive pets makes these behaviors worse.

These techniques rely on dominating the pet. The old style of training said you should correct a pet for showing aggression. But today behaviorists understand that aggression is caused by stress and anxiety, and punishing the cat or dog increases the stress and anxiety rather than diminishes it. Punishment causes aggression to escalate.

A NEW WAY TO TRAIN

In the 1970s, applied animal behavior became popular, with behaviorists, pet therapists, and behavior consultants offering advice on a variety of pet issues. Newer training methods used scientific methods that encouraged dogs and cats to think and want to perform a task, rather than being forced or punished into compliance.

"Modern trainers have less concern about the whole 'alpha' thing," says Pat Miller, a certified pet dog trainer and past president of the Association of Pet Dog Trainers. "We focus more on deference and 'say please' type programs that encourage the dog to offer behaviors in order to get all good things in life." The leader of the social group controls the good stuff, such as food and toys. Therefore, Miller explains that owners automatically give themselves a high-ranking status without having to intimidate or use force in any way.

"A dog's brain is too precious to waste," says Dr. Dunbar. He promotes a training philosophy that operates from the dog's point of view, making the experience fun for both the owner and pet. In 1994, Dr. Dunbar founded the Association of Pet Dog Trainers (see Appendixes), which encourages the use of positive reinforcement training methods. Modern training improves communication between you and your pet, and teaches him *to want to comply.*

Reward training means you allow your pet to discover the behavior you want him to do and then reward it. He may perform many bad behaviors (jumping up, barking, clawing the furniture) until finally he sits and is rewarded. The pet figures out the desired behavior from your body language, verbal praise, and the treat; he learns he only gets the reward when he does what you want. The more wrong behaviors he performs, the more he learns what *won't* work. This technique trains without giving commands or physical direction—no touching allowed—and works especially well with cats who dislike being moved into position.

One of the most popular modern training methods employs

THE SNIFFING REWARD

Not all dogs respond to treats. "Nonfood-motivated dogs force you to get more creative!" says Deborah Jones, dog trainer and assistant professor of psychology at Kent State University's, Stark Campus. For some dogs, sniffing proves the best incentive. Simply create something the dog wants to sniff and then control access to the object.

"I made a toy we call the 'stinky squirrel,' " she explains. The fleece jackpot toy contains a pouch for treats that she fills with freeze-dried salmon chunks and Cheerios. "The salmon stinks to high heaven, so I must keep the toy double-wrapped in plastic bags," she says. "When the dog gives a desirable behavior or response, I click and offer an opportunity to sniff the squirrel for a few seconds." The dog also gets a Cheerio (now salmon-flavored) to reinforce the behavior, which also helps make the dog more food-oriented.

clickers (as a secondary reinforcer) to communicate with the pet. The technique teaches pets to recognize the click as a signal you wanted him to do *that* (click!) behavior, such as fetch a ball or meow. A food reward linked to the click reinforces the message. This painless way to train puts no pressure on you or the pet, because you've not told him to do anything, so he's never wrong. He's only right, though, when he figures out the correct behavior. Clicker training encourages dogs and cats to think and figure out what pleases you to turn their owners into a treat machine.

Lure/reward training is the fastest, easiest, most effective, and enjoyable training technique of all. The basic sequence is request, response, reward. This training method teaches cats and dogs not only to respond to commands, but to listen and react to humans, and for humans to watch and react to their pet. It enhances communication as you teach pets your language while you learn their language.

EMOTIONAL HEALING

Various techniques help stifle arguments, calm hurt feelings, and build peace between pets. These tools also can positively impact your pets' emotions to help them feel better.

TTOUCH
Specialized massage, called TTouch, was developed by Linda Tellington-Jones and works particularly well to relieve dog and cat behavior problems, especially aggression and fearfulness. Tests show that TTouch changes the electrical activity in pets' brains. This helps them relax so they're open to learning new ways of coping, rather than just reacting out of fear. TTouch uses very specific circular stroke patterns on the surface of the skin all over the pet's body, with extra attention paid to the ears. The basic circle technique is called the Clouded Leopard TTouch because

the strokes follow the circle shape of leopard spots. For large dogs, make the circles with the side of your thumb, and use one or two fingers for smaller dogs and cats. Push the skin in a clockwise direction by "drawing" a complete circle with your thumb or fingers. Completing the circle changes the brain waves. After completing each circle, slide your hand on the pet's body an inch or two, and form another circle. *Never lose contact with the body.* Continue making "chains" of circles all over, as long as the dog or cat allows. A ten-to twenty-minute session is a good target. Let your pet be your guide, whether he wants a light touch or stronger pressure.

BACH FLOWERS

Dogs and cats don't have deadlines to meet or a mortgage to pay, but they suffer stress just the same—anything from meeting the new baby, hearing fireworks, or experiencing a change in your work schedule can leave tails in a twist. You can't always explain to them that there's nothing to fear, and when pets get emotional they can't learn. Behavior modification and training methods won't work until the pet gets his feelings under control.

Flower essence therapy can also help with behavior modification. These herbal remedies are made from plants, trees, and bushes. The essences are said to carry the imprint of the plant's energy, so the patient's body somehow "recognizes" this image, which wakes up the system so it can heal itself. In a percentage of cases, flower essence therapies work extraordinarily well. The most familiar products are Bach Flowers, composed of thirty-eight individual remedies. Each benefits a different emotional state and is sometimes used in combination with others for greater effect. Rescue Remedy, for instance, is a premixed combination of the essences Impatiens, Star of Bethlehem, Cherry Plum, Rock Rose, and Clematis, recommended for any kind of stress. Others recommended elsewhere in this book include Gentian for general depression, Gorse for severe depression, and Star of Bethlehem for grief.

Most health food stores carry Bach Flower remedies. They're safe to use alongside other medical treatments; and choosing the "wrong" essence won't cause harm. Once you've chosen your flower essences, here's how to put them to work.

- Maintain the original undiluted bottle as your stock bottle. It should last a very long time.

- Place two drops of the undiluted remedy in a one-ounce glass dropper bottle. Fill the bottle three-quarters full with spring water (don't use tap water or distilled water—they go stale too quickly). Shake one hundred times. Refrigerate the mixture, which lasts up to two weeks.

- Give the pet four drops, four times a day, from the treatment bottle until the behavior changes. This takes a few days to two weeks. Administer either straight from the treatment bottle dropper into the pet's mouth or on his nose (if this doesn't stress him out too much), add to yogurt and give as a treat, or mix several drops into the drinking water for all the pets to sip. Don't touch the dropper to the pet or that could contaminate the bottle.

PHEROMONE THERAPY

Pheromones are chemicals that communicate directly with the brain via the nose on an almost instinctive level They can be used to "talk" to your dog or cat in order to put them in a better state of mind to accept learning and training. Dr. Patrick Pageat identified D.A.P. (dog-appeasing pheromone), a chemical that mother dogs secrete from a sebaceous gland in the middle of the abdomen between the mammary glands, three to four days after giving birth. "This pheromone decreases the canine stress reaction in pups but also in adult dogs," says Dr. Pageat. He created an analogue of the pheromone, available as a plug-in product for indoors or as a spray. The D.A.P. plug-in lasts about four weeks and covers a 500 to 650 square foot area. It takes twenty-four to forty-eight hours for the ideal heating rate to spill the pheromone into the air and may take up to two weeks to see a difference in behavior. "It can be used as a tag to label an area safe," says Dr. Pageat. "It provides a reassuring effect for that location."

D.A.P. is particularly helpful for calming new pups and acts like "mom in a bottle" to make them feel at home. It also calms fears of any age dog. You can use the spray by treating a cloth or the dog's bed and placing it inside the car fifteen minutes before travel, or by scenting a bandana for the dog to wear. Your dog will still need behavior modification training, but this pheromone helps reduce his fear so he learns more easily and quickly.

Dr. Pageat also created Feliway, an analogue of the F3 fraction of the feline cheek pheromone, which cats use to identify and mark their physical environment. Basically, the substance tells the kitty brain, "Your environment is familiar and safe, so chill, calm down, everything's cool." Like D.A.P., Feliway comes as a plug-in product for indoors or in spray form, and is available at most pet product stores. You can use the spray by treating a cloth or bed and placing it inside the cat carrier during travel or use the plug-in to affect all the cats in a house during introductions. The plug-in lasts for about four weeks and works well in enclosed rooms (500 to 650 square feet). It is particularly helpful for dealing with stress-related marking behaviors such as scratching and urine spraying, and eases the fear of other felines or a new environment. Feliway spray helps redirect scratching and works best when combined with training to use a legal scratch object. It takes twenty-four to forty-eight hours for the plug-in to reach ideal heating rate to spill the pheromone into the air, and about one to two weeks before you'll see a difference in behavior (see pet product stores or www. felineway.com).

TEACHING THE BASICS

Ideally, every puppy and kitten learns the rules of the house, just as every child learns basic manners. Before anything else, agree with the rest of your family what rules apply. If pets know one human allows sofa digging but not the other, they capitalize on that information.

It's helpful for multiple pets to not only know their individual name but also respond to a group name, such as "dogs" or "kitties." Teach all the critters to pay attention by saying the word command, then treat every pet that looks at you. Make a huge deal over praising and giving special treats only to those pets that respond and come when called indoors, for example. Before long, all of the critters will compete with each other to see who gets the treat first—they won't want to be left out. This also saves time so you can call all the dogs inside at once, rather than reciting each name.

One of the keys to training involves breaking behaviors down into manageable components and working backward to train one thing at a time until you've "chained" all the components together. Trying too much all at once frustrates you and the pet. Pets chain their own behaviors naturally, repeating the same routines each day on the same schedule. Sheba wakes you at 6:30 A.M., follows you to the bathroom, leaps onto the sink, sits, then sips water from the faucet while you shower. Pay attention to the natural behaviors the cat or dog already performs, pick the ones you like, and reward for doing them—and voila! You've trick-trained Sheba to sit on command, for example. It helps in multipet homes to have one command (sit or down) that your cats or dogs will reliably perform.

Many very short training sessions (even five to fifteen seconds) work better than fewer marathon sessions that wear you both out. Concentrate on one behavior in each session to keep from confusing your pet. Repetition is very helpful and important in first trainings. Both you and your pets need the incentive and inspiration of ending with success, so if he doesn't "get it," build his confidence by asking for a behavior or trick he already knows—and reward him lavishly to end the session.

Give up on the idea of democracy or equality within your pet pack. Dogs and cats don't expect life to be fair all the time, and they need to learn how to cope with disappointments without throwing tantrums and being pushy or rude to get their way. Never reward rude behavior or you'll create a furry monster that rules the household. Instead, teach your dogs and cats that the only way they get access to treats, toys, and attention is with polite, patient behavior. You'll all enjoy each other more.

TEACHING "SIT"

Train one pet at a time. Situate other dogs or cats to watch from behind a baby gate so they get a preview and also learn by observation. Make the game unbelievably fun with a high-value reward for the first pet you work with so the others can't wait until it's their turn to train.

1. Say "sit."

2. Lure the cat or dog to sit, using his preferred reinforcer (treat, feather, stinky squirrel). Lift the treat upward in front of his nose so he must lift his head up to watch. His nose follows the treat; to keep his balance, his butt must hit the ground.

3. As soon as he sits, reward with the treat or toy.

4. Repeat steps 1 to 3, many times a day, every day. Within a short time, your pet will figure out he gets the treat even quicker if he simply plants his tail as soon as you say "sit." You won't have to lure any longer.

5. Once Rex and Sheba understand and know how to "sit" on command, it becomes the ticket to good things. To go outside, get fed, or receive attention, they must first "pay" with a sit.

GO TO YOUR ROOM!

Dogs and cats often need to be safely confined as part of re-learning bathroom protocol, being transported for veterinary treatment, or

TECHNIQUES TO AVOID

Throughout the years, a number of techniques have been recommended to deal with bad pet behaviors. Karen Overall, VMD, Ph.D., a behaviorist and researcher at the University of Pennsylvania, says many old-fashioned techniques are either ineffective or do more harm than good.

- The chin slap is not a species-appropriate communication. Dogs won't have a clue what this means, so it has no effect and may prompt the dog to bite back.

- The scruff shake may parallel the cognitive damage that results in shaken baby syndrome and results in an increased activity level in the pet and an inability to pay attention. In other words, it makes training more difficult.

- Chaining or tying dogs makes them more reactive. A dog that can't take "flight" and escape can only respond with fighting.

- A review of electronic training collars indicated that all the dogs took longer to train and that the training collars changed their play behavior.

- The "alpha roll," popularized as a way to establish dominance by acting like a wolf, makes fearful dogs more fearful and escalates aggression in aggressive dogs. Dominant wolves do *not* force others onto their backs; rather, subordinate wolves willingly offer the behavior in concert with a repertoire of other calming signals. Bottom line—dogs are not wolves.

- Hanging a dog (or cat) by a choke chain or "helicoptering" him by spinning him around by the leash from the throat causes brain damage and emotional changes, such as obsessive-compulsive disorders.

preventing destructive behavior that can result from boredom or panic attacks. Upset pets can injure themselves when they pull the drapes off walls, chew the legs off furniture, or break windows to escape.

To protect the pets from themselves and your house from destruction, confine the worst offenders in a small room. One bad apple often can cause everyone to indulge in the bad behavior, so separating the problem child from the rest helps keep everyone in check. Other times, you may wish to give a picked-on pet a safe place where the others can't reach him. It may not bother some pets to spend time alone, but others are more upset by being confined, so introduce the concept gradually. Pets should view necessary confinement as a happy and safe place, not as a punishment. Train one or two at a time (if they get along), but allow the others to watch so they'll want in on the fun.

 Play a game and have your pets run in and out of the area three to five times in a row to snarf up treats tossed inside. Do this every evening for several days, without shutting the door.

 Shut the door for one second once they enter without hesitation. Open it before they finish eating so they know the door always opens and won't trap them inside.

 After several sessions, swap the treat with a puzzle toy stuffed with peanut butter, cream cheese, or other tasty treats. Shut the door while they snack. Pets should only get this bonanza treat when the door is shut.

 After a week or so, leave Rex or Sheba for longer periods of time with puzzle treats. Once they really enjoy the game, walk away for thirty seconds. Come back before they finish so you can open the door and take the toy away. This teaches them that they *only* get the toy or treat when you aren't there, and the door shuts.

 Continue to extend time alone from thirty seconds, to a minute, and so on. Once you reach five minutes, you can jump to thirty minutes pretty easily. From there, extending time to an hour and then two hours goes pretty quickly. Use the same area or different ones for your various dogs and cats, whatever works best. If pets are happier confined together, do so—just provide enough treats and toys for everyone so there's no squabbling. *Don't* confine food-aggressive dogs together.

CRATE EXPECTATIONS

All cats and dogs need to travel at some point, if only to and from the veterinarian; crate training simplifies the process. There's nothing more dangerous than a loose dog or cat in the car—unless it's more than one! They can get under your brake pedal, distract you, and, in the worst situation, become furry projectiles if you have an accident. Crates can also be used to retrain and/or segregate cats or dogs if they aggress toward each other, or to provide safe havens for scared pets.

Crates come in different sizes. Up to two small adult pets or three kittens or pups that get along may be able to share facilities. Larger pets and those with prickly personalities do best with individual accommodations. You can find soft-sided zipper bags, hard carriers, and suitcase-style travelers with rollers. Cat and dog show enthusiasts stack carriers on wheeled carts and tow multiple pets from cars to the show hall and back again.

Train your pets to ride happily in a crate or carrier by making it appealing. Cats are especially reluctant to accept change, so go slowly and begin training at least four to six weeks before you must move them. You can train multiple pets at a time as long as you have enough crates to go around—otherwise, teach the lessons one on one. Once one claims the first carrier, the rest may become anxious to get in on the fun.

FOR CATS:

- Rub the inside of the carrier with catnip, or toss in a catnip toy while leaving the door open, to encourage feline exploration.

- Spray a bit of Feliway on a blanket or towel, and leave it inside the carrier for a kitty bed.

- Toss in a Ping-Pong ball to create a kitty playground. Play games with your cat in the crate every evening for a week, without shutting the door.

FOR DOGS:

- Place a T-shirt or pair of socks you've worn but not washed inside the crate; Rex then associates the area with your comforting scent.

You can also spray the pheromone product D.A.P. on a cloth to reduce any fearfulness.

 Leave a rawhide chew toy inside the carrier while leaving the door open, to tempt dogs to explore. When Rex enjoys games of chase and fetch, toss his tennis ball inside and praise him when he retrieves it. Play games in and around the open crate for a week.

FOR BOTH:

 Make the crate a part of the furniture, rather than a scary and strange object that only appears to herald a vet visit. Take the door off or unzipper the opening, then set the carrier on the floor in the living room.

 Turn the crate into a treat dispenser, by leaving tasty treats inside for the cat or dog to find.

 After Sheba or Rex goes into the crate without hesitation, shut the door for one second, then open as soon as the pet finishes eating the treat. That tells her the door always opens and won't trap her inside.

 After several sessions, trade the treat for a puzzle toy stuffed with tuna, cream cheese, liver, or other irresistible treats. Shut the door while the pets snack. Make sure they only get this special bonanza treat when they are in the carrier with the door shut.

 When Sheba and Rex begin to enjoy the treat and crate sessions, increase the time they spend inside. Carry the crate around the house before opening the door for her to come out.

 Try stuffing a Kong or kitty toy with goodies and tie it inside the crate, then close the door with the pet *outside*. Wait until the dog or cat begs to get in, then open the door. The pet must choose either to chew the treat inside the crate, or not at all. Most dogs and cats quickly learn that the crate is fun.

 Carry the crated cat or dog into the car and take short rides before returning home and letting her out. Each pet will have a different learning curve—some do better if they see each other, while others remain calmer if a cover shields the view.

PART TWO

THE MULTIDOG HOUSEHOLD
Common Problems and Practical

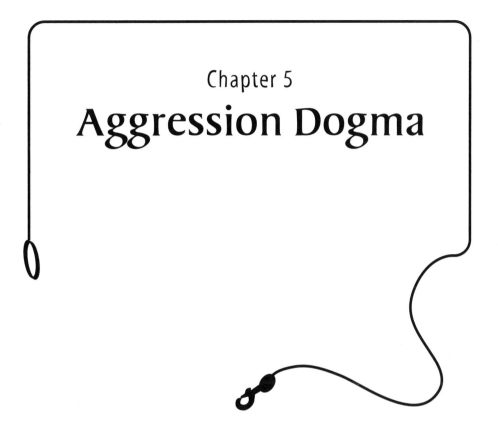

Chapter 5
Aggression Dogma

S narling, growling, or—heaven forbid!—biting canines are serious threats to owners, other pets, and any hope for a happy pack. We want dogs to love us, and this dangerous behavior makes it hard for us to love them back. Behaviorists characterize many kinds of aggression; some types may be normal for your dog's circumstances. Mother dogs instinctively protect puppies, shepherds attack predators that threaten their herd, and puppies naturally indulge in play aggression.

Your dogs aren't evil creatures and you are not a bad owner because you must deal with these problems. You aren't alone. Andrew U. Luescher, DVM, Ph.D., an associate professor of animal behavior at Purdue University, says forty percent or more of dogs have growled at owners at one time or another, and more than twenty percent of dogs have growled or snapped over food or objects. More than fifteen percent of dogs have bitten.

Certain behaviors just aren't acceptable, though, and even if your dog has not yet bitten anyone, you must deal with the situation. The P.E.T. test will help you to recognize the different types of aggression in order to safely deal with it.

Poor socialization increases the potential for all kinds of aggression later on in life. Shy puppies and dogs that never played with other dogs typically act fine until a first fight, which often arises out of fear or from being accidentally hurt. Thereafter, shy dogs inflict hard, dangerous bites because they never learned how to hold back.

People may not recognize warning signs or situations that prompt dogs to act badly. Other times, dogs bring aggression upon themselves by acting inappropriately around other pack members. A "gang mentality" can potentially develop in groups of otherwise well-behaved dogs when high arousal of one or more spreads throughout the entire pack. Most aggression has a stress or anxiety component, which increases during pet introductions and in multiple-dog households where dynamics often shift with age, health status, or living arrangements. To avoid or diffuse aggression, owners must understand what triggers the behavior, recognize warning signs, and know what constitutes an appropriate response.

Some owners accidentally teach and reward bad behavior. Talking softly to a dog that is growling out of fear conditions the growling behavior to continue. When a growl prompts you to get off or stay away from the sofa, Rex learns he can control the property. He may generalize that lesson and use growls to control other interactions, too. Dogs threatened or punished for aggressive displays learn to associate pain and/or fear with the trigger and become even more aggressive each time the situation recurs. Common situations when your dog may react with aggression include:

- When he is approached or disturbed while resting.

- When he is protecting resources (food, toys, family members).

- When he is physically and/or verbally disciplined.

- When he is stared at or forced into prolonged eye contact.

- When he experiences unwelcome handling (being lifted, patted, hugged).

- When he is restrained or otherwise forced into an unwelcome position.

- When people try to leave the room or family members enter the house.

- When he is physically forced into a subordinate posture onto his back by a human (alpha roll).

GROWLY DOGS

Canine (and human) aggression occurs most commonly in "middle management" from the members of the social group who have the ear of the CEO. These dogs position themselves as "second-in-command" to the human (or canine) pack leader. Keeping dogs from assuming this status helps eliminate group tension. Growls are warnings, and dogs often growl due to a lack of confidence or because they're upset. I much prefer a growled warning to back off to getting bit by a silent dog, but growly dogs that haven't progressed to biting can learn more acceptable ways to respond to their world.

- Use a treat or toy to lure Rex on and off the sofa. Give him lots of praise and rewards each time he follows direction.

- Shake the sofa until he gets off, if he ignores an "Off" command and growls. Say "Earthquake!" and don't give him a treat.

- Praise him and then instruct him to get onto the sofa again.

- Sit on the sofa, show the treat or toy, and invite Rex to snuggle with you. If he growls, say, "Shush," and praise with rewards if he stops growling.

 If he doesn't shush, "Earthquake" until he gets off. Repeat the invitation to snuggle and reward when he doesn't growl.

Dogs thinking about when the next treat appears usually forget to growl. These drills also build confidence so he's less likely to be worried and feel the need to growl. Every time you repeat the drills, the dog gets a food reward to cement the lesson.

MUZZLING PROBLEMS

Untrustworthy dogs with a history of biting should be prevented from future altercations by wearing a muzzle. Some dogs calm down once they know teeth can't be used, but they'll also lighten up if you relax. Being afraid makes your body pump out cortisol, a kind of steroid that tells the dog you are in a subordinate position. By having the dog wear a muzzle, you relax and feel less worried, which helps Rex relax, too.

"Put treats inside the basket muzzle so the dog goes into it after the treat, willingly," advises Dr. Pryor. For example, smear the inside of the muzzle with Cheez Whiz or peanut butter. Doing this twice a day will turn the exercise into a game; then, when Rex needs to wear a muzzle, such as for a vet visit, he can arrive with it already in place.

FIGHTS, BITES, AND ASSESSING DANGER

All dogs fight, just as all people sometimes get upset and argue, but that doesn't mean dangerous bites always result. Most dogs know how to fight without hurting each other, and it's important to figure out how well your dogs have learned this lesson.

Ultimately the issue is not whether dogs fight, but whether a dog causes damage to another dog during the fight. Canine jaws easily tear flesh and break bones. Dogs also know exactly how close they can come without making contact—snapping in the air acts as a warning when he could just as easily clamp down on the target. Learning to master the power of their jaws—bite inhibition—is key to dogs resolving differences without hurting each other.

To determine how good your dog's bite inhibition is, figure out the bite-to-fight ratio: how often do dogs fight, and how many fights need vet care? The more fights a dog has had with the least damage, the less the likelihood will be that he'll hurt another dog in the future. When noisy, furious squabbles have never required a vet visit, you're probably pretty safe letting the dogs work it out themselves. But lots of injury from a single incident means that at least one of the dogs has very poor bite inhibition—and has an extremely poor prognosis.

The success and safety of social interactions depend on the level of bite inhibitions. If dog-on-dog fighting has resulted in separate incidents requiring veterinary care, or the wounded dog must stay overnight at the clinic, then separate the two dogs for their own safety. It is next to impossible to teach dog-dog bite inhibition to adult dogs, so you may need to permanently segregate the fighting dogs to different parts of the house. Or, if that's not possible, you may need to find a new home for one. Although time-consuming, it is possible to safely teach dog-human bite inhibition to an adult dog.

PULLING PUNCHES:
TEACHING BITE INHIBITION

Just as we use our hands to gently grasp or explore objects, dogs naturally use their teeth for this same purpose. This mouthing behavior employs a soft, or inhibited, bite that causes no damage, but some dogs overdo mouthing even when they mean no harm. Bite inhibition doesn't mean stopping mouthing behavior altogether, but it teaches the dog to inhibit the force of the bite by explaining to the dog that his teeth can hurt. A dog with good bite inhibition will bite (if provoked) but cause no harm. Problem biting can be easily resolved by building the dog's confidence, while a dog with no bite inhibition causes damage and can be difficult to retrain.

Puppies learn bite inhibition by playing with other puppies and getting good feedback. Other dogs are the best teachers to train Rex to inhibit his bites, but owners can use exaggerated body language, facial expressions, and tone of voice to get the point across. Some puppies, like children, become more agitated when tired, and uncontrollable rough play may be a cue Rex needs a nap.

With an aggressive dog, yelling or physical punishment makes the aggression worse, and you won't win against teeth. Instead, whimper if you can manage. This works especially well with tough dogs. Allowing dogs to chew clothing teaches them to bite very hard very close to the skin, so treat your hair and clothing as an extension of human skin. Here's how to teach Rex as well as other adult dogs how to inhibit their bite with owners.

- If the dog mouths gently, praise him.

- If the mouthing becomes uncomfortable, say "Oooooooooh" in a gentle tone of voice, and follow with a sulking expression and attitude. Don't shout. Instead, say, "*I* don't like that, you hurt me" with as much emotion as possible.

- If the mouthing hurts, *yelp*! Another canine would announce pain similarly. Also *yelp* if the pup or dog chews, nips, or grabs hair or clothing.

- Immediately after you yelp, give the dog a ten-minute time out—no mouthing allowed—to teach him that hard bites make the fun stop.

Once the dog has a soft mouth, teach him to stop mouthing on request and never to initiate mouthing. To make sure your dog has a trustworthy mouth, periodic mouthing training sessions are essential throughout his life.

- Say "Off" and offer a food reward or toy for every ten to fifteen seconds of mouthing. He must stop mouthing to get the reward, which also pays him for stopping.

- Let the dog resume mouthing for another ten to fifteen seconds after he takes the reward.

BREAKING UP FIGHTS

Preventing fights works best. But how do you break up the wrangling when a pitched battle ensues? The technique depends on the size of the dogs, says Margaret Bonham, an expert in Northern dog breeds, dog sledding, and a dog book author. "If you try to break it up, you're probably going to get bit."

Avoid pulling collars, since excited dogs may turn and bite whoever grabs the collar. Also avoid yelling because that can escalate the arousal. In many cases, dogs scare owners with lots of show—but it's no less scary. "Most dogs snap or bite, somebody gives up, and that's it," says Bonham. So part of breaking up fights includes heading them off before blood is actually drawn. When you see aggressive posturing or hear warning snarls, don't wait for the fur to fly. Interrupt the action with these tips.

- Say, "No!" or "Hey" or "Off" in a calm, low voice. That may be enough for some dogs to stalk away and pretend each has won.

- Offer a pleasant distraction such as a favorite toy or activity. Use a cheerful voice to invite Rex to play a game or go for a car ride.

- Put obedience-trained dogs in a long down-stay. The posture keeps them separated and also serves as a canine calming signal that helps diffuse the angst.

When your dogs are already engaged in a pitched battle and the dogs will do great damage to each other if not stopped, don't be afraid to use extreme measures to save the dogs. Stop canine wars with one or more of these suggestions.

- Interrupt with a loud startling noise, such as a blast from an air horn.

- Separate small dogs by using your body to block access and distract them from each other.

- Set a chair over the top of the aggressor to stymie his attack. Take care the victim doesn't turn the tables and bite him back.

- Soak the combatants with water. If that doesn't work, aim a water hose at the dogs' open mouths so that they stop fighting in order to breathe.

- With the help of another person, pull the dogs apart. Each person grasps one dog by the back legs or base of the tail and lifts the dogs off the ground in a "wheelbarrow" to separate them.

- Toss one or both dogs in a swimming pool.

- Spray the dogs with a fire extinguisher if all else fails. "You'll need to bathe the dogs later to rinse off the chemicals, which can be an irritant," says Bonham.

After the fight, removing one dog from the area sends the message that the remaining dog "won" and chased that nasty canine out of sight. Instead, keep the dogs separated but in sight of each other. Crate both dogs or separate them by using a baby gate. Then ignore both dogs. Neither should get any attention or reward for

COMFORT ZONE

DirectStop, an aerosol citronella formula, interrupts dog-on-dog or dog-on-people attacks. The surprising, powerful scent is highly effective for dealing with low- to medium-level aggression. When tested with trained attack dogs, the product was found to be just as effective as ten percent pepper spray, but without harmful side effects. DirectStop, available at www.premier.com, causes the dog no pain and gives owners time to separate the dogs or move to a safe place.

fighting. A thirty-minute shunning works for mild transgression; for a serious fight, a whole day could be appropriate. Ignoring means you can be in the same room, but don't acknowledge their presence with any eye or physical contact. When the incidents are stopped, dogs learn that fighting doesn't get them what they want.

KING OF THE HILL

Dominance aggression includes guarding food and toys or other objects; the aggression gets worse if you punish the dog. First-time dog owners are more likely to have dogs with dominance aggression, perhaps due to their misunderstanding of canine communication. These behaviors erupt in situations where the dog believes his place in the family is threatened, causing him to try to put people back in line.

Dogs under a year of age are most likely to be reported, but ninety percent of dominance aggressors are males that develop problem behaviors by the time they reach eighteen to thirty-six months of age, which corresponds with canine social maturity. One survey showed that by two months of age, many puppies were aggressive over food. Female dominant aggression tends to develop during puppyhood.

Testosterone makes dogs react more intensely, more quickly, and for a longer period of time, so neutering males can cool their jets, but dominant aggressive intact female dogs tend to get *worse* if they are spayed. Dogs exhibiting dominance aggression often act submissively in other situations and stay friendly or submissive to other dogs. They keep their ears and tail down during the attack, tremble afterward, and act "remorseful." Behaviorists speculate that a first-time instinctive display may occur during play or food guarding, out of fear or conflict. Thereafter, the dog tries to avoid or prevent a repeat of the fearful or upsetting experience by being the first to aggress (scare off the person who might steal my food) when faced with similar triggers.

Picking him up or restraining (such as for nail clipping), or reaching "over top" of the dog near an "owned" object often triggers a dominant aggressive reaction. These dogs become possessive of furniture and refuse to get off when told. Furniture possessiveness only affects family members the dog feels are less dominant. Sleeping in bed with you elevates the dog's sense of status, and he's more likely to consider himself your equal—or even your boss.

Other predisposing factors include lack of training or exercise and playing tug-of-war games. Such dogs often live with teenagers in the home, have a history of a skin disorder, and suffered a serious illness in the first sixteen weeks of life. Dominant dogs may challenge the authority of young humans the same way adult dogs harass adolescent puppies. If your dog has excellent bite inhibition (see the earlier "Pulling Punches" section in this chapter), you can begin working with him at home.

- Identify and avoid triggers to prevent confrontations. If the dog protects toys, remove them from the general environment so he has nothing to guard.

- Don't challenge the dog, and *don't* punish him.

- Avoid all casual interaction and touching.

- Require the dog to earn good stuff with good behavior. Create interactions based on your request (Sit!) and his payment (he sits), which will then earn him what he wants (treat/attention/verbal praise). He should get *nothing* unless he earns it by responding in a positive way to your command.

- Make the furniture off-limits when the dog reacts around it.

- Prevent access to problem areas by placing clear plastic carpet runners, nub-side up, on top of sofas or beds—or simply shut the bedroom door.

Use happy words or phrases to change his mood. For example, if he's growling or posturing, ask, "Want to go for a car ride?" and watch his mood change. It's hard for dogs to be happy and aggressive at the same time.

 Confine problem dogs to a single room, an X-pen (wire-exercise pen), or a crate to better control their movements and access to trigger areas.

TOO MUCH FUN

Dogs can become so aroused from happiness that their excitement turns into aggression. One of the most reactive areas of the home, especially in multiple-dog households, is the doorway. The leader gets to go out the doorway first, and therefore dogs rush ahead of the pack (and you). This not only endangers people when a big dog (or pack) knocks them off their feet, but it allows Rex to believe that he is in charge. It can set a precedent so he may decide to control other interactions with you as well.

When you expect guests, separate the dogs into different rooms or crates until visitors have settled, then allow the dogs to meet and greet. Teaching the dog to sit and stay, or redirecting

---

VET ALERT!

Recently behavior specialists have focused on the role of protein in behavior problems. The quantity, quality, and method of processing commercial dog food may influence canine aggression.

Low levels of serotonin, a natural hormone and neurotransmitter, have been associated with canine dominance aggression. The way a dog's body processes amino acids, which make up proteins in dog food, may interfere with tryptophan, from which the body makes serotonin. Dr. Lansberg says that studies indicate that supplementing the diet of a dog with dominance aggression with tryptophan and changing to a low-protein diet may reduce aggression.

Dr. Overall further explains that some dogs have an impaired ability to use protein and can develop hepatoencephalopathy, a liver condition that causes them to act demented, frantic, and aggressive. Feeding a very low-protein diet returns dogs to their former sweet natures.

excitement by asking him to fetch a toy, also works well. Turn the doorbell into the "trigger" that prompts Rex to search for and bring you his ball.

In these situations, it will help greatly if the dog understands the "wait" command. "Wait" is different from "stay" because wait means Rex can't move forward until you give permission; stay means don't move in any direction until released. This reinforces your position as leader and also helps your dogs learn deference and polite behavior. It can prevent arousal and doorway excitement that sometimes leads to aggression between dogs. You can use a combination of leash control and natural dog body language to teach the wait command, but you should only train one dog at a time.

- Face your dog, using your body to block his pathway to the door.

- Move slowly toward him so he gives way to your approach. "Herd" him about four feet from the doorway. Don't shout or yell—that increases his excitement.

- Say "Wait" in a low voice.

- Open the door a bit. Body block or shut it if he leaps for the opening and herd him again with your body. Say "Wait" and open the door again.

- Go through the doorway first, then step back, as long as he doesn't lunge forward.

- Give the release command, such as "Okay" or his name in a high-pitched, happy voice, and allow the dog to proceed through the opening.

Repeat the exercise three or four times each training session. The dog only gets to go through the door when he no longer charges, but instead waits for you to go first; then, release him. Going outside rewards the "wait," so treats or toys aren't needed. Always end the training on a successful note. Once all of your dogs have been individually trained to wait, teach the group wait, beginning with two dogs at a time. Sometimes they want to race each other through the door, so treat this like a new trick.

- Say, "Dogs wait."

- Give the "Okay" release to only one dog at a time. Alternate who gets to go first during these sessions.

- Initially let the dog who does the best "wait" go first. Dogs catch on quickly, and you'll love it when your pack competes to see who acts most polite.

FRIGHT CLUB

While bites can happen for many reasons, most dogs bite out of fear aggression. Humans can inherit a tendency to be anxious and so can dogs, but environment, life experience, and breed tendencies also play a role. (See also "Bashful Behavior" in Chapter 7.)

When dogs fear something, it triggers the instinctive "fight-or-flight" response. When Rex can't escape whatever scares him, he lashes out with teeth. Fear-biters think they must fight their way out of the situation and become so panicked they aren't able to think in a reasonable manner. When the aggressive behavior makes the scary "thing" go away, Rex learns that acting aggressively works and uses it time after time.

Fear aggression causes severe damage to the target because usually the biter had poor socialization and never learned to inhibit his bites. These dogs don't fight other dogs over status, only fear, and punishing them with harsh physical or verbal reprimands will make the behavior worse.

Fearful dogs show displacement behaviors, such as licking or chewing themselves, sniffing, lip licking, and yawning. Common vocalizations include growls mixed with whines. Body language includes whale-eye—showing the whites of the eyes in an exaggerated sideways glance. The ultimate appeasement gestures are crouching or rolling onto his back with submissive urination (see also Chapter 6).

Most normal dogs tolerate a distance of one dog length and a half (of their own length) before feeling uncomfortable. A fearful dog's sensitive distance may be much greater, and if another dog or person approaches within that range, he attacks. Cage aggression occurs when a dog can't back away from your reaching hands when the cage or crate door opens; he therefore defends the space with snarls and teeth. Here are ways to diffuse the fear.

- Don't stare. Strong eye contact signals dominance and intensifies the intimidation.

- Use Rex's own language to calm him down. Glance away and pretend to yawn.

- Make note of the distance at which the scared dog becomes agitated and stay beyond that range whenever possible.

- Avoid cage aggression by opening the door and backing away, using a food lure to tempt the dog to exit on his own.

- Avoid reaching for his collar, which almost always precipitates a bite.

- Avoid petting on the top of the head because a descending hand looks threatening and makes the fear worse. Instead, pet the dog on his sides or chest.

- Practice obedience training to build confidence in frightened dogs. The Gentle Leader head halter works quite well with these dogs.

- Use the "nothing in life is free" concept to teach Rex that he must "pay" for everything. Once he recognizes that you are in charge, so he doesn't need to be responsible, much of the fear goes away.

- Create a house of plenty. Provide lots of toys and treats to reduce competition with other dogs for the good stuff.

- Play builds confidence. Teach Rex to play "fetch," but avoid tug-of-war games with fear biters, which can encourage the biting behavior.

Add several drops of Rescue Remedy to the dog's water. It won't hurt the other pets to sip at it, too.

 Use D.A.P. pheromone therapy to calm fears.

UNKNOWN MYSTERIES

Idiopathic aggression means we can't identify a cause of the aggression. It's characterized by the dog transforming from being happy into Cujo in a heartbeat. He may show clear signs of submission but still attacks with excessive aggression that is out of sync with the situation. This condition most often affects dogs that are one to three years old and is frequently misdiagnosed as dominant aggression. Dr. Luescher believes idiopathic aggression more closely resembles status-related aggression (see also "Sibling Rivalry" in this chapter), but that the (poorly socialized?) aggressor misunderstands canine communication and attacks inappropriately. In such cases, pet owners must be vigilant and always supervise the dog. Manage with muzzles and teach the dog to "go to bed" into a crate or other safe time-out area. Drug therapy from a veterinary behaviorist may benefit the dog.

THE HUNTING MYSTIQUE

All dogs display predatory aggression, a normal instinct that involves stalking, chasing, catching, biting, killing, and eating, and is mimicked during play. In most domestic dogs, these behaviors have been modified to a level that stops short of doing damage to other animals.

In play aggression, the context changes. Dogs tell each other it's all fun and games by using certain body gestures, termed "meta signals," which change the meaning of the behavior that follows, so that growls, chasing, and soft-bite mouthing are meant in play. Common signals that say, "Let's play!" include the play bow (tail and butt up, with the front end down). When your puppy or dog indulges in play aggression, teach the proper limits. Punishment—hitting, thumping the nose, scruff shakes, ramming your fist into the dog's mouth, or harsh alpha rolls—make play problems worse or create other sorts of aggression. (See also "Playing Around" in Chapter 2.)

Movement and sound triggers the behavior. Joggers, bicyclists, playing children, and moving cars stimulate the prey drive, as do high-pitched cries of puppies, babies, and young children. A sudden silence (such as when a prey animal "freezes") also provokes attack. Predatory aggressive dogs don't use meta signals—no play bows for them, because they're deadly serious and extremely dangerous. Predatory behavior is found in dogs of any age or sex, and dogs that show an extremely unwavering focus directed toward movements and vocalizations of a baby or other pet (some dogs drool!) should be suspect and watched closely. They may go through the whole predatory sequence or stop at any stage.

Prognosis is variable. Often predatory aggressiveness toward young pets or babies diminishes as the youngsters grow up. In the meantime, take precautions to keep targets safe from doggy teeth and help teach Rex to control his natural impulses.

- Identify all the triggers that prompt predatory aggression and avoid them, except during training sessions when you have control.

- Work on obedience training so your dog has automatic default commands he'll do at the drop of a hat—or toss of a treat. "Sit" or "Down" work well and can help distract him from instinctive predatory aggression, as well as get him to think about what he's doing.

- Use desensitization and counter-conditioning to change the dog's response by using a *happy* word he can't resist that improves his attitude, such as "Ball," "Frisbee," "Cookie" or "Ride."

- Ask an accomplice to ride a bike or jog past the house, and use your *happy* word every time to interrupt the predatory response. Before long, the dog will see the "prey" target, then switch attention to you for the cue word and reward.

Stop games when Rex goes too far and play turns into aggression. Walk away or give the dog a time-out in a room alone for five minutes, to teach him that crossing the line makes all the fun go away.

SIBLING RIVALRY

Dog-on-dog or status-related aggression relates to social standing and typically involves same-gender interactions. There are many potential causes, but a typical status-related aggression involves two or more dogs with nearly equal social status. Dogs usually resolve the issues through social posturing and minor skirmishes, but if the owner interferes or punishes the dog that wins, the aggression can escalate. Puppies often act like jerks and test their limits, prompting older dogs to put the delinquent in his place. These altercations look deadly serious, but as long as both dogs have good bite inhibition, they won't endanger each other. Problems arise when a dominant dog uses excessive and inappropriate aggression to control another dog or the submissive animal uses overly fearful displays that feed the aggression and make it continue.

Aggression can result when social status changes by a new dog being introduced; by dogs returning home after surgery, boarding, or vacation; by the dominant animal becoming ill, aging, or dying, which leaves a void the other dogs squabble to fill; by a family member considered by the dog to be his "leader" leaving home; or by a younger dog maturing and challenging the status of the current dominant dog.

Intact male dogs have the greatest problems with aggression toward other dogs, and while the behavior often results from hormone-driven competition, dominance or fear can also play roles. Interdog aggression typically first appears in males one to three years old. Castration decreases the problem in about two-thirds of the cases. Female-female aggression more often involves intact females one to three years old that live together in the same home, and results from an unstable social hierarchy. Female-female fights typically include uninhibited bites and severe injuries. Opposite-sex rivalry occurs rarely and is most often initiated by the female dog. They can be very severe and usually instigated by the younger, larger, more recent addition to the house.

Dogs challenge each other with stares, shoulder or hip bumps and shoves, mounting behavior, or blocking access to food, play, or attention. They bark, growl, and try to bite other male dogs they live with or encounter outside the home. Prognosis remains guarded for males that aren't neutered or for males that still have problems after neutering. In the latter case, you may ultimately need to manage the dogs separately. If your dog has good bite inhibition, the tips that follow can be useful.

- Neuter both dogs if they are intact males.

- Spay your female dog to reduce aggression if she only fights when she's in heat. If your intact female fights whether she's in heat or not, *spaying makes aggression worse!*

- Separate the dogs when you cannot supervise. Place a baby gate in a long hallway so each dog has access to one end of the house.

- Leave the two dogs together while wearing muzzles and on leash but *only* when you supervise. Dogs can get muzzles off.

- Provide leash walks for both dogs at the same time (but with two different people) and reward with food treats for behaving well.

- Support the ranking of the two dogs to prevent confusion and help them sort out who has priority (see also Chapter 2 to identify subordinate and dominant individuals).

- Treat the dominant dog preferentially by feeding him first, giving him the best resting places, and letting him in and out of doors first. Be prepared to support the younger dog as he matures and usurps the place of beloved old Rex.

🐾 Discourage the subordinate dog from challenging and encourage him to defer to the dominant dog. Cut the privileges of the subordinate dog so he has no privileges that the dominant dog has.

Rather than simply managing and/or avoiding situations that prompt aggression, teach your dogs an alternative response by desensitizing them to each other and counter-conditioning them with reward-based training. When the two (muzzled) dogs approach each other and the aggressor growls, give him a time-out. Perhaps say, "Uh oh, you're fired!" and, using the leash, walk the growler to the bathroom and leave him there for thirty seconds. With repeated trials, Rex learns that acting growly means being locked up alone, away from you. Be consistent; eventually, when Rex sees the other dog approach, he will look away instead of growling, thereby substituting an acceptable alternative behavior that doesn't prompt a time-out. When that happens, *reward* Rex with a cookie to reinforce the alternative behavior and to teach him that he gets paid for being good.

WALKING DOG-AGGRESSIVE DOGS

All dogs feel protective of their own turf and may not welcome a strange dog trespassing in your yard. Some dogs turn on the aggression at the mere sight of *any* other dog, even a familiar pack mate, when approached off their own territory. Picking up and holding a small dog in your arms often provokes bigger dogs to jump up to reach the little one—it's safer for you to keep the little dog's four feet on the floor. Dog trainers recommend teaching Rex a new way to react by helping him associate the presence of the other dog with a benefit.

🐾 Be sure your dog accepts and pays attention to leash control. A flat-buckle collar and leash, a head halter such as the Gentle Leader, or a body harness such as the SENSE-ation are ideal. Keep the leash loose because a tight grip communicates stress and can make your dog feel even more aggressive.

- Fill your pockets with the smelliest, tastiest treats you can find before starting the walk. Liverwurst works well, or you can see if Rex likes stinky cat treats. Break them up into tiny morsels, so you have a large supply.

- Use a high-pitched, happy voice to say, "It's a cookie dog!" when you see the first dog on the walk. Immediately shove a smelly treat right in front of his nose. Keep repeating the phrase in the happy voice, feeding Rex treats as long as the other dog remains in sight. Once the other dog goes away, so should the treats.

- Expect your dog to act confused, growl, or become aggressive, but he should eventually accept the treat. Continue to use the singsong phrase and offer a bonanza of treats whenever you see a dog, to associate the other canine's presence with good stuff.

- Keep the treat under his nose even if he continues to growl and ignore it. Then, once he pays attention to it (since the other dog left), hang on to the treat, and put it back in your pocket so he knows he blew it. He could have had the treat, but growled instead. Before long he'll realize he has a choice—growl and get no treat, or ignore the other dog and get paid for it.

- Watch for Rex to anticipate the treat. He will see other dogs and then look at you for a reward. The sight of another canine that used to trigger aggression has been changed to trigger the expectation of treats. Done with consistency, one-time dog-aggressive dogs may eventually eagerly go on walks and look around to find a "cookie dog" in order to get goodies.

PROTECTING PROPERTY

Dogs most prone to territorial aggression include those bred for herding and protection, such as shepherds and terriers. They protect their property (the house, other animals, car, yard, you) no matter who is present. For instance, Rex may "protect" your bedroom so vigorously that you can't make a trip to the bathroom at night without risking his teeth. Boundary confinement, such as a fence or chain, makes the aggression worse. Territorial-aggressive dogs can trigger on family members or strangers and can be part of a pack that learns to mimic the bad actor's behavior en masse.

 Change the dog's mood with pleasant words and commands that prompt him to concentrate on something else.

 Ask him to "Sit" or perform another command; reward with the ball.

 Make high-trigger areas, such as the front door, bedroom, or kitchen, off-limits. Use a baby gate to keep him out from underfoot, but allow him to see into the room to "protect" you or the other pets.

 Enlist the aid of delivery people, neighbors, or the paperboy to stage interactions so dogs are not rewarded when the "intruder" (the mailman, new dog, or your roommate) leaves (see also Chapter 9). Give the approaching stranger a handful of treats, (something irresistible the dog only gets during these sessions, such as liverwurst) and ask him or her to toss the treats to the dog without making eye contact. Once the dog's mouth is full (so he's no longer making noise), the stranger can say, "Good Rex!" and walk away. He or she should *not* walk away as long as the dog barks and lunges.

 If Rex ignores the treat and continues to bark and lunge, then *you* go out the door, call him, and reward with a treat or toy for coming. The stranger leaves as the dog retreats—so essentially, neither won.

Chapter 6
Bathroom Challenges

Owners expect dogs to know what's acceptable bathroom behavior as soon as they arrive in the house. We wouldn't expect human toddlers to know it all, and dogs also need instruction to understand the basics. Doggy instincts often prompt Rex to act contrary to human protocol, and it takes solid training to undo his natural tendencies. When he leg-lifts against the side of your bed to mark it (and you!) as the most important territory, owners rarely see that as a compliment. Angry shouts and punishment make dogs fear a normal function, causing them to hide deposits or avoid eliminating in front of you until they must "do" something or burst.

Living with multiple dogs increases this house-training

COMFORT ZONE: CANINE INDOOR POTTIES

Pups and adult dogs weighing less than thirty pounds may be candidates for indoor potty facilities. Make sure the doggy indoor toilet isn't up or down stairs or too far for your little dog to reach when he's in a hurry. A laundry room, baby playpen, or small bathroom may be ideal—just be careful a scary dryer buzzer or other noise doesn't frighten him during his "business," or he may have trouble becoming loyal to the box.

Dog litter boxes use pellets that absorb urine, control odor, and don't track. Other products catch waste through a grid system that keeps the dog's feet clean. These products often include training tips, and are available at pet product stores, including

- Puppy Go Potty (made from recycled paper fibers at www. puppygopotty.com).
- Secondnature (recycled newspaper product) at www.doglitter.com.
- WizDog housetraining system for dogs (flat tray with plastic grid) at http://wizdog.com.

challenge. Scheduling potty breaks and placement of the canine

toilet depends on the ages and breeds of the dogs involved as well as your house situation. Even if puppies know what to do, they don't always have the physical capacity to hold it for hours at a time.

A pack of small dogs may fit your apartment size better than a couple of Great Danes, but toy dog breeds often object to outdoor toilets especially during icy winters, when they must brave snow deeper than they are tall. Rescue dogs that have been confined in cages for months or years go where they sleep and eat because they had no other option. If you welcome one of these dogs into your pack, it may be a challenge but very rewarding to retrain these needy canines.

ACCIDENTS HAPPEN

If you share your home with a dog or two, you *will* be faced with an accident now and then. Duke and Prince may be royalty, but they aren't perfect; together, you can do something about it. With puppies, house soiling stems from them not yet knowing the proper place or time for deposits. Adult dogs soil the house for a variety of reasons, but the most common is inadequate house training. Adult dogs that have been house soiling for years may take several months before they're dependable. To determine other causes, take another look at the P.E.T. test. In addition, keep these tips in mind.

- Crate-train dogs of any age that lose housetraining, regardless of reason. A small bathroom rarely works because puppies or adults can get creative in one corner and sleep in the other, where the waste doesn't bother them. Any time you cannot supervise the miscreants, confine each dog in a small crate or carrier just large enough to serve as a bed.

- Leash Rex to your belt so he cannot hide a deposit without your knowledge—one dog per person, or they'll likely trip you.

- Time bathroom outings after meals, playtime, and naps.

- Don't yell, hit, push his nose in the mess, or otherwise punish Rex for accidents. That just makes him more diligent in hiding his waste.

- Watch for circling or sniffing early warnings and chant, "Outside, outside, outside" in an urgent but bright, cheerful voice to encourage dogs to be productive in the right spot. If you catch one of your dogs in the act, do the same thing: chant, "Outside, outside, outside."

- Use a cue word such as "hurry" or "potty" once he's in the designated potty spot and repeat it until he goes. During training, take dogs to the same location each time so they associate the area and scent with elimination.

- Avoid picking dogs up during or immediately after an accident, or they'll identify making a mess with getting attention. Thereafter, they may produce an accident on purpose rather than risk being ignored.

- Clean the spot thoroughly with an odor neutralizer or the smell will draw your dogs back to the scene of the crime—even those who know better. Try Nature's Miracle (aka Petastic), Simple Solution, or Anti-Icky-Poo.

- Pay your dogs for going in the right spot with the most scrumptious treat you can find—liver or smoked turkey, for instance. This teaches them they can cash in waste for goodies. Dogs watch other canines getting paid for doing the right thing and learn faster.

 Make sure to empty all your dogs before they eat, after they eat, and every hour afterward. A dog with a full bladder is an accident waiting to happen.

 Add straw to the designated spot or pick a corner of the driveway for elimination if your dog was rescued as an adult. These dogs may have learned to go on odd surfaces, such as straw or cement, and may need some extra guidance until they learn the new rules.

DUNG EATING

Dogs commonly eat their own or another animal's feces (coprophagia), usually as an attention-seeking behavior or a bad habit prompted by boredom. Dung eating first develops in puppies from four to nine months old, possibly as a result of copying mom-dogs that clean up after the babies. The frequency increases after one year of age, and while most pups outgrow the habit, it can persist throughout the dog's life. Not enough exercise or a lack of environmental stimulation leaves dogs feeling bored and more likely to do this. Manage the dog's bathroom activities and retrain him to leave deposits alone.

 Increase play time with your dogs to a minimum of twenty minutes aerobic exercise, twice each day. You may need to do this in shifts to accommodate all your dogs, particularly if they're different sizes and like different styles of play.

 Increase the number of toys to keep dogs busy when you're away. A treat-spiked toy such as a Kong filled with peanut butter offers a tastier alternative.

 Prevent the muncher's access to feces. Walk him on a leash until he's reliable.

 Reward him for leaving stools alone. Teach him to "come" and sit in front of you after each bowel movement—his or the other dog's—and give him a treat while you pick up the waste.

- Try a higher-protein, lower-carbohydrate diet that's more digestible. You may need to feed it to all the dogs if the snacking Rex follows them all around. Ask your veterinarian for a recommendation.

- Add a spoonful of canned pineapple, canned pumpkin, or spinach to the dogs' meals, or a dash of MSG. These change the taste or consistency of the stool and make it less appealing.

- Add papain digestive enzyme capsules (from health food stores) or a product called For-Bid (from pet product stores) to the food to make feces taste bad.

- Avoid giving too much attention. If dogs do this to get your notice, even yelling at them reinforces the behavior. If you catch Rex in the act, don't make eye contact or speak to him, but use an interruption to stop the behavior. Shake a can full of pennies or use a remote-controlled citronella collar.

- Muzzle the miscreants if you can't be around to supervise.

LEG LIFTING

Dogs mark important territory with urine by lifting one rear leg to aim a stream at vertical landmarks, such as a tree or fire hydrant, to leave a sort of doggy pee-mail other dogs can read via the scent/pheromone message. This normal behavior becomes a problem if your pack takes turns staining the side of the house, wilts the shrubbery, or marks your bedspread. Intact males are the most common culprits, and castration reduces male marking in seventy to eighty percent of dogs. But some females also leg

VET ALERT!

Diabetes and kidney disease make dogs so thirsty they drink too much water; as a result, they often wet in the house. Aging spayed dogs sometimes develop urinary incontinence due to loss of bladder sphincter control. These conditions have nothing to do with lack of house training and everything to do with medical conditions that often can be managed. See your veterinarian immediately.

lift, especially when in heat, and other dogs urine-mark out of fearful reactions and use leg lifting to bolster their courage. When territory must be shared, as in multipet households, leg lifting may appear or increase dramatically.

 Neuter your male dogs. If they still leg lift when your female dog is in heat, spay her or board her during estrus to cool everyone's jets.

- Prevent the leg-lifting pet from watching other dogs through the window, which prompts the behavior. Draw the blinds and move furniture to block the view.

- Remove the urine residue with odor neutralizers or the smell will draw your dogs—even the innocent ones—back to the scene of the crime.

- Give dogs a legal opportunity to leg lift. Drive a few stakes in the yard for them to mark so they'll ignore your rose bushes.

- Teach your dogs the "Don't touch" command. Dogs typically sniff the target before they leg lift, and that can cue you to interrupt him before he lets fly. Use a high-pitched, happy voice to get his attention; when he looks up at you, give a treat as you say, "Yes!"

 Give Rex a toy to carry when in tempting leg-lifting situations, such as at the veterinary clinic, so he concentrates on his pacifier. A toy in the mouth also makes it harder for them to sniff out a likely target.

 Use D.A.P. for very reactive dogs that leg lift out of fear. The plug-in affects all the dogs, or you can spray it on a bandana for individual dogs to wear.

YOU'RE THE BOSS

Normal canine submissive signals include wetting as the ultimate doggy deference—think of this as "crying uncle." Puppies usually outgrow the behavior, but some very submissive dogs continue as adults. The dog typically throws himself at your feet, wiggles and averts his eyes, squats, and wets. Sometimes he turns onto his back before wetting. The behavior commonly happens during greetings when you return after an absence. Angry reactions make it worse. Yelling, shaming, touching, or even making eye contact are dominance signals that tell the dog he's not yet submissive enough, and that makes him pee even more. Dominant dogs put a paw across Rex's shoulders or chin themselves on his neck to show they're in charge, and you patting Rex on the head equates to these dominant moves. You can teach him better control and more confidence so he doesn't feel the urge to wet.

- Ignore the behavior and clean up the mess without making eye contact or saying a word. When he wets for another dog, let the dominant canine make his point before calling him away.

- Don't pay attention to Rex for the first ten minutes after your homecoming, if your arrival tends to trigger submissive wetting. Turn your back and walk away to give him time to calm down and gain control. Avoid paying attention to any of the dogs if they're nearby, or your tone of voice will still influence Rex's emotions.

- Scratch his chest or beneath his chin once he's calmed down, but avoid head pats.

- Speak in a gentle voice. Men can unintentionally sound gruff and dominant to the dog, so practice expressing your inner softie nature.

- Don't be emotional. Avoid baby talk, which actually rewards the behavior and encourages the dog to continue peeing.

- Avoid "looming" over the top of the dog the way dominant dogs do. Instead, give the dog space by backing up and asking the dog to come and sit, over and over. Repetitive obedience commands take his mind off wetting. If other dogs also perform and are rewarded, that helps Rex model good behavior.

- Keep backing up, ignore the "wet" sits, and gently praise and offer food rewards for dry sits so Rex learns that *not* wetting prompts the payoff.

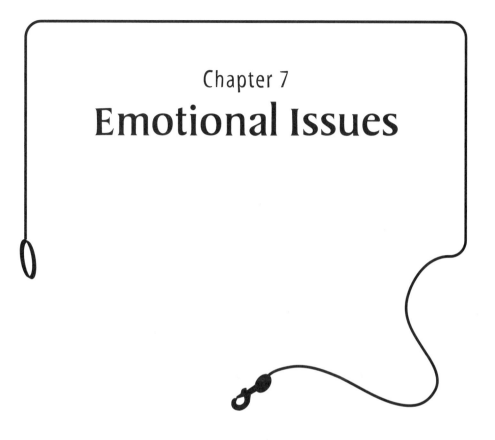

Chapter 7
Emotional Issues

L ike humans, dogs are emotional beings. We can't read their
minds or feelings, but canine behavior changes mirror those
of owners in similar situations. People who feel depressed
sleep more, want to be left alone, and may eat more (or less);
depressed dogs act the same way.

The feelings that dogs experience are often tied directly to
the emotions their human companions feel. Adding (or losing)
other pets or people to the household creates an emotionally
charged atmosphere. Kids going off to college, a divorce, the
death of a pet, or the addition of a new dog to the mix prompts
a strong emotional reaction. Changing jobs and work schedules,
or moving to a new home can also be particularly stressful. When

a single dog has an emotional problem, it impacts how the rest of the pack relates to him. Learn how to recognize your dog's emotional state and understand its causes; this will enable you to provide options for calming your pets' bruised feelings.

BOREDOM

Dogs are so social, they easily get bored, especially the smart ones. Having more than one canine prevents or reduces the potential for going stir-crazy because the pack keeps each other entertained. However, when your dogs vary greatly in age or activity level and don't have the ability or inclination to interact socially, one or more dogs often feels frustrated. Rex needs things to occupy his mind and keep him active, just as you do, or he'll vegetate and become a lump or aggravate you to death. While older dogs and lap pooches may not require much stimulation, some dogs thrive on outside activity. The Border Collie and similar working breeds look for things to do, such as rearranging the sofa pillows, herding the neighborhood kids, or chewing through the baseboard.

A large percentage of bad behaviors result from boredom, including excessive barking, chewing, and digging (see also Chapter 20). Use the following tips to keep your bored canine engaged in more productive endeavors.

🐾 Give your pack two or three toys per dog to ensure they always have something fresh. Rotate them to keep it interesting.

COMFORTS ZONE: TOYS FOR BOREDOM

The Best Ball comes in a ten-inch size and can be filled with water, sand, or fine gravel to change the way it sounds and rolls and can entertain several dogs for hours. Tennis ball tuggers and rope toys such as Ropeheads are perfect for multidog homes for interactive tug games. The vanilla-scented Hol-ee Mol-ee Extreme hollow ball can be filled with dry treats and works great as a rolling, bouncing, and fetching toy. These and similar toys are available at pet products stores or online at www.drsfostersmith.com

Organize a treasure hunt for your dogs to keep them engaged for hours. Kong toys stuffed with peanut butter, liverwurst, or other canine delicacies provide the incentive. Hide stuffed Kongs or dry dog biscuits around the house (or yard) before you leave for the day. The first time, show your dogs where you hid the treats; after that, noses will do the rest. This works particularly well with hunting dogs such as Golden Retrievers and Labradors.

 Replace the closed door with a see-through baby gate or screen so pets can commune but still be separate. This will prevent dogs from getting lonely and bored and also cuts down on howling, scratching, or digging at the door.

DOGGY DEPRESSION

Dogs get depressed for the same reasons we do, but unfortunately, we can't comfort them with words as we would a grieving person. Losing a family member or adding somebody new can leave dogs feeling blue, so it's up to you to recognize the signals.

Depressed dogs may sleep more than usual. They either want to eat all the time, become finicky, or refuse to eat altogether. Depressed pets often act lethargic, and many retreat from the world by hiding in the basement. These feelings are as natural for dogs as they are for owners, but they can cause health problems or upset feelings in the rest of the pack if they go on too long.

GRIEVING A LOST LOVE

Losing a pet to age, illness, or accident impacts the whole family, even the other pets. Although it sounds macabre, it can be helpful to allow the surviving dogs to "Say goodbye" to the body after a furry friend has died. Dogs may sniff and examine the body, ignore it, cry, or show no reaction whatsoever. Any reaction is normal. By offering surviving pets the gift of a last look, they'll recognize that Rex won't come back, and you'll be saved the tortured cries and pointless searching for the lost friend.

A human family member's absence also depresses dogs. Whether he's missing a human or furry friend, Rex must work through the grieving process. A number of things can help.

- Talk to your dogs. Be positive around mourning dogs and, when you can't, simply say, "I'm sad, but it's not your fault." They'll understand and it will help.

- Remove the favorite toys or bed of the absent loved one so the surviving pack doesn't have that sad, scented reminder that he's gone.

- Spend a weekend away at a different place to help a dog make the transition to a new life without the missing friend.

INTERLOPER DEPRESSION

- Give Rex special attention such as alone time with you or a TTouch massage (described in Chapter 4) when he feels depressed by the new puppy's presence, to show he's not been replaced and is still your best friend.

- Counteract depression with games or "canine work" so the dogs must think about something else. Playing a game with your new family member helps the pair bond and reduces the reason for Rex's depression.

GENERAL DEPRESSION

- Avoid babying. Your natural urge to pamper rewards and encourages the behaviors to continue or even become worse. Give Rex attention but in an upbeat, enthusiastic manner.

- Make sure depressed pets have a private place to retreat and not be pestered by other dogs, until they feel better. While losing a loved one or adding a new pet depresses some dogs, others may conduct business as usual, while a few dogs actually pick on those who act morose.

- Offer your pet a sunbath on the back porch every day for twenty minutes or so. Light therapy has been shown to be beneficial to people suffering from depression because it affects the production of hormones from the pituitary and endocrine glands. Similarly, it can help raise canine spirits.

🐾 Play music, such as Pet Melodies, to soothe the depression. Music that reminds your pet of happier times—perhaps associated with a loved one who has gone away—can free up the emotional responses in your pets so they can heal and come out of the depression.

🐾 Offer Bach Flowers remedies (see Chapter 4). Gentian helps general depression, Gorse lifts severe depression, and Star of Bethlehem relieves sorrow and grief. Give the affected dog two to four drops directly into his mouth two or three times a day until the depression lifts. When the whole pack is feeling blue, add the drops to a communal water bowl.

🐾 Talk to your veterinarian. Antidepressant drugs can be prescribed for severe cases of depression. The herb Saint-John's-Wort, a natural antidepressant that can take the edge off your pet's grief, should only be given for a very short time. The dosage depends on the individual dog.

BASHFUL BEHAVIOR

To survive in the wild, doggy ancestors needed to be cautious, but if taken to extremes it can result in fear aggression that endangers you and the rest of your pack. Studies indicate that up to twenty percent of any population of a given species will be born prone to introversion and fear, conditions that are worsened by abuse or lack of proper socialization. These experiences short-circuit the confidence-building that puppies need, so they become anxiety-ridden adults. Pain or illness that makes the dog hurt or just feel crummy also can cause anxiety. Such dogs begin to associate an owner's or vet's handling with discomfort and react with fear.

Extreme fear prompted by a sound, smell, or sight can cause a panic attack, in which the dog loses his mind. One study showed that eighty-seven percent of thunderstorm-fearful dogs also suffered from separation anxiety, and some behaviorists estimate up to twenty percent of dogs suffer from noise phobias, especially to thunder and fireworks, which can cause panic attacks. Even normally friendly pets can become dangerous to you and the rest of the pack when they are terrified. They try to get away from the threat, even going through glass windows or over other dogs, but will get over the fear in ten to twenty minutes. Until the panic goes away, talking or touching him can make the panic continue, so stay out of his way and let Rex hide and calm down.

Signs of anxiety include staring, panting, shaking, crouching, squinting, a furrowed brow, and whale eye. Fearfulness prompts increased heart and breathing rate; scared dogs signal unease with yawns, pinning their ears back, tucking their tail, urinating, or even defecating. Besides being unhealthy, nervous and fearful dogs aren't happy pets or fun to be around; above all, we want our dogs to enjoy life.

Recovery time for dogs with anxiety requires a great deal of commitment, time, and patience. You may not see positive changes for up to six months, and it could take as long as one and one-half to three years for the dog's fearful behavior to disappear. Some types of fear will never go away, but usually can be helped so the dog feels better most of the time.

- Identify all the different sights, places, sounds, odors, people, or other things that cause your dogs to feel fearful, such as thunder, car rides, strange men, or other dogs. Before you can help, you must know what prompts the fear.

- Choose a bold, happy, nonaggressive dog of similar size but of the opposite sex and younger than the resident shy dog. A canine friend gives a sense of security and can be a role model for your shrinking violet.

- Treat the shy dog the same as you do your confident dogs. Speak in a calm, happy tone as if he's already well-adjusted. Avoid yelling, which can prompt submissive urination (see also Chapter 6).

Never pet or speak in baby talk when dogs act shy or fearful. This can reward and encourage the behavior to continue. Instead, ignore shivers and praise for outgoing, confident behavior such as relaxed breathing, calm expressions, and body postures.

 Play builds confidence. When Rex is fearful of the other dogs, encourage him to play tug-of-war games with a gentle canine playmate. Limit the shy guy's interaction to only one or two other dogs at a time, not the entire six-pack, so Rex isn't totally overwhelmed.

 Let a shy dog see how much the other dogs enjoy being handled to help him learn by their example. Fearful dogs can be hand-shy, especially if they've been abused, so avoid petting doggy heads and instead pet the chest and ears.

 Don't stare. Strong eye contact is a dominant dog behavior and can be intimidating. Glance away while petting your shy dogs and pretend to yawn, which is a canine calming signal that tells him you mean no harm.

 Add several drops of the Rescue Remedy to the pack's water for everyone to sip.

 Use the pheromone product D.A.P. to relieve your dogs' fear. The plug-in diffuses in the air to benefit all the dogs, or spray it on a kerchief for Rex to wear.

 Provide lots of direction and create a schedule. This way your pack knows when to expect meals, a walk, potty breaks, and everything else. Routine builds security that allows shy dogs to become more relaxed and fit into the pack.

FOR SMALL DOGS

 Sit on the floor some distance away and ignore your dog. Let him come to you if he is shy of people. Standing over the top of small dogs intimidates them, but squatting can also seem scary. If Rex feels shy of the other dogs, have your pack lie down, which is another calming signal that helps ease the tension.

 Don't feel so protective of lap-sized breeds that you must carry them everywhere. This encourages shyness and tells tiny dogs the danger is real. Allow small dogs to keep four paws on the ground, and they'll be more confident as a result.

🐾 If your shy dog becomes fearful when another dog approaches, reproduce the trigger in gradually increasing increments to help Rex learn other dogs are nothing to fear. Ask a friend to help you stage counter-conditioning sessions by having one of your other dogs on leash.

🐾 Measure Rex's tolerance limit—maybe he remains confident as long as your other dog stays twenty feet away. Reward Rex for remaining calm when the scary dog stays at the twenty-foot zone limit.

🐾 Ask your friend to bring the leashed dog inside the twenty-foot mark to eighteen feet while you watch Rex's reaction. Use a treat to keep Rex's attention on you; if necessary, yawn several times to cue him all is well—and then give him the treat for maintaining his calm. Only proceed to the next level when your dog stays comfortable with the last gradient, and *don't* give a reward if he acts fearful.

You can also modify your dogs' fear of car rides by making the car the best place in the world. Open the door and have a bowl full of treats inside, a favorite toy, or a buddy dog who loves riding so the car becomes a happy place before ever starting the engine. Once your car-scared dog acts calmly inside the car, turn on the engine and ride around the block, then get out and play a favorite game. It may take a week of car rides that go nowhere—or end up at a dog park, or fast food restaurant for French fries—before dogs learn cars aren't so scary.

INSOMNIACS

Dogs don't have trouble sleeping very often. When they do, arthritis pain, metabolic diseases, or plain old stress can keep them awake. Other times, dogs get plenty of snooze time while you're at work and this lack of exercise means they are ready to patrol all night long, to keep you safe from intruders. Even if a single dog stays awake, his activity keeps all the others up, too. There are a number of methods you can use to help hit the snooze button on your pack's pacing, collar-jingling behaviors.

- Play games of tag-and-chase before bedtime to wear out the night owls so they settle down more quickly. Also, schedule additional walks and Frisbee-chasing sessions.

- Feed a meal late at night to keep your dogs from waking up hungry and pestering you for more food. Balance the timing of the last meal with their need for a potty break, though. It may take a bit of experimentation to find the best time.

- Move doggy beds to a location away from noisy appliances that switch on and off during the night. Dogs that have recently moved to a new house may hear unusual sounds or feel uncomfortable in the assigned "bedroom."

- Provide a nightlight so aging dogs sleep more soundly. They naturally lose some of their hearing and vision, and when darkness falls, they feel insecure.

- Harp music works as a natural, nondrug sedative, but any slow, calm, instrumental arrangement can help soothe pets. The Canine Lullabies CD also acts as a natural sedative and affects the entire pack at once.

- The hormone melatonin, available at health food stores, can counter canine insomniacs. Ask your vet for the proper dosage.

- A product designed specifically for dogs may be an easier, better option. Calm Pet (www.nutribest.com) contains melatonin along with a combination of other herbs known to help calm and soothe.

- Offer your pack a warm milk treat before bedtime. Milk contains the chemical tryptophan, which helps promote sleep. A quarter to half-cup of warm milk per dog for a bedtime snack may help them snooze more soundly. However, some dogs don't digest milk easily, so lay off the treat if diarrhea develops.

VET ALERT!

Some dogs develop memory problems similar to those suffered by human Alzheimer's patients. Dogs over the age of nine are most susceptible. Signs include disorientation, interaction changes (with people or other pets), sleep cycle changes, housetraining lapses, and anxiety. We can't stop time and aging altogether. However, a percentage of dogs suffering from these cognitive disorders are helped with drug and/or nutritional therapy prescribed by the veterinarian, which reverses the symptoms for a time.

- The drug Anipryl (selegiline hydrochloride) is FDA-approved for treatment of canine cognitive disorder, and helps up to seventy percent of dogs.
- Hill's Prescription Diet Canine b/d includes a combination of proprietary vitamins and other antioxidants to improve canine memory.
- Cholodin, a nutritional supplement, contains choline and phosphatidylcholine, which help brain cells work more efficiently, and may benefit dogs with cognitive dysfunction. More information is available at www.mvplabs.com.

JEALOUSY

Multiple-dog families often arise from literally combining households, and many owners have experienced how quickly these dogs get their noses out of joint when a new family member (human or canine) enters the picture. Dogs truly believe you belong to them and may not want to share. The more dogs you have, the greater the chance that at least one of them will turn into a green-eyed monster over your new love, roommate, puppy, or human infant. It is the people they love that will be most desired and guarded.

Jealous dogs can act depressed and mope around the house, or become more rambunctious or destructive to get attention. Moderate jealousy usually goes away once Rex adjusts to the new person or pet, but serious cases can escalate to aggression to keep that "interloper" in the proper place. Proper introductions go a long way toward keeping the peace between dogs; use these tips to avoid people jealousy.

Maintain the old, familiar schedule. If you must change the routine, do so gradually several weeks before the newcomer arrives. Get the dog acclimated to the new schedule *before* you bring home someone new.

 Introduce your dogs to the new person on neutral territory, such as at a dog park, in the same way you'd introduce Rex to a new canine friend, one dog at a time. Give the person a chance to play ball and make friends with Rex before entering your house and becoming a threat.

 Ask your new housemate to feed the dogs and play special fun games. You want jealous dogs to associate the new person in your life with only good things, and be the key to tasty treats and Frisbee. Once he or she wins over one of the pack, the others often see the light and start competing for equal time and attention.

 Make special time for your dogs when you pay attention to the newcomer in the house. Ignoring the pack in favor of the new person tells your dogs they must compete for your attention. Instead, find a way to give the dogs *extra* attention whenever the new person or pet comes near. When you're nursing the baby, toss dog treats; while holding hands on the sofa with your new love, play fetch with Rex.

KIDDING AROUND

 Prepare for a new baby ahead of time. If the nursery will be off-limits, get your pack used to that now. Don't shut them out the instant the baby comes home. A baby gate works well to allow the dogs to be a part of things by watching, while keeping them safely out of the room.

 Get your dogs used to baby smells and sounds. Use baby powder and lotion on yourself so it becomes a familiar, safe, and beloved association. Bring home a T-shirt or baby blanket the baby has worn for the pack to get an early warning sniff.

 Encourage the child to give tasty treats for sitting on command. Some dogs act jealous of children, especially toddlers and young kids, and they may not recognize "little people" as humans because they speak, move, and behave very differently than adults. Having the child always ask for a sit also teaches the dogs to keep their paws on ground, not knock down the little one, and also to expect good things around kids. Gentle dogs can take treats from the child's hand, while nippy dogs do best having a treat tossed to the ground.

 Be sure your dogs always have a "dogs only" retreat they can escape to, and can get away from pestering children. Your pets will feel much more willing to interact nicely with new people when they can sleep and relax in peace.

DOG-TO-DOG JEALOUSY

Alliance aggression results when a dog protects owners from other dogs. Quick moves or embraces stimulate the aggression, but these dogs aren't aggressive in the absence of their owners. Alliance aggression develops when a low-ranking dog becomes aggressive toward a higher-ranking dog, but only in the presence of the owner. The lower-ranking dog (we'll call her Sweetie) wants to keep the higher-ranking dog (Rex) away from her human (you). She uses snarls, snaps, growls, and fights to accomplish this.

When you aren't around, the two dogs get along fine because their hierarchy is clear and Sweetie defers to Rex. Your presence seems to elevate Sweetie's status, maybe she's your favorite. In any event, if Sweetie becomes overly attached, she'll feel justified in using aggression to keep Rex away from you. Rex usually slinks

---

VET ALERT!

Human panic attack research indicates it's not the event or circumstances that cause continuing or escalating attacks, but the memory of how awful the person felt during the attacks. For that reason, behaviorists believe anti-anxiety drugs would help control the condition in dogs. The drug wouldn't cure the problem, but could help in behavior modification to allow dogs to learn better ways to react.

Clomicalm (clomipramine, Novartis Animal Health) has been approved to treat dogs who suffer from separation anxiety. The drug prevents the metabolism of serotonin, a natural hormone produced by the brain that affects behavior.

off to a corner when you're all in the same room together rather than deal with Sweetie's nasty temper, but sometimes they fight. To cure alliance aggression, reduce Sweetie's dependence on you by practicing tough doggy love. The prognosis for fixing this type of jealous behavior is poor, but it can be done if you follow the steps behaviorists recommend.

- *Ignore* both dogs for three to four weeks. Don't speak to them, look directly at, pet, or play with either dog. This reduces Sweetie's dependence and avoids aggravating her aggression toward Rex.

- Identify the top dog and treat him preferentially. Rex should eat first, be the first let outside for bathroom breaks, receive the best treats first, and be allowed the best sleeping places (on the bed, for example).

- Keep the dogs together as much as possible. They should be fine, since alliance aggression by definition means they get along when alone together. If the dogs aggress toward each other when you are *not* there, the behavior is not alliance aggression (see also Chapter 5).

- Leave the dogs together when you are present, but with Sweetie wearing a muzzle to protect Rex from attack. Alternatively, Sweetie can wear a Gentle Leader or a leash so you can safely and easily separate the dogs should trouble arise.

- Interrupt any altercation with a loud noise—and then walk out of room. Sweetie won't continue to squabble when you aren't there.

- Walk the dogs at the same time, together, with two people. This way, neither receives preferential treatment. It's vital that you walk Rex while somebody else walks Sweetie.

- Begin a program of counter-conditioning once the "ignore period" has ended. This helps Sweetie learn to accept and tolerate the close proximity of Rex in the same room with you. First, tie the dependent dog (Sweetie) at one end of the room so she can't reach you or Rex. Conduct obedience drills with Rex in front of Sweetie, from the other end of the room. Have lots of treats ready to give to Sweetie for putting up with this. Don't forget to reward Rex. Reduce the distance between the two dogs slowly.

SEPARATION ANXIETY

About fourteen percent of pet dogs seen in veterinary hospitals in the U.S. suffer from separation anxiety. If you have more than one dog, chances increase at least one will be affected. Mixed breeds and dogs adopted from shelters or the streets are most commonly affected, and aging dogs (ten years and older) or puppies adopted prior to eight weeks of age also have a higher incidence.

The dog feels overattachment to one or more family member. Problems arise when the amount of time you spend with the pet changes, perhaps due to a new job or baby. The dog follows you about the house and becomes increasingly distraught as you prepare to leave. When left alone, affected dogs become anxious and distressed, extremely vocal, and sometimes forget house training or destroy property either to escape or as a way to relieve tension. Just one dog acting out can prompt the rest of the pack to join in the destruction.

Dogs don't retaliate for being left alone. Personal objects that are targeted smell like you and the contact reminds Rex of you, which may trigger anxiety that causes destructive displacement behaviors. As with other fearful behaviors, punishment makes the problem worse. The most intensive acting out occurs during the first twenty to thirty minutes after you leave. How long you're gone doesn't seem to matter. If you can distract Rex during this critical period, much of the destructive behavior and angst will be relieved.

🐾 Desensitize the affected dogs to the triggers of departure. Pick up the car keys fifty times a day, then set them down. Put on your coat or open the front door dozens of times, but don't go outside. Repetition makes these cues lose their meaning so the dogs no longer identify them as the signal that you're going away—and, consequently, they remain calmer when you do leave.

Stage absences of one minute, three minutes, five minutes, and so on in incremental doses to help build the dogs' tolerance. As with the key-rattling exercise, leave the house ten, fifteen, or twenty times in a row, immediately coming back inside. Rex may howl at your departure and leap for joy upon your return for the first fifteen trips, but thereafter, he will suddenly realize—hey, he's coming back, so what's to worry? Once you get the single canine instigator calmed down, the rest of the pack won't have a leader to follow to tear up the house.

 Give your dogs a long romp in the back yard before you must leave for the day. Tired dogs have less energy to burn up in destructive ways, and a worn-out pack may even snooze while you're gone.

 Play soothing music such as Pet Melodies while you're gone to calm pets.

 Offer a puzzle toy that contains a treat. This will distract dogs enough during the critical first twenty minutes after you leave, reducing the chance of a full-blown panic attack.

 Desensitize dogs to suitcases by leaving the bags out all the time. Encourage small dogs to jump in and out of the suitcase, put toys in it or a food bowl, and let them identify the bags with fun times.

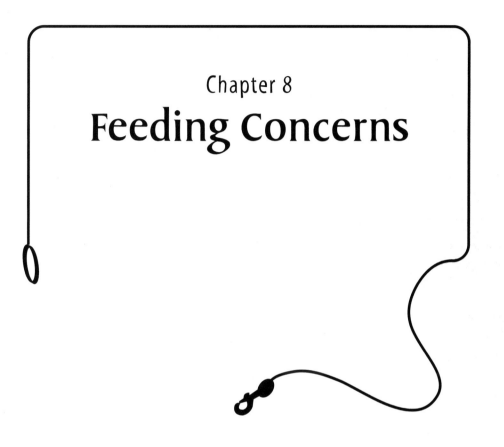

Chapter 8
Feeding Concerns

Dogs love to eat and breeds with a hunting heritage, such as Labradors, try to eat anything that doesn't get out of their way. Dogs are scavengers by nature, and as a result, owners must fill the bowl with the appropriate food. One-size-fits-all diets aren't appropriate, and in multidog homes, owners must be sure to cater diets to the dogs' breeds, ages, and sizes. Commercial diets fit the needs of the broadest categories of pet dogs, based on lifestage: diets for growth for puppies, maintenance for adult dogs, and a relatively new category for aging dogs termed senior foods. As your pack matures, individuals pass through each lifestage and need to transition to a new food made to fit their particular category. You can look for specialized diets to satisfy the higher-energy needs of performance dogs or for weight-loss diets or foods designed for small dogs that provide a smaller, more manageable kibble size. Dogs suffering from medical challenges may require a therapeutic diet to support their failing organs. Veterinarians dispense therapeutic diets based on diagnosis and needs of the individual dog. Choosing the right diet for your dogs and making sure the right dog eats from the correct bowl can be a challenge in the multidog household.

APPETITE LOSS

When a doggy glutton snubs the bowl, you know something's wrong. You must pay attention to intake, though, especially if you offer communal meals where the entire pack munches from one big bowl. Even when each dog has his own plate (a much better idea), if Rex leaves food in the bowl the other dogs likely will clean up after him, and you may not know about the problem immediately. Most dogs subscribe to the "grass is greener" philosophy and eagerly take advantage of grazing from the other bowls. If more than one of your pack leaves food behind, chances are they've all been exposed to the same bug, toxin, or emotional cause. Whatever the reason, the following techniques help tempt your pack's appetite.

- Feed the dogs together. To canines, eating is a communal event, and healthy competition can prompt Rex to clean his plate if he knows others gobble leftovers. If a glutton bullies another dog into leaving food behind, feed the dogs separately (see also page 148 for feeding multiple diets to several dogs).

- Stimulate doggy appetite with smell and temperature. Turn unappealing refrigerated leftover canned food into a taste sensation by zapping it in the microwave.

- Moisten dry food with warm water or low-fat, no-salt meat broth or bullion. The warmth and scent spark the dogs' appetites.

Use canned food or meat baby food as a top dressing on the dry diet, or switch to a very pungent, smelly canned food to get him eating again.

 Canned foods, especially the gourmet diets, contain more fat and flavor enhancers and may spur the reluctant eater's appetite.

 Offer canned cat food, which is much higher in protein than regular dog food.

 Serve baby food, which appeals to dogs even when they feel sick to their tummies. Add a dressing of fresh fruit puree (mashed apple or banana) or artificial sweetener such as aspartame to tempt the canine sweet tooth.

 Feed him small amounts every hour or so. This way he won't try to eat too much at one time.

 Transition slowly from an old diet to a new one, as a sudden change in diet upsets the digestion of many dogs. Begin by mixing one-quarter of the new diet with three-quarters of the old for a week. The second week, mix the two diets 50/50. The third week, mix three-quarters of the new with one-quarter of the old until finally Rex eats one hundred percent of the new food.

RELIEVING DENTAL PAIN

 Eighty percent of dogs develop dental disease by age three, and the pain can prompt dogs to refuse to eat. He'll need the attention of a veterinarian dentist, but in the meantime, offer soft foods he can chew more easily. Blend one part dry food with two parts flavored liquid in a food processor for easy chewing.

VET ALERT!

Hypoglycemia (low blood sugar) happens when the levels of glucose become too low in the bloodstream. Signs include weakness and "drunken" behavior—and, ultimately, seizures. Toy breed puppies are particularly prone to hypoglycemia because they have few fat stores and their tiny livers aren't mature enough to make sugar in adequate amounts. They need to eat frequently to maintain a healthy blood/glucose level to prevent hypoglycemia. If your puppy develops hypoglycemia, simply feed him a meal—and if he can't eat, smear some Karo Syrup, honey, or sugar water on his gums so it quickly absorbs into his system to counteract the problem.

MANAGING MULTIPLE DIETS

When your pack consists of similar size and age dogs, the same diet may be appropriate—one for large breed puppies, for instance, or an adult performance dog formulation for your agility crew. More often, the dogs' different personalities, social interactions, and health issues rule appetite, feeding schedule, and diet. That offers challenges to feeding multiple dogs.

For example, an overweight couch potato on a weight-loss food shouldn't be grazing from the puppy's high-calorie kibble. Other times, the pushy glutton bullies the other dogs out of their share. The larger your pack, the greater the chance that one or more dogs will need a special food the others shouldn't eat. If you're lucky, your dogs eat only from their assigned bowls. If not, use any combination of these tips.

- Stagger feedings ten minutes apart so you can oversee the dogs who shouldn't nibble from a particular formula.

- Avoid feeding from one big bowl. Each dog should have his own dish.

- Assign each dog a specific place to eat. Feed the dogs on opposite sides of the kitchen or at each end of a long hallway. Stand in the middle to keep them apart.

- Teach your dogs to go to a specific place as soon as they empty their own bowl, whereupon you give them a *bonus* reward or treat unbelievably better than anything in the other dog's bowl. To receive the treat, Rex must leave Sweetie's food alone.

- Feed a problem dog in a different room from the others. If you don't have enough rooms or doors to go around, use baby gates to separate them.

- Provide a treat ball for a problem dog. This dispenses a single meal to one dog as he plays, one kibble at a time. That keeps a problem dog occupied with "hunting" for his food rather than scrounging from another canine's bowl.

Place a large ball or heavy chain in the food dish to slow the gulper's intake.

 When the dogs are quite different in size, place the smaller one's food inside a closet or cupboard that's secured with a safety chain so it only opens wide enough for the small pet to access the food.

 Provide pet doors with electronic "key" collars that allow the dog wearing the special collar to access the door that leads to the location where his special food awaits, while the rest of the furry crew can't get through.

INCREDIBLE INEDIBLES: THE HOOVER COMPLEX

Veterinarians and behaviorists don't know why some dogs eat dirt or chew rocks, but they think it may be a type of obsessive-compulsive behavior. Pica (eating nonedible objects) in humans has been associated with a nutritional deficiency and occasionally linked to anemia. Teeth can be painfully broken or worn down, and if foreign material blocks the digestive tract, your dog could die. Some behaviorists suspect canine pica results from conflict, anxiety, and/or a lack of positive stimulation. In other words, your dog gets bored or feels anxious, so she bites rocks to release her pent-up emotion (see also Chapter 7).

When your veterinarian diagnoses a compulsive disorder, drug therapy may be prescribed. Prescription medications such as clomipramine, paroxetine, or fluoxetine may help. When the dog gets a clean bill of health from the veterinarian, you must decide how to manage the situation. Younger dogs or pups that observe this behavior may develop the same bad habit, so dealing with a single dog benefits the whole pack.

 Feed the dog a higher-fiber diet. Commercial products designed for weight loss can work, or supplement the regular food with raw vegetables such as lettuce, carrots, or green beans. It won't hurt the whole pack to munch on raw veggies as a treat, either, even if only one pet exhibits pica.

🐾 Search the yard and clear it of stones, sticks, or dirt pits, and supervise your dogs' outside activity. If the problem dog stays in the yard alone for much of the day, it can help to either bring him inside or have one of the housedogs spend more time with him in the yard. A "buddy" dog that gets along well and plays with the rock chewer offers Rex something better to do.

🐾 Offer safe, legal chewing outlets. Rawhide dog toys are ideal and come in flavors attractive to dogs. Make sure you have at least two or three available for each dog so one canine doesn't hog all the toys and leave Rex with only rocks to chew.

RESOURCE GUARDING

Dogs become possessive over valuable objects, such as toys or food. Even in homes where kibble endlessly fills the bowl, some dogs take great pains to protect this resource from other dogs—or even from the owner. Resource guarding, also called possessive aggression, stems from insecurity and may even include your possession. "I own that person, the person owns the briefcase, therefore I own the briefcase and will protect it from other dogs/humans," thinks the dog.

The behavior poses a danger to other pets, people, and especially children in your home. A dog might guard only his bowl or generalize that he owns the area and guard the entire kitchen. Dogs can be possessive of anything that hits the floor, but especially food. A child dropping a treat or toy, then reaching for it at the same moment the dogs decide it belongs to them, could spell disaster.

The level of danger depends greatly on the dog's tolerance level and how well he inhibits his bite. If your pack argues over a particular toy, throw it out and provide new ones—lots of them—to counter the behavior. Rotate the toys so Rex and the gang won't become overly attached to one. Never bully or take the toy from a dog that has possession or you risk getting bit. Instead, offer a swap with another toy or treat to distract him from the behavior. You'll see other dogs do this, and it works.

Food bowl guarding tends to be most serious. Growls and snaps in midair at the food bowl are scary and could escalate into more serious situations. Such dogs already feel defensive, and punishment actually accelerates the response. When one of your dogs reacts in this fashion to the rest of the pack during meals, use the tips on page 148 for feeding multiple diets to design a safe dinnertime. But when one or more of a pack guards the food bowl from you, a special program of systemic desensitization works best. You want all your dogs to feel comfortable and nonthreatened about somebody approaching during meals, or you won't be able to properly care for them. If you have more than one food-possessive dog, address each one separately.

- Throw out the old bowl and choose a new location for meals. Create a new routine without any of the old associations.

- Block off the designated area with baby gates to keep the other dogs out of range, to reduce the dog's reactivity. If you have other food-guarding dogs waiting their turn for training, let them watch from a distance to reinforce the lessons.

- Feed the dog from your hand for the next five to ten days.

- Use leash control if the dog still lunges to get the food. Attach Rex's leash to a stationary object to keep him confined to only the length of the tether. This protects you from his teeth and also teaches him that you control the situation.

- Place the new feeding dish in the new location within leash-reach of the dog.

- Measure a meal-size portion of food into a separate "control bowl" that *you* hold and the dog can't access. Ask Rex to sit. When he does, toss three or four kibbles into his dish to reward the behavior. Feed the entire meal three kibbles at a time, alternating "sit" with "down" until finished. This teaches the dog that he must earn the food to be paid. Feed this way for the next ten days.

- Walk away with the control bowl of food if at any time he becomes aggressive. When you have other pack members watching, give them a treat from the bowl to show Rex that when he acts aggressively, he not only gets no food but his cronies get a taste of his dinner.

- Give him a five- to ten-minute time-out to think about things, and then try again. If he still aggresses, leave with the food. Rex shouldn't be offered food again until the next scheduled meal. Missing a meal won't hurt him, but can teach that if he aggresses, the food goes away and he only gets fed with good behavior.

- Gradually increase the amount of food tossed into the bowl as long as he's calm. You can use a gravy ladle to safely transfer kibble from your handheld bowl to the dish within reach of the dog.

- Have other adult family members perform this technique so he begins to generalize the fact that humans near his bowl mean good things for him.

- Toss in smelly treats when he gets more comfortable so he learns that allowing you to approach doesn't mean food goes away but that he gets bonuses.

TEACHING DOGS "OFF" OR "LEAVE IT"

Preventing food aggression by training puppies saves you both heartache. Make mealtime a happy event for new pups. Don't just set down the bowl; be part of the mealtime experience. Sit beside the dogs, pet them, talk to them as they eat, dangle your hand in the bowl without taking anything out. Drop tasty treats into the bowl, or pick up the bowl and add cottage cheese, yogurt, or some other bonanza tasty. This teaches the youngsters that a bowl + human = yummies and that food will not be taken away.

You should also teach a command that means "back away" from whatever the item might be. That saves you from fighting with your pack over the dropped pot roast, rat poison, visiting skunk, or your son's shoe. Teach the "off" exercise to puppies as well as to adult dogs who do not already have problems with possessive aggression.

 Teach the "off" command to each dog individually. Hold the treat securely in your fingers and sit beside your dog with your treat-filled hand at his nose level.

 Say "Off," then move your hand directly to his nose (not above it), and hold it half an inch from his nose.

 Touch the dog's nose with your closed hand to induce him to back away if he reaches for it. Don't pull back (or he'll chase it) and don't repeat "Off." Use your hand to protect the treat.

 Say Rex's name with a cheerful voice and let him come forward to collect the treat, if he backs up and stops pressuring for it. This teaches him to move forward to get something *only* when you give permission.

 Repeat the exercise a half-dozen times in a row and end on a good note.

 Look for the doggy lightbulb to go off when he backs away or hesitates upon hearing "off" without your tapping hand body-blocking his nose. Once he reaches that stage, go to the next training level of food on the floor.

 Place your dog on one side of your body, drop food on the other side, and say "Off." Don't actually block the food, but be ready to do so if he moves toward the treat.

 Work in pairs once each dog understands "off" on his own. Release one dog by saying his name. Only the dog whose name is said can get the treat. Alternate dogs—or perhaps the dog offering the best "off"—get the treat first.

 Work with the whole group after pairs have successfully mastered the "off" exercise. Ideally, your pack will compete with each other to see who does the best "off" and wins your highest approval.

Chapter 9
Dog-to-Dog Introductions

Dog personalities vary a great deal, and while some "never met a stranger" and immediately fit into the furry pack, others need coaxing and lots of help. Introductions represent great change in a new dog's—and your existing pack's—life. Rex must not only meet, make friends with, and fit into the current canine family, but he must also adjust to a new house and yard, human family, and rules. Consider Rex to be a foreign exchange student with only a basic understanding of the customs and language. Be kind, patient, and ready to run interference for him and your resident canines.

Choose your new dog carefully so he or she will more easily fit into your existing pack. Current canines should be your first responsibility; they've been there the longest and you're already "family," so make sure any change won't disrupt their happiness. Dogs tend to be very accepting of new friends, but don't expect another dog to cure existing canine behavior problems. If one or more of your existing pack causes trouble, chances are additional dogs may aggravate the situation.

UNDERSTANDING DOGGY DYNAMICS

Refer to the L.E.A.S.H. technique in the Introduction to recall the five major considerations to take into account when choosing your new canine friend. After you've found your pick of the litter, remember that introductions go more smoothly when the resident pet already knows the rules of the house and basic obedience commands. At a minimum, your pack should understand "no" and each dog be leash-trained. Resident canines feel protective when on their own turf, so arrange for first meetings to take place on neutral territory.

Dogs properly socialized as puppies most readily accept new canines as friends, so don't be shy about quizzing the shelter staff or breeder/owner about these lessons. Also, the longer a pup stays with mom and siblings before being adopted, the better he learns "dog language" and bite control and the more easily he will accept living with other dogs later in life. That said, young pups adopted into a home with savvy adult canines benefit greatly from lessons taught at the paws of these "uncle" dogs.

It can be harder to predict personalities in puppies, but in adult dog adoptions, choosing complementary pet personalities promotes better relationships. Choose a confident newcomer for the fewest potential problems. Also, try to choose complementary activity types. A canine athlete partnered with a lap-sitter won't infringe on each's preferred way of life. Be patient, and don't rush. Introduce your new dog to one resident dog at a time or you'll overwhelm the newcomer and potentially prompt aggressive outbursts if Rex gets scared. Remember to *always* pay more attention to the resident pets during these initial meetings, at least when he is within view. Once all the dogs, old and new, mingle together, you should feed, pet, and groom the top dog first. Give him any other preferential treatment necessary to ensure peace and harmony in the multidog household. Avoid giving preferential attention to a new, lower-ranking dog. That prompts confusion and may inspire the dominant dog to kick furry tail to put the lower-ranking dog back in his place. Resident canines will be much more willing to accept a newcomer as long as your affections aren't usurped. Most dogs eventually make friends. In rare instances, it takes days or weeks for them to get along. A few dogs never become friends, but you can strive for tolerance.

STEP-BY-STEP INTRODUCTIONS

The information below assumes that both the resident dog(s) and the new pooch are confident, healthy canines that have been properly socialized. Use the same steps whether you're dealing with puppy-to-puppy, puppy-to-adult, or adult-to-adult introductions. Follow *all* the steps, although with pup-to-pup introductions you may be able to go directly to inside-the-house meetings. The adult-to-multiple-adult introductions will take the longest. Remember that each "pair" must meet individually, and every dog in the house must work out his or her own feelings about the interloper.

 Spay or neuter the newcomer *before* introductions. Fixed dogs have a less difficult time fitting into the household and aren't as great a threat to the status quo of the established hierarchy.

- Introduce one resident dog at a time to the newcomer, starting with the top dog. That allows you to more safely supervise the interactions and prevent your resident canines from overwhelming him.

- If you anticipate trouble, condition the new dog and other problem canines to the muzzle prior to introductions (see page 102). Using muzzles not only prevents potential injury, but also helps you relax and makes the dogs feel more at ease.

- Arrange first meetings on neutral ground, such as a neighbor's yard, a dog training center, or a tennis court. Meeting a strange dog on home turf can cause fear and possibly territorial aggression in your resident dogs.

- Give unleashed dogs a thirty-minute sniffing opportunity through a safe barrier, such as a fence. That helps the novelty of "new dog" wear off before a true nose-to-nose meeting and eases the tension brought on by a leash restraint.

- Use a nearby park or common area many dogs visit and none "own" if you can't go to a neutral area. Your resident dogs have less territorial claims in such a location and should be more willing to meet the new guy.

- Put both dogs on leashes and take them for a walk, if you don't have a park. Walk them parallel to each other, with a different person handling each dog. Remember to keep the leashes loose and give them room to move.

- Keep them far enough apart (ten feet) so they can't sniff or greet each other. Prevent them from staring at each other by using a toy or treat to keep each dog's attention. Walk the pair in tandem for five or ten minutes before allowing a head-to-head meeting.

- Allow the dogs to meet once they have shown positive interest in each other on-leash. Dogs naturally sniff nose-to-nose first and then work down to the anal-genital region. Let them be rude; that's the way they say "Howdy."

- Keep the dogs away from gates, doorways, or closely confined spaces during this first meeting. Choose an area with open space to reduce tension. Interrupt sniffing every now and then by calling them away and moving around to break tension and keep the mood light. Limit these initial meetings to ten minutes or so to keep from tiring the dogs.

- Distract the dogs from any hierarchical challenges (paw over the back, mounting, or chinning) by offering each a ball to redirect their attention.

- Allow any play to continue a few minutes, and then break up the play to end the session on a good note.

- Have the dogs repeat the meeting in your yard, off-leash, if it's fenced. Again, monitor the situation and call the dogs apart every few minutes to ensure they don't become too aroused.

- Once the new guy has met all your resident dogs, you can begin letting them co-mingle in the yard with one or two of the "old guys" at a time paired with the new dog. Pay attention to how each dog handles the situation before adding others.

- Place the new dog inside the house while the resident dogs are out. Discovering the new dog already inside reduces Rex's level of arousal.

- Segregate the new dog in a room alone with a baby gate barrier when you are not there to directly supervise and if you have concerns about safety issues (dogs of a greater size or age disparity, for example).

PART THREE

THE MULTICAT HOUSEHOLD
Common Problems
and Practical Solutions

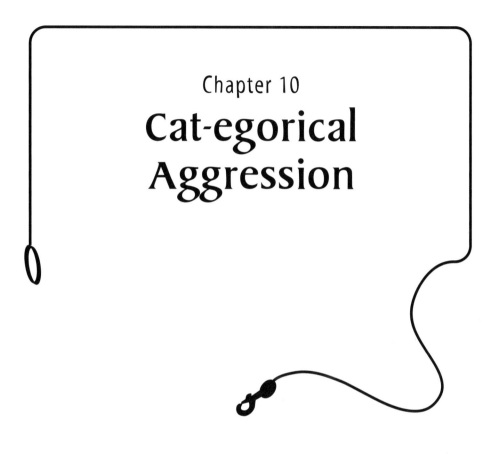

Chapter 10
Cat-egorical Aggression

In multicat homes, cats usually aggress toward other cats and rarely toward owners. Signs include outright attacks to urine spraying to staring at another cat until he moves. Adult cats normally aggress toward strange animals that trespass on their territory, which makes new cat introductions a challenge for owners. There are several categories of feline aggression, and more than one can happen concurrently. The more kinds the cat expresses, the poorer is the prognosis for improvement.

Cats bluff incredibly well and fur rarely flies. Dominance displays can be so subtle that you may never know any controversy took place. Almost all types have a fear or anxiety component. This holds true especially during pet introductions, or in multiple-cat households where dynamics often shift with age, health status, and stress levels.

Oftentimes people accidentally teach aggression when they reward bad behavior by allowing the cat to get his way. For instance, if they cut short the grooming when the cat hisses, Sheba subsequently "generalizes" the lesson and uses a hiss or bite to control other interactions. Owners who act anxious or threatening in the cat's presence further aggravate feline aggression. Recognizing potential triggers and understanding the warning signs of aggression will help you to avoid or diffuse aggression. Common situations during which your cat may react with aggression include:

- When feeling pain.
- When a deaf or blind cat is startled.
- When approached or disturbed while resting.
- When overcrowded by too many cats for the space.
- When protecting resources (bed, territory, kittens).
- When physically and/or verbally disciplined.
- When forced to make prolonged eye contact.
- When experiencing unwelcome handling (being held, petted, lifted).
- When restrained or forced into an unwelcome position.
- When hearing certain music frequencies or high-pitched sounds (a baby crying, a violin playing).

WHEN THE FUR FLIES: CALCULATING RISK

Most cats learn early on how to wrangle without physically hurting each other. Kitties have exquisite control of their teeth and claws and know how to pull punches to keep damage to a

COMFORT ZONE: BOTTLED FRIENDSHIP

Dr. Patrick Pageat, a researcher in the field of pheromones, discovered five "fractions" of the feline cheek pheromone. Three of these fractions have been identified: F2, communicates information about sexual behavior and the F3 fraction marks the physical environment and has been marketed as the product Feliway.

"The F4 is a collection of specific molecules, common to all cats, that says friend," says Dr. Daniel Mills, a veterinary and professor conducting trials on new pheromone products. "It's used to identify friend from foe so they don't shoot down their own plane." Dr. Pageat has created an analogue of the F4 fraction, marketed as Felifriend, useful in countering cat-on-cat aggression and soothing new cat introductions. The product communicates to all the cats that they already know the individual, have a good relationship, and don't need to fight.

"A problem has been that F4 smells like a very old cheese," says Dr. Pageat. "Even for a French guy, a very strong odor. Our first product was not so comfortable for humans." The new version of Felifriend, already marketed overseas, should be available in the United States in the near future and help enormously with cat-on-cat aggression.

minimum. They posture, show teeth, and swipe claws near (but not in contact with) the target, rather than biting. This allows them to resolve differences without hurting each other.

Thunder and fury with no blood spilled indicates they have excellent bite inhibition, but few fights resulting in lots of damage indicate that at least one of the cats either has very poor inhibitions or seriously wants to kill the other cat. Cats that hate each other and draw blood during fights have an extremely poor prognosis.

Kittens develop good manners through interaction with other kittens and mom-cat's discipline. Too often, though, kittens go to new homes before they've learned these important lessons and you'll need to teach them.

TEACHING LIMITS

Cats use mouths and paws to explore their world. You can't stop it nor should you try. Bite inhibition teaches kitty to inhibit the *force* of the bite and keep claws unfurled by explaining to her in terms she understands that teeth and claws hurt. She can still make an emphatic point bopping another cat (or human) with a soft paw. Begin training as soon as you get your kitten or cat. A well-socialized adult cat teaches the best lessons to kittens, but you can help, with these tips.

 Don't allow your kitten or cat to play with your hands, fingers, or toes.

 Offer a legal toy for the cat to bite and bunny kick.

 Gently praise Sheba for soft paws (claws withheld) or a soft mouth, by saying, "Good paws, good mouth!"

 Hiss if the claws come out or the mouthing hurts, just as another cat or kitten would to stop the games.

 Push your hand or arm *in* toward a bite if she won't let go to prompt Sheba to release you. Pulling away from the bite stimulates her to bite even more.

 Treat your clothing as an extension of skin and make it off-limits, or the kitten won't learn the difference between clawing jeans and nailing your bare legs.

 Use a very short, loud, high-pitched *Eeeek* if the *hiss* does not discourage a bite or claw attempt. Warn the rest of your family before doing this, though, so they won't call for help.

 Tell Sheba, "You hurt me," with as much angst and tears as you can muster. Physical punishment only makes cats more determined to fight back and protect themselves, but they often understand the emotion of hurt feelings.

 Send her into a room alone for five minutes to tell her she exceeded the proper bounds and needs to contain her teeth and claws.

COMBAT INTERVENTION

Screaming felines facing off for battle keep the faint at heart—and savvy owners—a safe distance away. In fact, you likely will get bitten by physically interceding. Dr. McConnell also warns against shouting or yelling. "That can escalate the arousal and make it worse," she says. Most caterwauling is for show, though, and can be headed off before the teeth and claws engage.

 Interrupt the hissing with a favorite toy, such as a fishing pole lure or flashlight beam. Don't wait until the cats fight. The earlier you intervene, the quicker the cats will chill. Choose toys that keep you a safe distance away.

 Use a loud noise like an air horn or hiss of aerosol spray to startle the combatants apart.

 Toss a half-glass of ice-cold water at them if the noise doesn't stop them. Aim for their bodies and avoid the face and eyes.

 Throw a thick blanket over top of both cats if you can't get them wet. That usually separates the pair.

 Wrap up the aggressor cat in the blanket to protect yourself and bundle him into a room alone for a time-out. It takes cats twenty-four to forty-eight hours to settle down after arousal. Just the sight of each other can start the fight all over again.

 Be sure all the other cats seem calm. Catfights may trigger other cats to join in or fight among themselves, so segregate any other agitated cats into a different room or crate until all have settled down.

CAT BASHING

Any two cats can develop a dislike for each other, but most intercat aggression involves intact same-gender cats and worsens during mating season. Neutering before twelve months decreases or prevents up to ninety percent of cat-on-cat aggression. Cats

---

VET ALERT!

Changes in a cat's thyroid hormone production can prompt changes in behavior, especially aggression. Dr. Beaver characterizes hyperthyroid aggression as "nasty" and hypothyroid aggressive cats as "grumpy." A routine blood test screening for thyroid function, especially in middle-aged to older cats, diagnoses this treatable condition.

typically work out their place in the hierarchy through posturing without injury to either party. The lowest-ranking cat may be targeted and picked on by the other felines. Acting like a victim can bring out the bully in the dominant feline and prompt additional aggression. Never allow cats to "fight it out," as that rarely settles conflicts but makes matters worse.

Cat-on-cat fights can result from any other kind of aggression. Increased conflicts arise due to changes in the social group as people or animals become part of the household or leave the family group. Major changes to environment, such as moving, or subtle changes such as where cats sleep, eat, perch, and eliminate can cause the fur to fly. Cats reach social maturity at two to four years of age, when many cats first challenge others for status.

Not enough space predisposes cats to territorial disputes. Cats mark property with cheek rubs, patrolling, and urine marking. Some diabolical felines lure others into their territory and then "discipline" the other cat for trespassing. Feline territorial aggression is notoriously hard to correct, and marking behavior is a hallmark of potential aggression. Outdoor cats are more aggressive on their home turf, and the cat closest to home usually wins the dispute. When all tactics have failed to stop two indoor cats from fighting, then ultimately one cat may need to be placed in a new home or permanently segregated from the other in another part of the house.

When trying to establish authority, cats employ a variety of signals to elevate their status in the eyes of the other felines. They challenge each other with stares, forward-facing body position, hisses and growls, mounting behavior and nape bites, or blocking access to food, play, or attention. Some dominant cats use "power grooming" behavior—energetically licking the other cat—to make her move away. Often, older or weaker cats are victimized and picked on by healthier felines. Manage with behavior modification, counter-conditioning, and sometimes drug therapy. The tips that follow can ease the strain and, in some instances, resolve intercat aggression.

Increase the territorial space to reduce the urge to wrangle by providing sufficient climbing, hiding, and perching areas.

 Implement electronic cat doors that can only be opened by the collared victim cat. This allows her to access the entire home yet retreat to a safe area where the aggressor can't follow.

 Don't reward undesirable behavior by offering the aggressive cat food or attention to calm down. If you can catch Sheba before she gets hissy, you can redirect her behavior with an interactive toy, such as a flashlight beam, to lure her into play in another direction and help her associate good things with the other cat.

 Interrupt with an aerosol hiss if the toy doesn't work. Reinforce the desirable response—acting calmly—by offering a treat, toy, or attention.

 Treat them as though they are meeting each other for the first time, as long as the cats act aggressively toward each other (see also Chapter 14). With reintroductions, it's best to give the victim cat the choice location of the house and sequester the bully cat to the isolation room.

 Talk with your veterinary behaviorist if you see no significant improvement within a week. Drugs along with a counter-conditioning program may help control the aggressive behavior and decrease the defensive posturing and vocalizing of the threatened cat.

COUNTER-CONDITIONING THE AGGRESSIVE CAT

 Expose the cats to each other gradually and in very controlled situations once the signs of aggression, anxiety, and/or hypervigilance fade. Begin with the cats in carriers or controlled with a harness and leash, at opposite ends of your largest room or longest hallway.

 Feed cats tasty foods or engage in play during each session. This helps both cats learn to associate each other with fun, positive rewards.

 Interrupt unacceptable behavior by the aggressor cat with a squirt of compressed air or water. Toss small treats to reinforce good behavior. Counter-conditioning can take months and require much patience and time.

☙ Create at least two feeding stations and two bathroom locations once cats have learned to tolerate each other and are allowed to freely roam. Locate them so cats won't be trapped or surprised when using either.

SCAREDY CATS

Fear is the most common reason for feline aggression. Influenced by heredity and shyness, some cats aggress every time they become frightened. Punishment and poor socialization can also cause fear aggression and will make it worse. Cats may develop fear of people, places, other cats, certain noises, or even odors, and react with aggression, making it difficult for them to enjoy their lives and hard for you to enjoy their company.

Cats often learn to associate one scary experience—a car ride to the vet—with all future car rides. A single bad episode with a longtime feline friend can turn the relationship sour. Scared cats quickly learn that aggressive behavior makes the scary "thing" go away and use it repeatedly, such as to warn off strangers. Affected cats may turn from offense to defense and back again during the arousal. They display a mix of defensive body signals (ears flattened sideways, tail tucked, crouching, and leaning away) and aggressive signals (fluffed fur, showing teeth, hissing, growling, swatting, biting, and scratching). Usually the pupils of their eyes dilate wide, unrelated to the amount of light present. If the cat's aggression is mild and you can keep Sheba away from triggers, no other treatment may be necessary. These tips can help.

☙ Identify the reactive distance at which the scared cat becomes agitated if another cat approaches. Avoid situations by maintaining appropriate distance between the fearful cat and potential triggers.

Provide additional quiet areas and/or hiding places in the home. Elevated perches such as cat trees, shelf space, and small boxes can help Sheba feel more secure.

 Separate aggressive cats so they can't see each other. Visual contact heightens cat arousal and can increase aggressive episodes or make them worse.

 Use Feliway, in plug-in or spray form.

 Create a house of plenty by providing lots of toys, scratching posts, and litter boxes (at least one per cat, plus one) to reduce competition with other cats.

 Use interactive play to build feline confidence. A fishing pole toy or the beam of a light pointer allows the cat to have fun with you, but from a distance not likely to trigger an attack.

 Train cats to do tricks. This will help to build confidence and improve the bond you share (see also Chapter 4).

 Add several drops of Rescue Remedy to their water bowl for a calming effect.

COUNTER CONDITIONING THE FEARFUL CAT

Fearful cats can't think or learn new behaviors while afraid. Instead, they turn aggression "on" immediately at the sight of another cat with which they've argued. Behavior modification using counter-conditioning teaches Sheba to manage her fear and so better tolerate the other feline.

 Segregate each cat in a separate room.

 Create a fifteen-minute routine and repeat three to four times every day, with each cat in private. This could include the cat's meal, a special playtime, grooming session, or other pastime Sheba enjoys, to reduce fear of the unexpected.

 In a single room or long hallway, measure a length a bit beyond the cats' reactive distance. Place two cages/carriers at each end or use a pair of baby gates to keep the cats separated outside of that reactive distance. When using carriers, spray a bit of Feliway on a cloth and leave it inside before inserting the cat.

Feed each cat lots of treats, talk in a happy, upbeat voice, and scratch their cheeks and chins through the crate to make the experience pleasant. Cats willing to take treats while seeing each other are not as fearful. Do this several times a day for three to five minutes at a time before returning them to their private rooms.

 Slowly decrease the distance between the carriers, continuing with the treats, praise, and petting. This teaches the fearful cat to associate the other kitty's presence with good things while she feels protected inside the carrier.

 Remove the nonfearful cat once the fearful cat no longer shows arousal within that critical distance. Leave the scared kitty inside her carrier, and continue to treat, treat, treat. Take turns bringing one cat out while the other gets treats in the cage. The cats may never become buddies, but over time they may be able to tolerate each other without resorting to violence.

IT FEELS TOO GOOD

Owners of multiple cats often experience "petting aggression," also referred to as status-related aggression, especially when these cats don't have the "clout" to boss other felines around but want to control their world. Cats avoid the behavior with those who resist

CALMING SIGNALS: FELINE RESTRAINTS

Fearful cats often bite without thinking and pin-wheeling paws cause lots of claw damage. When you know a particular situation (*i.e.*, vet visit) prompts an aggressive outburst, contain the cat's claws and teeth to protect yourself and others.

 Mesh cat muzzles are available from veterinarians and pet product suppliers. They cover the face and eyes, contain the teeth, and help calm the cat by shutting out the view. Make sure you choose one that fits properly (they come in several sizes) and that allows air to circulate for appropriate breathing. Flat-faced cats such as Persians can be more difficult to fit and also often have more trouble with breathing.

 Commercial "cat bags" typically contain the whole body while the head sticks out and can keep claws at bay particularly when something on the cat's head needs attention. A pillowcase can work well in a pinch.

but get pushy with people who give in to demands. They often ask for petting, especially when you're cuddling another cat, but then bite you to stop the interaction. That may, in part, be due to the location of the strokes, since cats accept grooming from other cats on the head and neck and may prefer this to body contact. Physical correction makes the behavior worse. Petting aggression can be explosive and dangerous and is typical of young, energetic cats taken early from their litter and left alone for long periods during the day. The following tips also can help.

- Identify and avoid situations that might lead to aggression. Use a treat or toy to bribe cats off furniture or out of the way, rather than physically move them.

- Say, "Move," and toss the treat on the floor or entice the cat down with a feather. Eventually just say the word "Move" and offer a sweeping gesture for the cat to obey—with this, you've avoided an encounter that could otherwise cause a bite.

- Stand up to dump the cat off your lap before she bites. When you're petting other cats, ignore her when she solicits attention, unless she behaves.

- Limit petting to the cat's head or back of the neck and identify the cat's petting threshold. Count the number of strokes Sheba enjoys before her ears flatten, tail becomes active, and eyes dilate. In the future, stop before you reach her limit.

- Desensitize the cat. If she tolerates three strokes before her ears go back, add one more stroke and then stop and dump her off your lap before she can bite. Add one stroke each week to gradually increase her petting threshold.

ALL WOUND UP

Both predatory and play aggressions include components of stealth, silence, alert posture, hunting postures, and lunging or springing at "prey" that moves suddenly after being still. Nearly any type of movement, from walking to picking up an object, triggers the behavior. Predation directed toward a human infant or smaller pets represents the greatest danger, but over-the-top play is normal and hand-raised kittens and those weaned early seem to have increased risk. They'll terrorize shy cats, bully smaller kittens, and pester geriatric felines as well as target their owners. Confident adult cats usually put these obnoxious felines in their place, young kittens outgrow the behavior, and tips found in the section on "Teaching Limits" in this chapter help a great deal. In addition, the following will help you deal with very playful or predatory aggressive cats.

 Provide safe areas where the picked-on felines won't be molested, such as high perches or separate rooms.

 Place a bell on the attack cat to warn victims in time to escape and so you can interrupt and stop the behavior.

 Using the hiss from an aerosol can, a squirt from a water gun, citronella sprays, and other interruptions may stop the attack cold. Experiment to find what works best for Sheba.

 Attach a leash and harness to the cat for control and interruption of undesirable behavior.

 Play interactive games with all your cats to burn off energy. Move toys perpendicular to their line of sight—across the cat's field of vision rather than toward or away from her—to spark the greatest interest. Interactive play encourages confidence in shy cats so they'll kick Sheba's furry tail and teach her manners.

 Create a regular routine that includes specific playtimes so the cats learn to expect fun interactive times.

 Adopt a second kitten of the same age, size, and temperament. This provides a legal target and playmate as well as an outlet for teaching bite and claw inhibition.

THE BLAME GAME

Redirected aggression happens as a result of Sheba being unable to respond to a physical or verbal correction or the thwarting of a desire. This affects adult male cats most often and arises from territorial, fear-induced, intermale, or defensive aggression.

When Tom can't reach the squirrel tap-dancing on the trees out the window, he instead nails the closest available victim. That may be another cat or the owner who wanders by at the wrong time, and such attacks seem unprovoked if you never see the squirrel. Owners often think the cat has gone nuts when Tom attacks out of the blue or when cats who previously got along become hostile to each other.

Common triggers include the sight, sound, or odor of another cat, other animals, unusual noises, unfamiliar people or environment, and pain. While people only become the accidental victims in the presence of the trigger, a housemate cat can become a permanent scapegoat after just one "accidental" response. After a first episode, the aggressing cat "remembers" and launches an attack whenever he sees the scapegoat cat. The poor scapegoat anticipates

VET ALERT!

Aggressive behavior without an identifiable cause is referred to as "idiopathic" aggression, but a relatively rare physical condition could be the culprit. Hyperesthesia syndrome, an excessive sensitivity to touch, refers to several odd behaviors (including aggression) that have no recognizable stimulus.

The syndrome first appears in cats one to four years old; Siamese, Burmese, Himalayans, and Abyssinians seem to have the highest incidence. Affected cats indulge in excessive grooming that targets their own tail and lower back and may ultimately result in self-mutilation when Sheba attacks herself. Inexplicable aggression is the second pattern of behavior. Cats seem friendly and even beg for attention, then furiously attack when the owner attempts to pet them. The final pattern reported by the veterinary literature is seizure.

Some behaviorists believe stress triggers psychomotor seizures that cause the behaviors. Other researchers believe the syndrome parallels human panic attacks and obsessive/compulsive disorders that occur due to the individual cat's personality, in combination with the pressures of her environment, frustrations, and stress levels.

If you can identify and avoid stress factors that trigger incidents, the syndrome may be eliminated. Some cats can be jarred from the behavior by an unexpected sudden noise, such as clapping your hands or slapping a newspaper against a table. Cats may also respond to anti-seizure medication or human anti-anxiety drugs and antidepressants that act on the cat's brain to put on the behavior brakes.

these attacks and, acting like a victim, stimulates the aggressor to continue the behavior. Refer to the section on "Cat Bashing" to help stop the cat aggressor/victim pattern. The following suggestions also help prevent future cases of redirected aggression.

 Leave the cat alone when you know he's aroused or you notice chittering teeth and an active tail. Try to keep the other cats from bothering him as well, especially when he lounges in the windowsill.

 Keep stray cats and strange animals away from window sight of your property. Eliminate hiding and perching places that draw animals, and don't leave food outside.

 Invest in the Scarecrow, available at home and garden stores. A water sprinkler, activated via a motion detector, scats stray critters with a spray of water. The Garden Ghost uses a safe, nontoxic spray technology to keep unwanted animals away from your property.

 Prevent access to windows or partly cover them to keep your cats from seeing the triggers. Pull the blinds and move furniture away from windows. Double-sided tape products such as Sticky Paws, applied to windowsills, make the surface uncomfortable so cats avoid lounging.

 Separate cats that show aggression toward each other. It may take several days or weeks for the aroused cat to "forget" the association and stop picking on the victim cat. Time away helps the scapegoat stop acting like a victim, too, which helps reduce the chance of being picked on.

 Bell the aggressor cat so the victim kitty can avoid encounters.

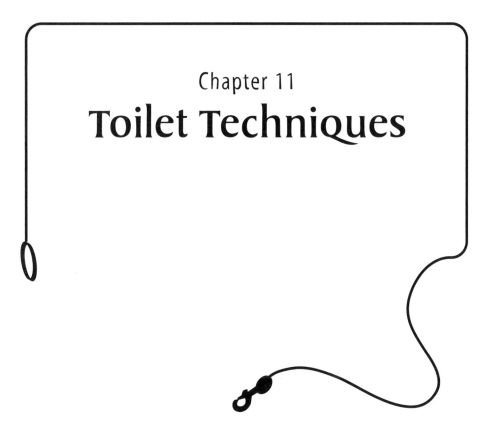

Chapter 11
Toilet Techniques

Cats have a reputation for being fastidious, clean creatures so we expect kittens to be born knowing toilet etiquette. Doing what comes naturally often gets Sheba in trouble with owners when neither party understands what the other wants out of the deal.

The dirt in the potted palm offers the perfect place to make a feline deposit, especially if the "legal" toilet isn't up to kitty standards. Spraying urine on the door frame or on your purse makes perfect sense—or, actually, scents—especially when other cats are around. To the dominant kitty, urine labels the object as hers and dampens the territorial ardor of other felines. Shouts or inappropriate punishment increase the cat's stress level and frequently prompt an increase in bathroom indiscretions.

On average, an adult cat without elimination problems uses the litter box five times per day. The more cats you have, the greater your chances of having bathroom problems. Felines have very specific ideas about who should go where and which cat owns what litter box. Ages of cats and placement of facilities also have a great impact. Strays rescued from the neighborhood or shelter that have spent years outdoors may not have a clue about using an indoor litter box.

HAIRBALL HORRORS

Barefoot owners discover wads of wet fur—hairballs—decorating the most stainable portions of the carpet during the wee hours of the night. Hairballs challenge all cat owners, but multicat homes must manage more hair. Cats spend up to fifty percent of awake-time grooming themselves. Friendly cats also groom each other, so the more cats, the greater the problem. Swallowed fur that doesn't pass into the litter box becomes hotdog or cigar-shaped wads when vomited. An occasional hairball, especially from long-haired cats during shedding season, isn't unusual. But large amounts of swallowed fur can block the digestive tract. Fifty percent of feline constipation is due to hairballs, and when cats suffer painful bowel movements they often "blame" the box and stop using it. There are inexpensive and effective means to prevent hairballs.

CALMING SIGNALS: WHO DID THE DIRTY DEED?

In multiple-cat households, you must identify the culprit(s) in order to treat the right cat. Confinement may help, or ask your veterinarian about "pilling" each cat in turn with fluorescein dye, suggests Dr. Seskel. Six dye strips placed in a gelatin capsule given orally to the cat causes the urine to fluoresce a bright yellow-green color (under a black light) for twenty-four hours after ingestion. For inappropriate defecation, add shavings of different-colored non-toxic crayons to the food of each cat.

- Comb and brush your cats regularly to reduce the amount they swallow through grooming themselves and each other.

- Feed a "hairball diet." Commercial formulas include added nondigestible fiber that helps push swallowed hair through the digestive tract and into the litter box.

- Mix a teaspoon of plain bran or Metamucil into canned meals. Some cats enjoy grazing on wheat grass, available in grow kits from pet product stores. Flaxseeds or psyllium husks, available in health food stores, also act as natural laxatives and work well. Add one-quarter teaspoon of flaxseeds or psyllium for every meal.

- Spread nonmedicated petroleum jelly on Sheba's forepaw for her to lick off. This slicks down the hairball and lubricates it to help the cat pass the mass into the litter box. Avoid digestible fats such as butter, which can cause diarrhea.

- Serve a teaspoonful of canned pumpkin over the cat's regular food a couple of times a week. It is high in fiber and cats like it as a treat. Divide the can into teaspoon-size dollops and freeze in an ice cube tray so you can thaw one serving at a time. Commercial products also help the hairball pass more readily.

MISSING THE MARK

In multicat households, hit-or-miss bathroom behavior can be a real problem as cats wrangle to claim position and territory. Problems are split evenly between spraying (urine marking) and urination/defecation misbehavior. Cats squat to empty their bladder and urinate downward on horizontal surfaces; urinating outside the litter box constitutes "house soiling." Normal marking behavior (spraying) consists of backing up to the target to spray urine on a vertical object and almost never takes place in the litter box.

Cats do *not* target owner belongings to "get back" at some imagined slight. For some cats, problems result from leaving mom-cat too early before learning proper bathroom manners.

Handraised orphan kittens or those adopted younger than eight to ten weeks must be taught the basics by owners, and transitioning adult outdoor cats to an indoor lifestyle also requires retraining. Many cats develop a routine and defecate once or twice a day, usually at the same time—and urinate two to six times a day. However, it's not unusual for some adult cats to urinate only once every thirty-six hours or so. You can use this information to monitor and manage your cats' bathroom activities. A sudden loss of litter box allegiance means either the litter box is unacceptable, the cat feels bad, or the other cats make her avoid the bathroom.

More than one-third of cats with elimination problems have an underlying health condition. If Sheba refuses to use the box to urinate (or defecate) but not both, look for a medical problem. Cats are instinctively clean and want privacy, so they "go" elsewhere if the box is dirty or in a high-traffic area. Changing litter brands also may prompt Sheba to snub the box. When one cat guards the bathroom facilities, the others leave deposits under the potted palm. A bully may dominate access to the litter box by sleeping in or near the pathway that leads to the toilet or glaring to keep hopefuls at bay. Punishment won't work. You must first identify and then remove the cause, reestablish good habits, and prevent a return to the scene of the crime.

> 🐾 Solve litter box woes with the 1+1 rule: provide one litter box for each cat, plus one (that's three boxes for two cats, for example). Many cats don't want to "go" after another cat. Others demand a separate box for urine and another for feces, and some dominant cats guard the facilities and won't let the others use it.

VET ALERT!

Cats have been known to suffer hairballs as big as baseballs, which require surgery to be removed. Frequent vomiting signals intestinal blockage. Hairballs also can cause diarrhea, loss of appetite, wheezing cough or dry retching, or a bloated abdomen. See your veterinarian immediately if your cat exhibits one or more of these signs.

Keep the toilet clean by scooping waste and discarding it at least twice a day. The more cats you have, the greater the amount of waste and ensuing smell, which offends you and the cats.

 Maintain product loyalty. A new litter often prompts Sheba to snub the box.

 Add an automatic litter box to keep the litter constantly clean. Be aware that it may take some training to teach cats to use this facility.

 Empty and clean the entire box at least once a week. Use scalding hot water but no harsh-smelling disinfectant because the detergent smell can be just as off-putting to the cats.

 Clean soiled areas thoroughly or the scent will draw Sheba (or even innocent bystanders!) back to the scene of the crime. Avoid using ammonia-based products, as cats think that it smells like the ammonia in their own urine. Use an enzymatic odor neutralizer, such as Petastic, Tuff-Oxy, or Anti-Icky-Poo, which literally eats the odor.

 Use a quality "black light" to find hidden urine accidents. Shine it around after you've turned off lights in the suspect areas; the cat urine glows under the black light.

 Toss out any plastic or rubber-backed bath mats that the cats target with their urine. The backing hosts various microorganisms designed to keep the carpet stain-resistant, but it smells like urine to cats. Many felines eliminate on these because they already smell like a litter box.

 Offer a "smorgasbord" of litter substrates for cats to choose their ideal texture, granularity, and coarseness. Provide sand and potting soil mix for cats used to doing their "duty" outside.

 Use Cat Attract (www.preciouscat.com) brand litter to help reestablish litter box allegiance when all else fails. This proprietary herbal blend proves irresistible to even hard-case cats.

 Change the depth of litter (increase or decrease) or remove the plastic liner to make the box more attractive. Cats that scratch to cover their waste may dislike catching their claws in the plastic liner.

- Offer an empty litter box and gradually add litter to cats that prefer the linoleum, wood floor, or bathtub surfaces.

- Buy a new box. Plastic holds odor and smelly old boxes offend cats even when you've scrubbed them. Cats that "blame" the old box for a scare or discomfort often eagerly embrace a new facility.

- Offer different types of toilets—uncovered or covered—to encourage kitty to choose one. Covered boxes help contain litter when energetic diggers throw sand everywhere, but they hold odors too, and your shy cats may fear being trapped inside and avoid using them. Very large cats may not be able to pose in a standard-size box without dropping deposits or urinating over the edge. Provide a much bigger container such as a clear plastic storage bin to accommodate these cats.

- Reduce the total number of boxes by purchasing storage-bin type containers, which work well for up to three small to medium cats who are willing to share.

- Provide a toilet on each floor of a multistory home or at each end of a single-story home. Very young, elderly, or ill cats may have trouble reaching the box in time, and this gives these felines a better opportunity for a pit stop.

- Use a cookie sheet or cut down the sides of the box for tiny kittens or very arthritic older cats that struggle to climb in and out.

- Position litter boxes in more than one location. With multiple options, a territorial kitty can't guard them all at once, leaving at least one available to the rest of the cats at all times.

- Be sure boxes are in a low-traffic area and a quiet location such as a closet or storeroom. Laundry rooms where a dryer buzzer frightens the cat in mid-squat may be less than ideal.

- Put the new litter box right on top of the soiled area. This encourages cats to use the box in that location; once they use the box again, gradually move it to a more appropriate area a foot or so a day.

- Make the illegal location unattractive so they willingly use the proper toilet. Give the soiled area a different connotation by placing favorite cat toys, food bowls, a bed, or a scratching post on top of the soiled area once it's been cleaned.

Confine problem cats who can't be supervised to a small area with a litter box if house soiling goes on for too long. Usually cats prefer to use a box rather than having to live with the accident. Behaviorists recommend one week's confinement for every month Sheba has been soiling, but that ratio can be decreased if the problem has been in existence more than six months.

TARGET PRACTICE

Urine spraying almost always involves problems between cats. While only about twenty-five percent of households with a single cat deal with this, every household with ten or more cats suffers this problem. The more cats you have, the greater the likelihood of tiffs, resulting in one or more cats "baptizing" your belongings. Common targets include vertical objects such as windows, computer equipment, curtains, and sliding glass doors. Horizontal targets often include clothes, beds, backpacks, briefcases, and plastic bags. Spraying arises out of anxiety. You must figure out why the cat sprays before you can fix the problem, so determine the social significance of the target's location. Draw a map or videotape the cat-to-cat interactions to find clues. Perhaps a cat dominates territory with stares and posturing, strays trespass in the yard, or you spend extra time at the computer.

If you can't pinpoint the reason, try many things all at once to manage the environment. After the spraying stops, you can try reducing these options one by one to find the least amount that works.

VET ALERT!

"Sixty-five percent of cats with blood in their urine are diagnosed with idiopathic [unknown origin] cystitis," says Dr. Elsey. According to research done at Ohio State, although the urine looks normal, the bladder lining is inflamed. That makes the cat hurt when urinating, so she blames the box and goes elsewhere. "We can't routinely detect the inflammation," he says, "so owners just think they have a bad cat." The drug amitriptyline won't cure but can help cats feel better by reducing their stress levels. "Switch from dry to canned food," suggests Dr. Elsey. That doubles the amount of water intake and helps dilute urine to ease the condition.

- Fix your cats! Neutering eliminates spraying behavior in ninety percent of the boys; spaying eliminates the behavior in ninety-five percent of the girls.

- Create a "house of plenty" with lots of food, toys, and territory available so less squabbling occurs.

- Add cat trees, bookcases, window perches, and other second-story real estate to reduce the anxiety between cats in small apartments or homes.

- Generate a routine. Cats thrive on the status quo, and anything unexpected sends stress levels soaring, potentially increasing the urge to spray.

- Clean illegal targets with an odor neutralizer to help prevent the cat from refreshing the scent again and again. Use Anti-Icky-Poo to eliminate pet odor problems.

- Cover scents with Feliway, a pheromone product that helps calm stress related to the environment. After you've cleaned the illegal targets, spray them with the Feliway and use the plug-in in the room where the cat most often sprays.

- Make frequent targets unattractive by covering them with aluminum foil. When the urine hits, the sound startles the cat and stops her in her tracts. It also tends to splash urine back onto the kitty and she'll not like that. The foil lining also makes cleanup easier.

- Interrupt any cat's "spray pose" behavior (backing up with tail erect). Don't yell. Ideally, the interruption should come out of the blue, with the cat unaware it came from you. Toss a beanbag, Ping-Pong balls, or other toy near the cat (don't hit her) to startle and stop the pose.

- Redirect the behavior. When you see the cat sniffing a danger zone, engage her with a favorite toy. Place toys, a scratching post, or a food bowl in the area to give it a different association instead of the "potty" place.

- Employ the ssscat aerosol when you can't be there. This helps to keep cats away from high-risk targets.

VET ALERT!

Not all cats respond to environmental management, and this can be a challenge to owners who love their cats but hate living with urine. When spraying arises due to fearfulness, stress, and/or anxiety, Dr. Pryor suggests you discuss drug therapy options with your veterinarian.

- Two studies have reported that eighty percent of treated cats improved using clomipramine (Clomical). However, there are serious side effects to consider, including potential toxicities.

- An equally effective drug called fluoxetine (Prozac) works well with less serious side effects, but spraying behavior returns if the cat goes off the drug. Behavioral and environmental management must continue, along with any drug therapy. Some cats respond as early as the first or second week of treatment, while others require three weeks or more to see results.

CALMING SIGNALS—PET DOOR TRAINING

When you have a safe outside enclosure for your cat to play and go potty, installing a cat flap in a window or patio door allows your cats to come and go rather than you becoming the doorman. Cats naturally rub against objects to leave behind their scent. Use this natural inclination to teach Sheba to push through the cat flap.

Prop the door flap open so the cats can see through to the other side. Use a favorite treat or toy to repeatedly lure her back and forth through the opening until she becomes used to the idea. Next, leave the flap closed, but find an alluring scent that cats can't resist. Catnip, peppermint, or tuna juice painted on the pet door may prompt a cheek rub or forehead butt.

Reward even a nose touch to encourage the behavior. When the first cat pushes through, have a favorite treat waiting and reward her while the others watch. Once they understand that there *may* be a treat waiting, they'll be more inclined to use the cat door (and the bathroom facilities or play opportunities) whether a treat awaits or not. Note: It's best for cat flaps to be translucent so Sheba can see through and not be ambushed by another cat.

Chapter 12
Upset Kitty Feelings

C ats are just as emotional as people and behavior changes mirror those of owners in similar situations. Stress may be expressed as depression and grief, fearful behavior, insomnia, jealousy, or any of a range of emotions. Some cats (most commonly Siamese, Burmese, Himalayan, and Abyssinians) relieve stress by overgrooming themselves until they go bald; once the stress goes away, the hair grows back. Physical health problems and instinct can also prompt cats to act out emotionally, so remember to use the P.E.T. test (in the Introduction) to figure out the cause.

Pets also react to the emotions their human companions feel. When a cat has bonded deeply with you, she'll react to your emotional state with purrs and snuggles. Changes in the routine almost always upset cats. Changing your work schedule, introducing a new cat to the household, or moving to a new home is particularly stressful. One cat feeling out of sorts makes the rest of the felines uneasy and can cause an emotional meltdown among all the cats. Recognizing your cat's emotional state and understanding why she feels that way allows you to help soothe upset feelings and ensure the entire feline family stays happy.

FELINE GRIEF

Depression and grief can be worse for cats because we can't explain why a beloved cat or human friend has gone away. Death, divorce, or just leaving for college often leaves one or more of your cats deeply affected, and that always causes a ripple effect that impacts the entire feline household. For instance, when your top cat becomes depressed, she'll be less patient with the other felines and may lash out with aggression. Or if she disappears under the bed, the other cats will argue over taking her top position. A new family member (husband, baby) who demands your attention also upsets the cat, because you are the most important part of Sheba's territory (see also "Green Eyed-Monsters" in Chapter 14).

Depressed cats sleep more than usual, avoid company, stop playing, and hide. They don't groom themselves as well, lose their appetite, and refuse to eat. Depression affects physical health by compromising the immune system, so pets become more susceptible to disease. Symptoms of depression may mimic other problems. Scratching or urine spraying increases, especially near and on items that you own (your bed, the laundry) because the scent comforts them (see also Chapter 20). Time heals grief, and cats who have bonded closely with other pets or people can become attached to new loved ones. Supporting the feelings of a grief-stricken cat helps her more quickly return to normal and interact with the rest of the felines in a healthy manner.

 Provide a sunbath for twenty minutes a day to raise kitty spirits. Light therapy benefits people suffering from depression and helps cats, too. A soft blanket on a table near a sunny window helps ease the cat's sadness.

 Play the radio or CDs that have a fast, upbeat tempo. Peppy music can improve the grieving cat's disposition.

 Use the TTouch massage technique (see Chapter 4) to reduce your cat's depression. Pay particular attention to her ears, face, and neck.

 Employ the Bach Flower remedy, Gentian for general depression or Gorse for severe depression. Star of Bethlehem commonly is recommended for sorrow and grief. Put four drops into the water bowl for all-day sipping, or add drops to a treat, such as a teaspoonful of plain yogurt.

LOSING A FURRY FRIEND

 Help the surviving cats to understand by letting them "say goodbye" to the deceased pet's body. Expect any sort of reaction, from sniffing the body, to ignoring it, to crying. A last look allows cats to understand the deceased won't return and prevents the tortured searching some grieving pets display.

 Remove those toys or beds used by the deceased pet so the lingering scent of the departed pet does not cause the remaining felines to avoid that area.

ABSENT HUMAN FRIENDS

 Be aware of how your sadness impacts the kitties. Cats act like sponges that soak up your emotion, so talk to them and be positive. Your cats won't understand the words but will recognize your intent.

 Keep scented items of human family members that have gone away. Seal a few unwashed socks in a baggy and bring one out now and then for Sheba to sleep or play with as a security blanket, until the beloved's return. The long-distance human can also mail scented objects home to the cat.

SHRINKING VIOLETS

Some cats grow up to be worrywarts, and acting fearful or shy is like wearing a "kick me" sign that prompts the other cats in your household to pick on them. Up to twenty percent of any population of a given species will be born prone to introversion and fear. Some cats acquire the traits from poor or missing socialization or from a lack of proper nutrition during gestation. Kittens whose mothers received poor nutrition prior to giving birth are more "reactive" than normal and often suffer fearfulness and shyness.

An intensely unpleasant experience can lead to a "memory" of the event, in which cats generalize the fear to similar future events. A onetime abuse situation or single bad experience with another cat or the car makes Sheba fearful of all cats, car rides, or men.

Signs of anxiety include decreased grooming, reduced social interactions, and loss of appetite. The fearful cat signals unease by looking away, holding the ears down and sideways, shaking, crouching, urinating, or defecating. Stress strains the immune system, and fearful felines are unhappy pets. Some types of fear never go away, but with lots of patience you can help the cat feel more comfortable in her home.

Identify all the different sights, places, sounds, odors, people, or other things that trigger fear. You need to know what she fears before you can address those issues. Some cats fear children, others act scared of one particular cat, and a few fear men. The strange sounds, odors, and sights of strays or other critters can also arouse fear.

PREVENTING FEAR

 Adopt pairs of kittens together or a mother with a baby. This gives the new pets an ally to build confidence and ward off shyness. Some kitties dislike other cats, but don't feel threatened by a friendly, gentle dog (see also Chapter 19).

 Create a schedule that frightened felines can rely on so they know when to expect meals, petting, or chase-the-feather game. Routines reduce a cat's fear caused by unpredictability.

MANAGING FEAR

- Purchase a white noise machine (or tune your radio to static) to cover up any distressing sounds, such as thunder, engine noises, or outside animals during the spring mating season.

- Provide Sheba with lots of places to stay out of sight. Kitty tents placed in strategic places and collapsible cat tunnels create safe pathways through the center of rooms, especially in open areas where Sheba feels exposed. This keeps her stress level low, can encourage her to move around the house more, and builds confidence.

- Give frightened cats space, and don't talk, touch, or follow them. When cats panic, they lash out at anything between them and perceived safety and stay aroused for at least an hour. Cat skin is so sensitive that any contact can make the feelings of panic even worse.

- Speed up the recovery time by shutting out any further stimulation for at least fifteen minutes. Turn off the lights in the room, draw the blinds, or toss a towel over the cat to muffle scary sounds.

- Praise and give treats for relaxed breathing and calm expressions and body postures to help build confidence. Avoid baby talk, as it encourages the behavior to continue.

FIGHTING FELINE FEAR

- Play with both the shy cat and a resident cat at the same time, with a different toy in each hand, to help teach them to get along.

- Use the pheromone product Feliway to help the cats feel more comfortable about their environment. The plug-in product helps all the cats "chill."

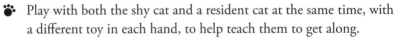

- Add several drops of the Rescue Remedy to water bowls for all of your cats to sip; it can help diffuse the other felines' aggression toward the shy kitty.

Use the TTouch technique (see Chapter 4) on the ears of shy cats for a positive effect.

CONQUERING PEOPLE FEAR

 Keep your temper. Yelling and punishment could prompt fear aggression. Low-pitched men's voices and a heavier walk often sound scary to cats, so take care to lighten your tone and your step.

 Encourage human guests to stay calm and sit quietly across the room from the fearful cats; allow the cats to retreat if they wish.

 Glance away from fearful cats and don't stare, as strong eye contact is a challenge that intimidates cats.

 Offer cats a closed fist or index finger to sniff, head butt, and cheek rub. Shy cats fear hands if they've been abused. Others have a petting "threshold" and become aggressive (see also Chapter 10). The closed hand is less intimidating, reminds Sheba of another cat's head, and allows the cats to be in control of the contact.

 Engage shy cats with a fishing pole toy or flashlight, which allows people to interact at a safe distance that doesn't threaten the fearful cat.

COUNTER-CONDITIONING FEARFUL CATS

 Counter-condition with incremental exposure to the known trigger, be that a person or another cat. This helps fearful cats to learn to tolerate a scary situation—whatever it may be.

 Stage "safe" exposures. Have the person or pet stand across the room while you give Sheba treats or play with a feather to reward her staying calm.

VET ALERT!

Middle-aged and older cats may develop hyperthyroidism, an endocrine (hormonal) disease that revs up the metabolism. The condition, caused by an overactive thyroid, spills too much hormone into the cat's system. Affected cats have an increased appetite but lose weight, pace a lot, become short-tempered, and often howl and yowl incessantly. A blood test diagnoses the condition, which can be treated, controlled, or even cured with ongoing drug therapy, surgery, or radioactive iodine treatment. Cats suffering from hyperthyroid disease often also have high blood pressure and/or kidney problems at the same time. Be sure to have your cat examined by a veterinarian, if he suddenly becomes hyperactive.

Position the scary trigger a bit closer—if human, ask the person to sit on the floor. If Kitty remains calm, offer another treat or game. Only go on to the next level when the cat remains okay with the last gradient.

THE "ZOOMS" AND MIDNIGHT MADNESS

For most cats, actual hyperactivity is rarely a problem. Since cats normally sleep up to sixteen hours a day, they almost never have problems with insomnia. Felines naturally become most active at dawn and dusk, and nocturnal behaviors that keep you awake are most common in kittens and usually decrease when they reach twelve to eighteen months of age. While the nonstop energy of one cat challenges owners, a houseful of galloping felines multiplies the problem. The high jinks not only disturbs you, especially at night, it can rub cranky cats the wrong way and prompt short tempers to flare or teach bad habits to more sedate, well-behaved felines.

Some breeds are more active than others. Persians tend to be more sedate, while Abyssinian and Siamese swing from the drapes. When active cats don't have legal outlets for energy, they get creative and empty your sock drawer.

You may reward unruly behavior without meaning to. Highly motivated cats hate being ignored and settle for your angry words if they can't get good attention. If you feed her to make Sheba stop biting your nose to wake you, she's trained you to fill the bowl.

Only reward good behavior. Teach Sheba she must pay for attention, food, or anything she wants with something *you* want, such as a quiet "sit." If she yowls, the food stays in the can. If Sheba learns opening kitchen cupboards or vaulting to door tops garners attention, she'll continue the antics. The following tips can help put the brakes on your cat's nonstop activity.

 Prevent access to the cats' favorite sleeping places during the day so they sleep at night.

- Tire the cats out in a constructive way and they'll leave your goldfish bowl alone. Twenty minutes of aerobics twice a day works well. Schedule playtime a half-hour before bedtime to tire your cats out so they'll sleep when you do.

- Feed your cats just before you go to bed to keep them from waking up hungry and pestering you at 3 A.M. to fill the bowl. You can put their last meal of the day in several "treat balls" filled with favorite kibble, so they must play and manipulate the ball to shake food out to eat.

- Play harp music or a selection from the Pet Music CD. Any slow, calm, instrumental music arrangement can be soothing.

- Purchase melatonin, a hormone that helps lull cats to sleep. Ask your vet for the proper dosage.

- Give one-quarter cup warm milk per cat to help your felines snooze more readily. Milk contains the chemical tryptophan, which helps promote sleep. Some cats don't digest milk easily, so lay off the treat if diarrhea develops.

- Adopt a second kitten if a new kitten pesters the adult felines in the house. A kitten closer to her age can more effectively wear her out.

VET ALERT!

As cats age, sight and hearing fade and they can become disoriented at night. A nightlight helps them more easily find their way around and calms the jitters so they sleep more soundly. Some very old cats develop memory problems similar to those suffered by human Alzheimer's patients. Signs include disorientation, interaction changes, (with people or other pets), sleep cycle changes, housetraining lapses, and anxiety. We can't stop again, but a percentage of cats suffering from these cognitive disorders are helped with drug and/or nutritional therapy prescribed by the veterinarian.

- The drug Anipriyl (selegiline hydrochloride) is FDA-approved for treatment of canine cognitive disorder, and helps up to seventy percent of dogs. it has been used off-label to help cats with similar cognitive disorders.

- Cholodin-Fel, a nutritional supplement, contains choline and phosphatidylcholine, which helps brain cells work more efficiently and may benifit cats with cognitive dysfunction. Find more information at www.mvplabs.com.

Find a behavior she already does, such as reach out with a paw toward the feather. Reward the behavior with a favorite treat, and you've taught her to "wave." Smart, active cats relish training, which gives them something constructive to do with their brains. Teaching one cat in front of the others prompts copycat behavior once they realize the "wave" gets a treat.

MOVING ANGST

Cats love routine so much that change leaves them outraged. Moving traumatizes many cats because they so strongly bond to territory and place. Those upset over a move often act out by scratching more and spraying urine to mark the new territory. Shy kitties may disappear for days or even weeks until they feel more comfortable with the new surroundings, and will worry themselves sick if you aren't careful. Plan ahead to calm cat fears and make the transition go as smoothly as possible.

 Schedule your move when you can be at home with the cats and spend several days together. Don't leave the cats alone to deal with fears by themselves.

 Move cats in carriers to prevent them from accidentally escaping during the trip or upon arrival (see also "Crate Expectations" in Chapter 4).

 Confine the cats that get along to a single room and shut the door once you have arrived at your new house. That keeps them safe while you unpack, arrange furniture, and open and shut doors. If you have a large number of felines, you may need two safe rooms.

 Bring all the familiar toys, cat furniture, bowls, and litter boxes along. Set these up in the safe room(s) to create a familiar "home base" they can become used to very quickly. Your cats should stay in the room for at least the first two or three days until they appear comfortable in *that* room.

 Add Rescue Remedy to the cats' drinking water to relieve feline stress.

Open the door calmly and allow them to explore at their leisure once they have cheek-rubbed territory in their safe room. Cats tend to take it slow and easy, checking out new territory a room at a time. If any of your cats don't get along, give low-ranking cats the opportunity to explore alone first, then switch out the more confident cats, before giving all the felines free rein in the new digs.

 Return to your old routine as soon as possible. It may be a new house, but a familiar feeding time, play periods, and your comings and goings should help remind the cats that all's well in their world.

 Use extra exercise to calm the cats during the transition period. Playing with them reassures that all is well, causing the tired cats to sleep more soundly and suffer less stress.

 Keep all cats confined indoors for at least one month after the move. Cats let outside too soon after a move try to find their way back to their old home and become lost, injured, or killed along the way. It takes time for the group to swear allegiance to the new residence and learn all the important feline landmarks inside the house and out. The first few visits outdoors are best done on a leash until the cats have mind-mapped the area and you are confident they can find their way back for dinner.

FEELING LONELY

Separation anxiety results when sensitive cats are apart from human loved ones, and most often happens when you spend less time with your cats due to a job change or vacation. In one study of cats with this condition, ninety percent had owners who worked long hours. In eighty percent of the cats, owner absence due to a vacation triggered the behavior or increased the frequency of problems. About one-quarter of the affected cats had been adopted from a shelter at less than three months of age. As a consequence, these kitties formed much stronger attachments to one or more family members.

Classic signs include urinating and defecating on owner-scented objects (see also Chapter 11). Some cats cry and become upset as you prepare to leave, while others don't seem to notice your departure but "act out" once left alone. Even if only one of your cats reacts to your absences with poor behaviors, separation anxiety affects the entire feline family because hit-or-miss bathroom behaviors upset the status quo. The scent of one cat's urine on your bedspread may draw other felines to also baptize the spot. In addition, when one cat becomes upset by your absence, the other kitties may react to her behavior by picking on her, or Sheba may take out her angst on the other cats.

Having other buddy cats may help the lonely feline feel less upset, but usually the anxious cat needs you to feel happy again and a furry substitute won't do. Use behavior modification to help the affected cat(s) feel better about missing you. This keeps the rest of the cats calm, too.

 Distract upset cats during the critical twenty-minute period after you leave so they won't dirty your bed. Ask another family member to play interactive games with a fishing pole toy so the cats don't focus on your absence.

 Leave a catnip treat to keep cats happy when you leave. Also, food-oriented cats can be distracted with a food-puzzle toy stuffed with a favorite smelly treat.

 Screen videos of fluttering birds, squirrels, and other critters for indoor cats. While cats that have been outside don't often react, homebody cats love these. There are a number of these videos available, including the original, Video Catnip.

 Play familiar music that cats associate with your presence to help ease the pain of your being gone. Harp music especially helps naturally sedate a whole room full of cats.

DESENSITIZE DEPARTURES

 Leave your overnight bag out all the time so your cats won't identify it with your departure. Toss a catnip mouse or other toy inside the suitcase, and turn it into a kitty playground to help her identify the suitcase with positives, rather than your absence.

Pick up the car keys fifty times a day, then set them down. Carry your purse over your arm for an hour or more. When you repeat these triggers often enough, cats stop caring about them and will remain calm when you do leave.

 Fake your departure by opening the door and going in and out twenty or more times in a row until the cats ignore you altogether. Then extend your "outside" time to one minute, three minutes, five minutes, and so on before returning inside. This gradual increase in absence helps build the cats' tolerance.

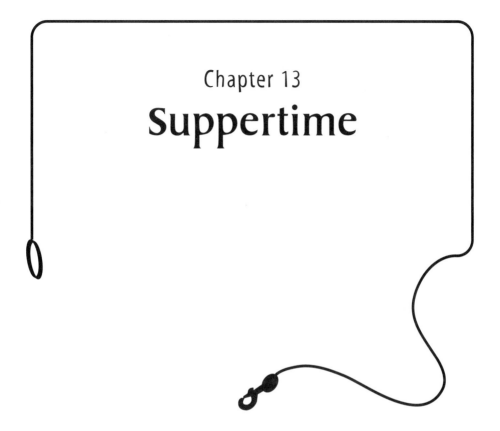

Chapter 13
Suppertime

Cats live longer these days because of properly prepared commercial foods, but not all work for every cat. Commercial foods fit the needs of broad categories of cats, including growth for kittens, maintenance for adult cats, and a senior category for aging kitties. As kittens and cats mature, they must transition to the food that best fits their particular lifestage. Some cats may require a therapeutic diet, such as for kidney disease or weight loss/control, dispensed by prescription from the veterinarian. Appetite is a barometer of your cat's health. A sudden increase in appetite, for example, may indicate hyperthyroid disease, while a loss of appetite may point to intestinal blockage or any number of other physical or emotional health issues.

SNUBBING THE BOWL

Anorexia—refusing to eat—or a reduced appetite, over the long term, can be deadly. A wide range of health challenges can make Sheba finicky, and the most common—upper respiratory infection—is so contagious that multiple cats can get sick at the same time. Cats won't eat if their noses stop up and they can't smell their food.

Territorial issues between cats also impact feline appetite. Stressful interactions make shy cats fearful so they avoid communal dining and miss out on the goodies. Dominant cats can guard the feeding station so even when kibble remains in the bowl, intimidated felines don't dare approach.

When you feed all the cats free-choice (from a single ever-full bowl), it can be hard to tell which cats have problems. The smallest or youngest cats in the home may not be able to eat all they need at one meal, especially if they compete with a glutton who gobbles up everything ahead of time.

Pay attention to how much *each* cat eats, if they show up for dinner or hide, and whether they feel "bony" under all that fur. Appetite loss goes beyond a finicky attitude. There are a number of techniques you can use to prompt Sheba's appetite to return.

- Offer soft foods that cats with mouth pain can eat until a veterinary dentist can be seen. Up to seventy-five percent of all cats develop some form of dental disease by the time they reach two years old.

- Use a warm, wet cloth to clean off gummy noses so sick cats can smell their food.

- Create a steamy room to aid the stuffy cats' breathing. Moist heat helps open up the clogged nose.

- Warm up leftover canned food in the microwave to mouse/prey body temperature. Heating helps unlock odors and makes food more pungent and appealing.

- Moisten dry kibble with warm water or low-fat, no-salt chicken broth to spark your cats' appetites.

Provide a top dressing of soft foods or meat baby food on the cats' regular diet. Canned and gourmet diets include more fat and flavor enhancers that tempt the reluctant eater, and human baby foods also appeal to sick cats. Avoid foods that contain onion, which can be problematic for cats.

 Offer small amounts of food every hour, with a break in between times. Leaving the food out all the time can wear out the appetite centers of sick cats.

 Set up more than one feeding station and serve meals separately when a gobbler outeats nibblers or a dominant cat keeps shy felines from feeding (see also "The Kitty Smorgasbord" in this chapter).

 Transition from old food to new food gradually. Mix one-quarter of the new diet with three-quarters of the old for a week. The second week, mix the two diets 50/50. The third week, mix three-quarters of the new with one-quarter of the old until finally Sheba eats one hundred percent of the new food.

 Feed Sheba from your finger while stroking her neck to stimulate her to eat. Pungent foods like tuna work best to tempt flagging feline appetites. In cases of long-term anorexia, it's "legal" to offer the cat anything just to get her to eat.

THE KITTY SMORGASBORD

Different personalities, social interactions, and health issues will impact appetite, diet, and feeding schedule and dictate how to manage the multiple-cat home. When cats are approximately the same age, the same diet may be appropriate. But when they are different ages, you may need one for kittens or a senior

VET ALERT!

Cats that stop eating for even a day or two can become very ill when the condition affects the liver. Fatty liver disease (hepatic lipidosis) may result when the body reflexively moves fat stores into the liver to counter the lost nutrition. The stored fat interferes with liver function and makes the cat feel even sicker and less willing to eat. This creates a vicious cycle and, in some cases, the kitty must be hospitalized and a feeding tube inserted to be force-fed before she'll regain her appetite.

formulation for your aging crew. The more cats you have, the greater the chance they'll require different foods. One adult may need a food to control lower urinary tract problems, which won't work for the new kitten. Another cat may eat reduced-calorie food, while his best cat-buddy requires a high-protein diet to control diabetes. Feeding multiple diets becomes a management issue of time, space, and personalities. Feel free to use one, all, or any combination of tips to design the best situation for your cats.

- Stagger feedings ten minutes apart so you can supervise each meal and "ride herd" on the kitties who shouldn't nibble from a particular formula.

- Make sure the cats' bowls are a safe distance apart. That way they don't feel their personal space has been invaded. Cats form good opinions of each other by eating within sight of one another because that creates a positive association for them. If a cat stops chewing to stare at another feline, move the bowls farther apart.

- Provide a separate eating area for cats that guard feeding stations or are afraid to eat when another kitty is present.

- Use treat balls to dispense a single meal to one cat or give treats to a group as the cats play. Dry food inserted into the ball or toy dispenses a kibble at a time. Some felines love to scrounge, "hunt," or swipe food, so give these cat burglars a legal outlet to keep them fed, entertained, and out of another feline's bowl.

- Assign a single bowl for each cat and an individual place for each bowl. Cats faithful to a routine are less likely to interrupt each other's mealtimes. Countertops, tables, various levels on the cat tree, or bookshelves all offer valuable kitty real estate for individual feeding locations each cat can "own."

- Spread kibble on a large flat pan so the cat must "chase" it to get each piece. This slows down glutton cats, which prevents food from getting gulped down too quickly and coming back up. There are also commercial foods that make larger kibbles/particles so the cat must chew rather than gulp mouthfuls at a time.

Separate cats that have different diets during meals or create a "boxed lunch." Cut a tiny cat-size opening in a cardboard or plastic storage box to fit the smaller cat, and place the small cat's food bowl inside the box, where he can access and nibble at his leisure.

 Install pet doors that open with electronic "key" collars. The cat wearing the special collar can access the door into the screened porch to eat, for example, while the rest of the furry crew can't get through.

 Set the food bowls of more agile cats on countertops, out of reach of geriatric felines that must eat a special diet.

 Use a baby gate to segregate feeding stations by allowing only the more nimble cats to pass through or jump over.

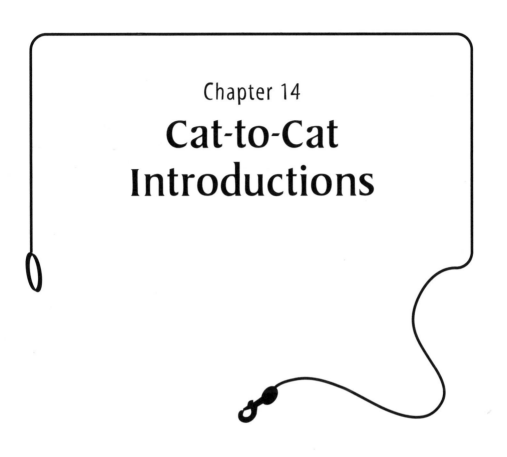

Chapter 14
Cat-to-Cat Introductions

Adopting a mom with one or two kittens can offer security and build confidence, particularly for the kittens. Similarly, adopting two kittens together can give them a "buddy" to depend on for fun and games and a furry security blanket when they feel fearful or stressed. When you have an existing cat family, choose the new member carefully so she will fit in with your other felines.

Because cats become so dependent upon routine and bond closely with "place," bringing a new feline into the mix disrupts the worlds of both the resident cats and the new cat. Pay special attention to your current cats. They've been around the longest, and their happiness must be considered first before any interloper's.

Existing cat hierarchies do not welcome strange felines with open paws. It's natural for your resident cats to try and drive off newcomers, or at least keep them at bay. Adding another kitty to the mix rarely solves existing behavior problems, either, and may make them worse or prompt new ones. A newcomer has a hard time being accepted under the best conditions, so keep these issues in mind to make the introductions run smoothly.

CAT COM-PET-ABILITY

There are five important components to consider when choosing a new feline to join your resident cats (also see the L.E.A.S.H. technique in the Introduction). Introductions take a great deal of patience, and you'll earn fewer gray hairs if your resident kitties already have basic manners, such as understanding the word "no."

If your current cat family gets along well, that improves the odds they'll welcome yet another feline into the mix because they already understand "cat language" and know how to fit into feline society. Adult cats more readily accept babies that don't challenge their social position. It's best to pick a kitten that's at least twelve to sixteen weeks old so she's had time to learn important cat lessons from siblings and mom.

Cats reach social maturity by age four and often become very set in their ways, so if they've never lived with another cat, extra patience will be needed to convince them to accept a newcomer. Watch the cat's tail and ears for cues. A low-held or swishing tail reveals agitation; ears turned to the side or backward indicate fear and/or aggression. Be prepared to break up serious altercations that include growls or hisses, and separate the cats.

All cats need space to claim as their own. Ideally, have no more cats than you have bedrooms—or, build *up* the potential territory by adding vertical space. If your cats get along and each has claimed a favorite resting/lookout spot, be sure to add several more options to accommodate the new felines. Don't expect cats to share with the new guy. They might become fast friends and want to sleep together, but that's a bonus if it happens and not something to count on.

While you know all your resident cats, the new feline feels insecure and defensive. Sheba won't be willing to meet anybody until she's familiar and comfortable with the new environment. To be fair, initial introductions should be one-on-one, a single new cat meeting a single resident cat. *Always* pay more attention to the resident pet. The resident kitty will be much more willing to accept a newcomer as long as your affections aren't usurped. Be patient. It may take days, weeks, or even months for the cats to get along. Rarely it's love at first sight, but some cats may never become friends.

STEP-BY-STEP INTRODUCTIONS

These basic principles of introduction apply no matter what type of cats share your home and heart. The assumption has been made that both the resident(s) and the new kitty are confident, healthy felines that have been properly socialized. Extra steps may be necessary to smooth upset feelings when one or more of the cats involved have a physical or emotional health issue.

Neuter new cats *before* you begin introductions. Neutering makes a cat's urine smell differently, and visiting the veterinarian also creates a "foreign" smell on the treated cat. This can make resident cats even more suspicious of the new kitty.

Be sure that your resident "king cat" gets fed first, petted first, groomed first, and receives preferential treatment over lower-ranking cats. Preferred attention to a lower-ranking cat may inspire Sheba to kick furry tail to teach the lower-ranking cat her place. If your top feline is geriatric, you may need to separate her during feeding and resting times so she's not bothered by a more energetic newcomer. Don't be surprised if neither the resident "king" nor the interloper end up on top. Adding a new feline could create a brave new kitty world and a fresh hierarchy as well.

STEP ONE: THE NEW CAT SANCTUARY

- Create a home base for the new cat in a small room with a door that shuts completely. New cats feel more secure when initially confined to small areas of the house. If you have more than one new cat and they already know each other, you may be able to confine them together and they'll comfort and give confidence to each other.

- Choose a room for the home base that the resident cats don't normally use so they won't feel upset being banned from it. Segregating newcomers to a single room reassures resident cats that only *part* of their territory has been invaded.

- Separate the new cats from the old with a solid door that allows them to meet via sound, smell, and paw pats under the door. Cats become more upset by the sight of a strange feline than by the smell or sound, and this avoids emotional overload by restricting sensory input.

- Stock the home base with thoroughly washed food and water bowls, *new* toys, and a *new* scratching post and litter box. Second-hand supplies that already smell like other cats make a new feline feel more insecure, so if your newcomer came with a favorite bed or toys, include these so the familiar smells calm her. Include hiding places, such as cat tunnels, so she feels more secure about navigating the strange new room.

- Don't be alarmed by initial posturing and hissing at the door. Also, resident cats may engage in redirected aggression toward each other when they can't reach the newcomer (see also Chapter 10).

- Be encouraged by paw pat games under the door, the new cat's willingness to emerge from hiding and interact with you, and your resident kitties maintaining their normal routine and not aggressing toward companion cats.

STEP TWO: NOSY INTRODUCTIONS

🐾 Gauge your cats' readiness by introducing individual cat scents. Bring something out of the home base that's scented by the new cat for the resident felines to smell, and vice versa. When you're dealing with only two or three kitties, a plate of food where each ate works well because it also has a positive food association. *Don't* switch bedding or the cats may urinate on it to show dominance. Hissing and growling after sniffing means they need more time segregated, but mild interest means you're on the right track.

🐾 Use individual cloths or socks to collect cheek pheromones when you have more than three cats to introduce. Begin by petting each cat's cheek, using one cloth per cat. Take a cheek-rubbed cloth from the friendliest, most laid-back of your resident kitties and leave that with the new cat for her to acclimate to one feline at a time—the one least likely to cause problems. Continue the scent exchange several times a day, offering only one resident cat "smell" to the newcomer at a time, until all the cats have had the opportunity to become familiar with signature odors.

🐾 Place a bit of the wet litter from the new cat's box in the resident kitties' facilities, and vice versa. Only use a tiny amount (think in terms of a pinch!) or you risk prompting a litter box avoidance.

STEP THREE: CROSSING THE THRESHOLD

🐾 Isolate your resident cats in another room of the house once the hissing fades, paw pats increase, or all the kitties act disinterested. Open the door to allow Sheba to wander around the rest of the house, cheek rub everywhere, and "map" the location of all the good hiding places. A new cat won't want to meet anybody nose to nose until she feels secure in the surroundings.

🐾 Place the new cat in a carrier or another area of the house to allow your resident felines to check out her room after she has fully explored the rest of the house. Don't force them into the new cat's home base; simply open the door. They may investigate all at once, in shifts, or some may ignore the invitation altogether.

STEP FOUR: WHISKER-TO-WHISKER GREETINGS

- Open the door with no fanfare and carefully (and silently) watch what happens once the new cat feels comfortable navigating your house. Remember, these initial introductions should be between the new cat and only *one* of your resident cats at a time (the friendliest first)—not the whole furry crew at once.

- Set food down in the new cat's room and offer the resident cat a meal at the same time outside the open door. Eating distracts both cats from the scary newness of the other animal while associating food with each other's presence, so feed both cats during these initial meetings.

- Have a second family member play with the new cat while the resident feline's favorite person plays with her during these initial meetings. With practice, you can learn to manipulate a fishing pole or other interactive toy in each hand, to wrangle two cats at once. *Always* use two toys, or the cats may compete for the single lure and develop negative associations.

- Speed up introductions by making all the cats in the household smell alike. Cats that live together and get along well create a group scent by sleeping together and grooming each other, while new cats are shunned because they smell foreign and scary. When dealing with only two cats, trade the collars they wear. For multiple resident cats, rub a towel over each cat in turn and then rub the new cat with the same towel. Alternatively, you can use a strong, pleasant scent like vanilla extract, a favorite perfume, or cologne, and dab just a tiny bit underneath the chin and at the base of the tail of each cat.

STEP FIVE: PATIENT INTEGRATION

- Watch for body language indicating the introductions are successful. Cats normally approach, circle a bit, and attempt to sniff each other's flank and tail region before moving to the head. A tail-up greeting from either cat signals friendly intensions. Hisses and growls mean you should cut the session short and send the new cat back to home base.

Use the pheromone product Feliway to signal cats that their environment is safe.

 Add several drops of Bach Flower Rescue Remedy to all the cats' drinking water to ease the emotional upheavals.

 Include the new cat(s) in your existing routine. Group activities like grooming or playing with a fishing pole toy are particularly helpful.

 Add hiding places, scratching opportunities, and litter boxes so they don't have to argue over the facilities. Cat tunnels work great to give shy felines "hidden" pathways across the middle of rooms or long hallways so they feel protected while traveling to dinner or the bathroom (see also Chapter 12).

 Confine the new cat in the home base whenever you can't directly supervise. Replace the door with stacked baby gates so the cats can still interact through the mesh.

 Consider introductions over the hump once cats begin sleeping or playing together. Be prepared to interrupt play that gets wild before it becomes aggressive.

 Start introductions over again if aggression develops (see also Chapter 10).

GREEN-EYED MONSTERS

Cats also often act jealous when a new boyfriend or baby steals their thunder. Just one cat with her tail in a twist can upset the rest of the feline family and make them suspicious of the person or act poorly with feline companions. The jealous cat's behavior changes confuse the other felines and make them act out as a result. In the most serious cases, jealousy escalates to aggression, when cats seek to throw the interloper out of the house. Keep the peace with proper introductions to new people in your life.

 Maintain the old schedule or introduce changes gradually so the cats can cling to that familiarity. Cats become jealous when they think they might lose your love, so make a point of spending special time with them even when you have a new person in your life.

- Make sure your cats feel safe and relaxed in a favorite place, such as on a cat tree, so they feel in control rather than fearful or defensive during introductions to new people.

- Introduce your cats to new people with the whole feline family present. When your cats get along well, they can give each other confidence, and friendly kitties can act as role models for the shy felines during these introductions.

- Allow cats to approach new people on their own. Ask guests to avoid eye contact and ignore the cat. That does more to spark kitty curiosity and creates an urge to investigate. If she check-rubs his pant leg, that's very positive.

- Use a bit of your favorite perfume, cologne, or vanilla extract, or spray Feliway on guests' pant cuffs or ankles to make new people smell like you—someone your cats already love. Also dab a bit of the perfume or cologne on the back of the cats' necks and at the base of their tails so they smell like the "scary stranger" and won't be so fearful.

- Let your new housemate fill the cats' bowls, but then s/he should leave so the cats won't feel reluctant to eat. The person who controls the resources garners trust and respect, so the new person (parent, spouse, child, etc.) wins lots of points with cats by feeding them.

- Have the new people play with the cats using fishing pole toys and flashlights, which are feline favorites because they can play from a safe distance.

- Do not banish cats from the room or ignore them in favor of the new person. This tells them they must compete for your attention. Instead, give cats *extra* attention whenever the new person is nearby. When you're nursing the baby, shine a flashlight for the cat to chase. While you snuggle with your beau, make room on your lap for a cat or two or toss tasty treats for them to fetch so they associate the new person with good things.

KIDDOS AND BABY BLUES

 Prepare for a new baby ahead of time. Excluding cats from the experience of your new baby causes confusion and prompts behavior problems when they feel snubbed. Let the cats examine cribs and other paraphernalia. A screen door or stacked baby gates to the nursery allows cats to see, smell, and hear what's going on, but keeps them out from underfoot.

 Make nursery items off-limits ahead of time so you don't have to fight about it when the baby arrives. Place a plastic carpet protector, nub-side up, on top of the baby's bed to keep Sheba from claiming the soft spot as her own.

 Use baby powder and lotion on yourself ahead of time to get Sheba used to baby smells. Bring home a scented T-shirt or baby blanket the baby has worn. Brush a bit of baby powder into the cats' fur, too, so they smell like each other and the cats know they are family.

 Ask a friend to visit with an infant, or play the tape of a baby crying so the sound won't startle her. Cats sometimes mistake baby cries for feline distress calls and the noise can be upsetting.

 Ask children to sit quietly on the floor and *not* reach out to pet or chase the cat. Cats often don't recognize little people as humans because babies, toddlers, and young children talk, move, and behave very differently than adults. Allow cats to approach at their own pace—lure them near with a fishing pole toy.

 Provide cats with a "kitty only" retreat they can escape to, such as a cat tree or hiding place, to avoid pestering children. They feel much more willing to interact nicely with new people when they can sleep and relax in peace.

PART FOUR

THE DOG-CAT HOUSEHOLD
Common Problems
and Practical Solutions

Chapter 15
Fighting Like Cats And Dogs

When cats and dogs live together, the potential for aggressive behavior increases, particularly if the pets don't understand each other's language. In a dog's world, a waving tail signals friendly interest; this means impending attack in cat language, so the cat strikes out to protect herself. A cat rolls to her back to ready claws and teeth to attack; in dog language, exposing the tummy signals submission and an invitation to sniff, so Rex gets a nose full of claws. A raised canine paw solicits attention and signals submission, but means the opposite in cat language.

Aggressiveness includes everything from subtle body postures and facial expressions to explosive attacks. Both dogs and cats signal threat with forward-facing body positions and stares and shifting their weight toward their shoulders to be ready to launch an all-out assault. Canine piloerection—fur standing on end, especially over the neck and shoulders (hackles)—indicates arousal, and feline urine spraying almost always results from kitty aggression issues. Fear, excitement, play, or any arousal increases the risk for aggression when the pet feels defensive or the games get out of hand. Cats and dogs that act like victims, using excessive submission, also invite aggressive behavior from the other animals (see also Chapters 2 and 3 for pet language tips).

Behaviorists have characterized many kinds of cat and dog aggression, based on the purpose of the behavior, and each may be treated differently. Dominance aggression tops the canine list, while fear aggression leads the cat aggression complaints. Common situations during which your cat or dog may react with aggression include:

- Experiencing pain.

- Losing sensory abilities—deaf or blind pets startle easily and bite out of reflex.

- Being approached or disturbed while resting.

- Feeling overcrowded (too many pets for the space).

- Protecting resources (bed, toys, food bowls, territory, offspring).

- Play/predatory response to chase/attack a smaller pet or portion of a pet (the cat play-attacking the dog's waving tail, or the dog chasing the cat).

- Being physically and/or verbally disciplined.

- Making prolonged eye contact.

- Handling that's unwelcome (being held, petted, lifted, restrained, or forced into a submissive pose).

In addition, cats can aggress if they hear certain music frequencies or high-pitched sounds, such as a baby crying or a violin playing. They may also take out their upset feelings on your dog instead of the stray cat they can't reach through the window.

Pets usually know how to settle disputes without physically hurting each other. They use snaps and air-slashes to warn other animals to back off. Pets know exactly how close they can come without making contact and how to use a "soft mouth" or unfurled claws during play so they do no harm. Learning to master tooth and claw is the key so they can resolve differences without hurting each other (see also Chapters 5 and 10).

CALLING A TRUCE

When Rex and Sheba really get their noses out of joint, you must break up the fight before either gets hurt. Altercations most often happen when the dog gets too close out of curiosity or a desire to play, and the cat acts defensively out of fear and scratches or bites him; the pain prompts doggy retaliation. Another common cause results from play-aggression gone bad. Either the cat chases the puppy, or the dog chases the cat, and the victim scampering away triggers predatory drive that escalates into aggression.

It doesn't matter whether the dog or cat is the instigator or the victim, since during altercations each pet may alternate between aggression and defensiveness and you really can't separate the two. The same strategies for breaking up fights work in either case, but some are more effective with cats or with dogs—or with smaller pets than larger ones. For example, while wrangling between a Chihuahua and Maine Coon cat might be stopped by setting an object between them, that won't help when dealing with an eighty-pound canine and a kitten.

FOILING FIGHTS

It's best to prevent fights before the fur flies. Watch for doggy and kitty cues that they mean business. Most times your pets offer plenty of warning, such as growls and hisses. Only when the other animal refuses to listen does the tension escalate. Even when they are on opposite sides of the room, or Sheba perches high above Rex on her cat tree, it's a good idea to diffuse the tension before either gets too wound up or else their next nose-to-nose may prompt a bloody mess. The earlier you intervene, the less likely there will be a repeat; it takes cats twenty-four to forty-eight hours to settle down after arousal, and just the sight of the dog may start the fight all over again. The tips outlined below have been categorized as to what works *best* to dissuade cats and small dogs, or the *best* options for stopping a big dog aggressor, but these are not absolutes. A cat deterrent might work for your big dog, too, little and giant dogs may respond to similar incentives, and many of the options work equally well for all situations. So don't limit yourself to what falls in a particular category. Take care you aren't injured, either. Pets that are fully into battle mode may not even know you're there, and physically pulling pets apart will almost always get you scratched or bitten.

FOR ALL

- Sound an air horn to break pets apart once they become fully engaged.

- Separate the pets into different rooms until both have calmed down—at least one hour or longer if you aren't able to supervise their interaction.

FOR CATS

- Use the loud, abrupt hissing of an aerosol spray. This sounds like an even bigger cat and can prompt felines to run.

FOR CATS AND SMALL DOGS

 Soak them with water, which usually sends smaller fighting pets to their corners when noise doesn't work. Use a garden hose or toss ice-cold water at the pets' bodies; avoid the face and eyes.

 Use a barrier to separate the pair long enough for one to run. A cookie sheet, TV tray, large coffee table book, flat sofa cushion, or notebook may work if carefully slid in between the two furry faces. Wear an oven mitt to protect your hand.

 Set a chair over the top of the dog or cat to stymie the attack and give the aggressor something else to think about; this allows the defensive pet to run. The chair also keeps you at a safe distance from the snarls.

 Toss a thick blanket on top of both pets. That entangles paws and teeth, shuts out the sight of each other, and usually breaks up the fight.

 Use the blanket to wrap up the aggressor (this protects you from teeth and claws) and bundle him into a room alone for a time-out.

FOR DOGS

 Pull Rex away using a leash if noise, water, or obedience commands don't faze him. Don't grab his collar, since that often prompts him to whip around and nail your hand.

 Grasp the dog by his back legs or his tail and lift him off the ground in a "wheelbarrow" maneuver. Keep moving backward to keep away from his teeth.

Once the fighting has stopped, ignore both pets so neither gets any attention or reward for fighting. A thirty-minute shunning works for a mild transgression; for a serious fight, a whole day could be appropriate.

CAT-TO-DOG AGGRESSION

Aggression of the cat toward the dog usually arises from fear or (occasionally) territorial issues; if a dog acts like a victim, that can escalate feline aggression. Kittens never exposed to positive canine encounters during socialization naturally fear the "strange" critter and react with defensiveness. Other times, large cats find small scurrying puppies or an adult dog's tail an irresistible toy, and their predatory instinct takes over.

Cats also turn hissy when the dog invades their territory and especially dislike any sort of change in routine. A new dog coming into the house often prompts feline aggression, especially if Sheba thinks you prefer the dog over her. When Rex comes home from the veterinarian or kennel he smells differently, so Sheba may not recognize him and start hissing. Starting over with introductions can be very helpful, so refer to Chapter 19 for tips.

Cats challenge with stares, forward-facing positions, hisses and growls, and blocking access to resources, and may victimize your ill, very young, or aged dogs. In most cases, cats bluff more often than engage in full battle. The following techniques can reduce Sheba's inclination to pick fights with your dog.

- Spay and neuter cats to reduce the pushy behavior that prompts them to act up.

- Don't yell or scream. That makes cats more upset and can worsen the battle.

- Separate your pets when they cannot be directly supervised—when you answer the phone, cook dinner, or can't have your eyes glued to the pair. If you don't have enough separate rooms, baby gates (singly or stacked) work well to cordon off rooms or hallways.

- Keep Rex away from the cat's food and bathroom stations so Sheba won't feel defensive (see also Chapters 16 and 18).

- Give your victim dog a retreat where he'll be safe from the ambushing cat. An electronic pet door that's opened only by the collar Rex wears allows him the ability to go out into the fenced yard, for instance, but the cat can't follow.

 Use D.A.P. to ease the fearful dog actions that prompt Sheba to continue the bullying behavior.

 Employ Feliway pheromone product to help Sheba feel more comfortable about her environment so she doesn't take her angst out on the dog.

 Bell the cat so Rex has an early warning and is less likely to be ambushed.

 Attach a leash or drag line to the dog and let him tow it around the house to give Sheba a better target to attack that won't hurt Rex. This also provides a positive, fun association for your cat.

 Interrupt unacceptable behavior by an aggressive cat with compressed air or a water gun, then toss small treats to reinforce "good" behavior.

 Change the cat's hissing to purrs with a favorite toy, such as a fishing pole lure or flashlight beam to draw her attention away from the dog. That also keeps you at a safe distance from teeth and claws and creates a positive association for the cat about the dog's presence.

DOG-TO-CAT AGGRESSION

Aggression of the dog toward the cat most often has to do with status-related issues or predatory instinct. If the dogs missed socialization to cats, they won't know how to react; the most common "default" behavior is to either run or attack. Running can prompt predatory aggression when the motion triggers the chase reflex.

A change in the dog's social standing can turn on the growls, especially if Rex feels your affection is being usurped. Social status can change when a new pet is introduced, an animal returns to the house after surgery, boarding, or vacation, or the dominant animal becomes ill, aged, or dies, leaving a void other pets seek to fill. When you're having difficulties between a resident pet and a furry invader, start from scratch and repeat introductions all over again (see also Chapter 19).

Dogs challenge with stares, shoulder or hip bumps and shoves, or placing paws or chins over the shoulders of the target animal. They may growl or snarl a warning. Weaker and shy cats often are victimized. The aggression can remain subtle, with only posturing, or can escalate into knock-down, drag-out chase and attack. The tips below can be useful for helping with the situation.

- Neuter or spay your dog to decrease dominance behaviors that predispose Rex to act aggressively.

- Make sure the cat is out of harm's way by separating the pair when you can't watch them.

- Muzzle Rex during cat interactions until you're satisfied the dog won't hurt your cat. Refer to page 102 for tips on training dogs to accept the muzzle.

- Give Sheba lots of vertical hiding and resting places that Rex can't reach to provide a safe retreat for the cat.

- Teach Rex not to chase the cat by desensitizing him (see Chapter 19).

- Use a calm, low, commanding voice and say, "No!" or "Hey" or "Off" when you see Rex eyeing the cat. That may be enough for the dog to stalk away and pretend he won.

- Distract Rex with an alternate behavior. In a cheerful voice ask, "Want to go for a walk?" or offer a favorite toy to change the context of the feline encounter.

- Put Rex in a long down-stay. Lying down, in canine language, is a "calming signal" that diffuses upset feelings.

- Locate at least two feeding stations where neither Rex nor Sheba can be surprised or trapped (see also Chapters 16 and 18).

FELINE FEAR AGGRESSION

Cats faced with strange dogs for the first time become terrified; some become aggressive every time they get scared. Punishment makes it worse. Heredity plays a large role in fear and shyness, as does environment and socialization (see also Chapter 17). Fear aggression results from your cat's instinctive "fight-or-flight" response. If Sheba can't get away from the dog, she will lash out, and if Rex runs away, your fearful cat learns that aggressing works and will repeat the behavior whenever she sees Rex or any other dog.

 Watch for the distance at which Sheba becomes agitated. Once you know her limits, avoid situations by maintaining an appropriate space away from Rex such as by using baby gates to make "safe areas" in the house.

 Attach a drag line to the dog's collar so, at a moment's notice, you can intervene by stepping on it or picking it up to keep him a safe distance from your fearful cat.

 Provide additional quiet areas and/or hiding places for cats. Elevated perches and small boxes to hide in make cats feel more secure. Lots of tunnels, especially across open areas of the rooms, are ideal and allow fearful cats to slink to their destination out of doggy sight. As long as Sheba has an escape route, she won't need to attack.

 Engage Sheba in fishing pole toys or a light pointer when the dog is in the room a safe distance away. That helps build her confidence and associate "good stuff" with Rex's presence.

 Add several drops of the Rescue Remedy to the pets' water for everybody to sip.

CANINE FEAR AGGRESSION

Rex also can suffer from fear aggression, and some families of dogs tend to be shyer than others because they inherit this tendency.

While fear aggression of cats toward dogs is more common, tiny dogs such as Chihuahuas or puppies that haven't been socialized to felines often react fearfully when faced with a pushy feline (see also Chapter 17).

You'll see aggressive behavior if Rex feels trapped and unable to get away from the bossy cat. Most normal dogs tolerate one dog length and a half (their own length) before feeling uncomfortable, and stay calm until the scary cat invades this personal space. Dogs can generalize a scary situation to all future similar events so if Sheba scares your pooch only once or twice, Rex may thereafter react with terror upon meeting any other kitty. You can help calm your dog's fears of the cat with the following tips.

- Keep Sheba a comfortable distance away.

- Attach a bell to the cat's collar so fearful dogs hear her coming and can stay out of her way.

- Enroll Rex in an obedience class, help build his confidence. Until then, give him lots of praise and treats for staying quietly in the same room with Sheba.

- Use play therapy to build canine confidence, with games of fetch and tug-of-war games. Let the dog win and praise him for his success. It's particularly helpful for these exercises to take place in the presence of the cat so Rex associates her nearness with positive benefits for himself.

- Create a "house of plenty" by providing lots of toys so Rex doesn't feel he must compete for the good stuff.

- Add two to four drops of Rescue Remedy to the pets' water to help ease fearfulness.

- Use the plug-in product D.A.P. with your fear-aggressive dog to reduce his negative reactions.

FELINE PREDATORY AND PLAY AGGRESSION

All cats are born with predatory aggression—instinctive hunting behaviors that are also used in play. Cats rarely indulge in true predatory aggression, but when it happens, adult cats target very small dogs or puppies. More often, Sheba play-attacks your dog's tail and ears or chases and ambushes doggy feet. Movement across the cat's plane of vision (rather than directly toward or away from her) stimulates play aggression, which intends no harm and should stop short of doing any real danger. Kittens indulge in play aggression more than adults, but even mature pets enjoy a rousing game of chase or wrestling (see also Chapter 3). Feline predatory and play aggression almost always diminishes as either the attacking kitten matures or the adult cat's small canine target grows up. In the meantime, you'll need to take precautions to keep your dog safe.

- Separate tiny pups from predatory cats whenever you can't supervise them one on one. Stack baby gates in a doorway to keep felines at bay, or put the puppy inside an upside-down baby playpen.

- Distract Sheba with a fishing lure toy or light pointer, and lure her away from the Chihuahua puppy or the German Shepherd's tail. That helps her learn to associate the dog's presence with fun times.

- Avoid yelling or screaming, which increases the arousal level and makes the aggression worse.

- Use interruptions to stop the behavior such as the hissing noise from an aerosol can, a squirt from a water gun, a blast of an air horn, or a spray of citronella. Not all will work in every situation— some cats like to be squirted with water—so find the technique that works best for your pets.

- Attach a leash and harness for control and interruption of undesirable behavior.

CANINE PREDATORY AND PLAY AGGRESSION

Natural hunting and play behaviors arise out of instinctive predatory aggression, but most dogs stop short of doing damage. Dogs chase joggers, bicyclists, playing children, and moving cars—and cats—out of instinct. Predatory aggressive dogs are extremely dangerous to kitties and give no warning other than sometimes drooling with anticipation. While there are exceptions, terrier breeds developed to be "varmint dogs," which hunt and kill small animals, and sighthounds such as Greyhounds, which can't resist chasing moving prey, are more prone to predatory aggression toward cats.

Other dogs, such as Shetland Sheepdogs, display many of the same predatory behaviors in play aggression but intend no harm. These dogs indulge in the "chase" impulse bred into their herding heritage, for instance, and try to "move" Sheba from one place to another, but will stop short of the capture/kill of the sequence. You can tell the difference between predatory behavior and play because dogs use "meta signals," such as a play bow, to announce that the following growls, chasing, and mouthing are meant in play (see also Chapter 2).

Any dog may get carried away with play and bite too hard, though, and a predatory adult dog may need to be permanently segregated from your cat to ensure Sheba's safety. Once a tiny kitten grows into a macho adult, the doggy predation tends to diminish. Until that happens, prevent accidents from happening with the following tips.

 Provide cat trees and elevated perches so Sheba can stay safely out of reach of canine teeth.

 Place a baby gate on the stairway to segregate the upstairs "cat territory" from the downstairs doggy domain.

 Work on obedience training so Rex doesn't have to think when he hears "sit" to get his butt on the ground. An automatic default command helps distract him from instinctive predatory aggression as well as helps him to think about what he's doing instead of following an impulse (see also Chapter 4).

 Attach a drag line to the dog's collar and use it to stop canine misbehavior.

Counter-condition to change the dog's response. Each time Rex drools and stares at the cat, create a new attitude with a *happy* word he can't resist, such as "car ride" or "ball." When he looks at you and away from the cat, toss him a treat. Before long, the mere sight of Sheba will prompt your dog to switch his attention to you for the cue word and reward (see also Chapter 19).

 Interrupt play between the dog and cat every few minutes to retain control and give either pet the opportunity for a break if they want it.

Interrupt bad behavior. A supersoaker water gun, air horn, or citronella spray from a remote collar may work. Pick the interruption that gets your dog's attention best. Avoid yelling, which makes aggression worse.

FINDING FAULT

Redirected aggression results when the cat is prevented from fulfilling some desire and takes out her temper on somebody else. If Sheba sees a stray cat through the window but can't chase it away, she instead attacks the dog even though he was sleeping across the room. Adult male cats are the most common perpetrators, and attacks seem unprovoked. You could also be a one-time victim, but only when the trigger is still present. Common triggers include the sight, sound, or odor of another animal. Redirected feline aggression may turn the dog into a permanent scapegoat after just one "accidental" response, when the cat associates Rex's presence with previous aggression. If the scapegoat dog anticipates these attacks and acts like a victim, the attack cat may continue the behavior. Refer to the section on cat-to-dog aggression to help stop the cat aggressor/victim pattern. The following suggestions also help prevent future cases of redirected aggression.

Leave the cat alone and watch her body language to gauge her emotional state. Cats wave their tails or chatter their teeth when they can't reach their quarry and often launch attacks after watching from a window perch, so call Rex into another room if you see these signs.

- Keep animals away from window sight of your property. Eliminate hiding and perching places that draw animals, and don't leave food available outside. The Garden Ghost uses a safe, nontoxic spray technology to keep unwanted animals (cats, raccoon, deer) away from your property.

- Cover window views during problem times or prevent access to windows by moving furniture or stepstools away. Tape white translucent paper to the bottom halves of windows to allow light in but block the view of the grass.

- Apply double-sided tape products, such as Sticky Paws, to windowsills to make the surface uncomfortable for cat lounging.

- Separate the victim dog from the aggressive cat until Sheba "forgets" the association and stops picking on him. It may take several days or even weeks. Time away helps the victim learn to stop acting like a victim, too, which helps reduce the chance of being picked on. You may need to reintroduce the pair to calm ruffled feelings so they become friends again.

Chapter 16
Potty Concerns

S avvy dog owners with a new cat may not understand the ins and out(puts) of litter box training, nor may longtime cat owners understand the basics of canine housetraining. Most people think of cats as immaculately tidy animals and are shocked when a cat misses the litter box. In a similar way, we expect dogs to read our minds and know better than to make a mess in the house.

The truth is, neither will know how to do the right thing, in the right place, unless you tell them. Cats and dogs living in the same house add challenges to house training. Dealing with potty schedules, bathroom placements, and cleanup duty becomes more complicated each time you add more pets to the mix. If the cat has never been around dogs before (or vice versa), all kinds of litterary problems may develop. I've provided information about some of the most common cat and dog bathroom issues, with techniques to keep everyone happy and stay faithful to proper potty protocol.

LITTER BOX SNACKS

Coprophagia, the fancy term for eating feces, may disgust you but must be dealt with, especially in homes with both dogs and cats. Dogs treat the litter box as a snack bar because cat food contains more protein than dog food; as a result, feline waste tastes good to dogs. Dung eating first develops in puppies age four to nine months, but even adult dogs indulge. Some dogs snack on their own or another dog's feces as well (see also Chapter 6). The nasty habit is not only unsanitary, but it puts Sheba's tail in a twist to have a dog messing with her toilet. Cats pestered in their bathroom look for another place to go such as behind the sofa, so use these steps to prevent doggy access.

- Scoop and clean the cat box as often as possible. Leaving droppings any length of time asks for trouble. Electronic cat boxes automatically sweep the feces into a bin within ten minutes of the cat's deposit.

- Place litter boxes on a table or countertop, out of reach of nosy dogs.

- Put the litter box in a small cabinet or closet. Make sure there's a door latch that allows it to open only wide enough for the cat, or use a baby gate that the smaller cat can either slink through or jump over, while keeping the dog at bay.

- Use a "covered" litter box, with an opening that the dog's head can't fit through.

- Add a tablespoon of vegetable oil to Sheba's food so her waste becomes softer and less attractive to snacking dogs. A spoonful of canned pumpkin added to her food also changes the taste or consistency of her stool to make it less appealing; many cats relish pumpkin as a treat.

A HAIRY SITUATION

Cats not only spend much of their time grooming themselves, they'll also groom the dog, and licking results in swallowed fur and hairballs. What doesn't naturally pass into the litter box or yard is vomited out the other end. Feline grooming can turn into a hairy nightmare, especially if Rex has lots of fur. Hairballs predispose cats to constipation, and painful bowel movements often prompt Sheba to "blame" the litter box and stop using it. Keeping the fur from flying will help maintain your cat's litter box allegiance (see also Chapter 11).

HOUSE SOILING

It's not unusual for dogs and cats to have accidents in the house. House soiling in dogs almost always results when puppies don't know any better or adult dogs haven't been adequately housetrained to begin with (see also Chapter 6 for dogs and Chapter 11 for cats).

But when dogs and cats live together for the first time, house soiling commonly results from emotional stress (see also Chapter 17). They also have accidents due to inadequate environmental adjustments; if one of the pets has poor toilet habits, that can lure the other to also make mistakes. Rex may find Sheba's "accident" and feel compelled to baptize it with urine to make a doggy point. Cats often potty in a corner of a room opposite a doorway or in the dining room with two entrances so they won't be surprised and have an escape route. Punishment makes house soiling worse because even if you catch them in the act, reprimands teach pets to *hide* the next time or to go when you aren't around. Use these techniques to help cure the problem.

FOR CATS

 Place litter boxes in areas with more than one exit, such as the dining room, so Sheba can see the dog coming and still get away in time.

 Offer different types of toilets, both uncovered and covered, to better meet Sheba's tastes. Covered boxes keep some dogs away, but they also hold odors offensive to many cats, and shy felines fear being trapped inside because they can't see out.

 Place litter boxes in at least two locations in the house—upstairs and down, or at either end of one floor—so Rex can't guard both at the same time.

 Get a new box. When Sheba "blames" the box for uncomfortable elimination or its association with a pestering dog, she may return to good habits in a new, pristine box that doesn't have any of the former negative associations (see also "Litter Box Snacks" in this chapter).

FOR BOTH

 Clean soiled areas with odor neutralizers available from pet product stores; they destroy the smell completely. Nature's Miracle or Anti-Icky-Poo works well.

 Make the illegal potty target unattractive to the pets. After cleaning the area, place a sheet of aluminum foil or plastic carpet runner nub side up over the top of the area to make it an uncomfortable place to pose.

 Create a new association for the soiled area. Cats and dogs won't go where they eat or sleep, so move the miscreant's food bowls or bed on top of the spot.

LEG LIFTING AND SUBMISSIVE WETTING

Male dogs, and sometimes females, lift one rear leg and aim a stream of urine at vertical landmarks, such as a tree or fire hydrant. This leaves important canine information for other dogs to sniff and understand. Leg lifting becomes a problem if Rex takes aim inside your house. Castration reduces male marking behavior in seventy to eighty percent of dogs. In some cases dogs continue to mark in the house, but this almost always has to do with multiple-dog relationships (see also Chapter 6).

Dogs use a variety of signals to show deference to other dogs, people, and intimidating cats. Squatting and wetting or rolling onto his back signal a dog's ultimate submission. When your "boss cat" glowers at your puppy, you'll likely see quite a lot of submissive wetting. Other dogs and cats understand and expect this behavior and know it means, "I am no threat, don't hurt me!" But it can be irksome for owners when Rex wets each time you arrive home. Puppies usually outgrow the behavior, but some very submissive dogs may continue the behavior as adults (see also Chapter 6).

URINE SPRAYING

Feline urine spraying has nothing to do with needing to go and is the feline equivalent of canine leg lifting/marking behavior. Spraying cats back up to the target, hold the tail erect with just the tip quivering, and release small amounts of urine in a directed spray, usually against a vertical target. More male cats do this, but females may occasionally spray, too. Breeding cats are most likely to urine spray, but spraying also arises out of anxiety. Spreading urine around helps calm the cat because this "self-scent" means safety and ownership. When your cat sprays the bed or your briefcase, consider it a backhanded compliment. The cat loves you so much she declares ownership of you and your belongings with urine.

When your cat becomes upset about the dog usurping her toys, resting place, food bowl, litter box—even your affections—or just taking up space in *her house*, then Sheba may spray. In addition to the tips you'll find in Chapter 11, include the following specific techniques for the dog-cat household. Once spraying stops, you can reduce options one by one to find the least amount that work to keep the house dry.

- Increase second-story real estate by adding cat trees and window perches out of reach of the family dog to reduce feline anxiety and spraying.

- Add cat tunnels to offer Sheba "hidden" pathways out of sight of pesky dogs; the urine spraying will reduce, along with her stress levels.

- Provide safe, dog-free zones for the cat to eat and potty (see also Chapters 16 and 18).

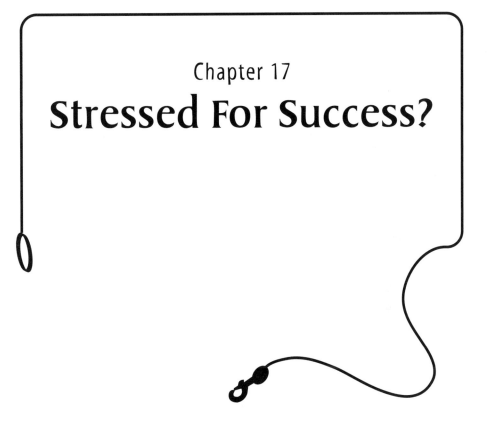

Chapter 17
Stressed For Success?

Pets seem to feel many of the same emotions we do. We can't know for sure if they experience jealousy or love in the same way, but they certainly react in a similar fashion. Excesses of any emotion take their toll, and the stress of cats and dogs living together can make upset feelings even worse and cause behaviors you don't appreciate.

Find more information about boredom and jealousy in Chapter 7 and moving angst or separation anxiety in Chapter 12. Use the tips in this chapter to deal with the stresses specific to cat-dog households. Recognize your pets' emotional upset and understand why he feels that way so that you can soothe furry distress.

DEPRESSION AND GRIEF

There are down times when pets feel depressed, just as owners do. But the loss of a furry companion or the addition of a new pet deeply affects sensitive dogs and cats.

Depressed pets sleep more, lose their appetite, stop playing, and retreat from the world. Dogs can become more vocal (see also Chapter 20). When Sheba becomes depressed, she stops grooming herself, hides, and uses more spraying and scratching to comfort herself (see Chapters 16 and 20).

We can't explain to pets what has happened, but they become confused and feel lost, especially if Sheba feels your affections have been displaced by the new dog or Rex mourns the death of a special cat friend (see also Chapters 7 and 12).

Cats and dogs can react to death in many ways. Just as some humans hide their pain, some pets show little reaction; other times, Sheba may cry and endlessly search for her deceased canine friend, while Rex howls his grief. Confusion and hurt are worse when the sick friend simply "disappears" from the house. And when you lose a beloved cat or dog, you also feel depressed and experience grief. Pets pay close attention to their owners' feelings and might think you're upset with them, and feel worse. Over several days or weeks, they'll start to feel better, but in the meantime help your pets deal with their grief with the following tips.

FOR BOTH

 Allow your surviving pet to view the body to say goodbye. That helps him understand his furry friend won't be coming back. Expect any sort of reaction—anything is normal in this situation.

 Tell pets how you feel. Talking about it also changes the way you act and react, so be positive and tell your pets, "I'm sad, but it's not your fault."

Use the herbal remedies from Bach Flowers to work on your pet's emotional level. Behaviorists recommend Star of Bethlehem to relieve grief. Give two to four drops directly into the mouth two or three times a day until the depression lifts. If they object to the taste, put the drops on a treat such as cheese or yogurt.

FOR DOGS

 Give Rex attention but in an upbeat, enthusiastic manner. Pampering a grief-stricken dog can reward the moping so it lasts even longer.

 Schedule a weekend away from home to visit new places that don't have the association of his missing feline buddy. Time away in a strange location gives Rex a fresh start once he returns home.

 Give your dog "work" to do to keep his brain busy so he doesn't worry so much. Spend time with him practicing obedience or tricks.

FOR CATS

 Remove Rex's toys or bed to eliminate these scent-reminders until your cat has gotten over the worst of the grief. His scent in the environment makes Sheba feel more depressed or fearful, as if she's encountering Rex's ghost.

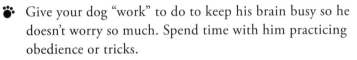 Offer extra smelly treats to tempt Sheba's appetite and make her feel special when she's upset. Depression and grief can kill the kitty appetite (see also Chapter 13).

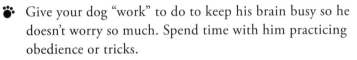 Lure her into activity with a fishing pole toy or flashlight. It's hard to feel blue while playing games, and just getting Sheba out from under the bed helps turn around negative feelings.

FEAR AND SHYNESS

When properly socialized to each other, dogs and cats interact with a happy, confident demeanor. But if they've not had this benefit, the "fear factor" can rear its ugly head. These pets may also fear new people or other situations; Rex may be shy of other dogs, while Sheba is terrified of other cats (see also Chapters 7 and 12).

Signs of slight fear—pinning their ears back—can escalate in both cats and dogs to extremes in which they shake, crouch, urinate, or even defecate in terror. If the frightened pet can't get away, he'll attack (see also Chapters 5 and 10). Fearful dogs also become very vigilant, act tense, and stare at the scary cat, but it's much more common for Sheba to feel uncomfortable around Rex. Terrified tabbies refuse to make eye contact with the frightening dog and usually hide, often stop grooming, and may lose their appetite and begin house soiling. It can take a great deal of time and patience to help frightened cats and dogs accept each other. Some types of fear never go away, but you can improve your pets' confidence with the following steps.

FOR BOTH

 Build a routine so both cats and dogs can predict what happens next. That way there are fewer scary unknowns and their fearfulness toward each other is reduced.

 Rescue Remedy, one of the Bach Flower essences, can help shy and fearful pets better deal with their emotions.

 Play fun games with the dog and cat at the same time, on opposite ends of the hallway, so neither feels threatened but appreciates the benefit of having the other one near—good stuff happens when that other critter makes an appearance.

FOR DOGS

 Don't reward poor behavior, or the attention encourages the fearfulness to continue. Instead, watch for relaxed breathing, calm expressions, and confident body postures when the cat is nearby and give Rex a treat to reward confidence.

 Play tug-of-war games to build confidence in shy dogs.

 Spray D.A.P. on a fashionable kerchief and tie it around your dog's neck, or use the plug-in product for indoor use to ease Rex's cat phobias.

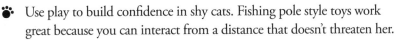 Expose your fearful dog to Sheba in gradually increasing increments. The dog's personal space tends to be about a dog length and a half (his own length); as long as the cat remains outside in the "safe zone," Rex should remain calm. Start from across the room, though, and reward Rex with treats any time the cat makes an appearance in the same room, as long as he remains cool.

FOR CATS

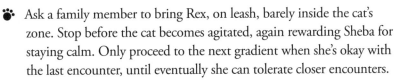 Provide Sheba with more second-story hiding or perching places, well out of dog sniffing range, to allow her to see "danger" coming and build confidence when she realizes she rules the elevations. Cat tunnels that offer "hidden" pathways for her to maneuver under the dog's radar also help.

Use play to build confidence in shy cats. Fishing pole style toys work great because you can interact from a distance that doesn't threaten her.

Have Rex lie down on the floor across the room to prevent him from looming over Sheba. Use treats to keep his attention focused on you so she can approach at her own pace.

Identify Sheba's "safe zone," in which she'll remain calm as long as Rex stays a safe distance away. Carefully expose Sheba to the dog's presence in gradually increasing increments. Reward her with petting or a favorite treat when she remains calm after Rex approaches this "safe zone."

Ask a family member to bring Rex, on leash, barely inside the cat's zone. Stop before the cat becomes agitated, again rewarding Sheba for staying calm. Only proceed to the next gradient when she's okay with the last encounter, until eventually she can tolerate closer encounters.

HYPER HOUNDS AND CRAZY CATS

High-energy youngsters play nonstop to practice grown-up "hunting" techniques and also because it's plain fun. This normal behavior becomes overwhelming to owners if cats and dogs turn your house into the Indy 500 at all hours of the day and night. Dogs and cats rarely suffer from insomnia, although a small percentage of aging pets develop cognitive disorders (senility) or other metabolic diseases that disrupt sleep cycles. More often the miscreants keep each other awake playing late into the night. Kitten and puppy energy calms down by the time they're eighteen months old or so, but many adult pets continue to act hyper and egg each other on.

Pets stuck indoors for eight hours want to cut loose when owners yearn to rest. Certain breeds are naturally more high energy than others. Dogs developed to herd sheep turn instincts to chasing the cat, while cats invite such games by playing tag-the-terrier. If you reward their high jinks with laughter or open the back door in response to whirling dervish behavior just to get them out of your hair, smart pets learn to use hyper behavior to get their way. Use the following tips to help cool their jets.

FOR BOTH

 Schedule playtimes and exercise, at least twenty minutes twice a day, to take the edge off hyperactive behavior. Both cats and dogs may react to the beam of a laser pointer—you can sit in an easy chair while they chase the light around and around. Avoid shining the light in the pets' eyes, though.

 Organize games before bedtime so they'll sleep on your schedule.

 Encourage your cat and dog to play together to wear each other out. Interrupt chase or wrestling games every few minutes to be sure both enjoy the activity, and stop the games when you've had enough. If necessary, separate the fur kids just as you would your human offspring.

 Play harp music or a selection from the Pet Music CD to calm pets' antics.

Feed them right before you go to bed so the meal lasts and they're less likely to pester you at 3 A.M. to fill the bowl.

 Give your pets melatonin to help them sleep. Ask your vet for the proper dosage.

 Provide each pet with a quarter cup of warm milk as a bedtime snack to help them snooze. Milk contains the natural sleep aid tryptophan, but some dogs and cats don't digest milk easily; discontinue it if diarrhea develops.

FOR AGING PETS

 A nightlight helps aging cats and dogs with fading sight and hearing to find their way around and calms the jitters, whimpers, and yowls so they sleep better.

FOR DOGS

 Enroll Rex in an obedience class, agility, or other canine events to keep smart, high-energy dogs busy in a more productive fashion.

 Teach Rex that he only gets attention when he "pays" with a "sit" before you open the door for an outside romp. Rex often prefers you yelling at him to being ignored; he may behave badly on purpose just to get attention (see also Chapter 4).

 Try the herbal preparation Calm Pet (www.nutribest.com) to reduce hyperactivity behavior.

FOR CATS

 Teach your cat tricks. Engaging her brain as well as muscles helps wear Sheba out and keeps her healthier and happier (see also Chapter 4).

Chapter 18
Ringing The Dinner Bell

Dogs and cats choose the tastiest, but not necessarily most nutritious, food to eat. When they live in the same house, you may catch Rex and Sheba snacking from each other's bowls. Simply put, dogs shouldn't eat cat food and cats shouldn't eat dog food. While we love them the same, their nutritional needs are not created equally.

Besides nutritional differences, cats and dogs also have different eating styles and preferences—cats tend to nibble, while dogs like to gulp. Even their bodies process food at different rates. It takes twenty-four hours from eating a meal for the dog

> **VET ALERT!**
>
> Adult dogs can go three or even four days without eating and suffer no permanent problems. But puppies, kittens and tiny dogs shouldn't go longer than twelve hours without a meal, and adult cats shouldn't go longer than twenty-four to thirty-six hours. If toy dog breeds don't eat regularly, they can develop hypoglycemia (low blood sugar). Anorectic cats suffer hepatic lipidosis (fatty liver disease) within a very short period of time and die. Check with your veterinarian if your pets stop eating for a dangerous period of time.

to fully process the food, but the same sequences only takes about thirteen hours in the cat. (It can take up to fifty-six hours in people.) Because their digestive systems work differently, cats and dogs need to eat on different schedules.

Choose foods based on the cat or dog's lifestage and health needs, such as for growth (puppies or kittens), maintenance (for adult dogs or cats), or for senior diets. There is also a host of therapeutic diets your veterinarian may dispense for certain health challenges. That makes offering the right food to your cat and dog even more important.

DOGGY DINING DEMEANOR

Dogs, like people, are considered omnivores. They can eat and use a wide variety of both animal and plant food nutrition. Rex can live quite happily eating cat food but can get fat because it contains more protein and calories than his regular chow.

Canines are group-oriented creatures that consider mealtime a social event, and they want to eat with their pack—including the cat. Group meals can lead to competition for the bowl, though. Dogs often eat more food when in the company of other dogs or family members, probably because of a perceived notion of competition—"I'll eat it so *she* doesn't get it!" mentality. Dogs inherited the glutton gene from ancestors that hunted in packs and killed large animals, which provided them with massive amounts of food. The rule was to eat it all or risk having interlopers steal the leftovers. Many dogs don't chew; they grab and swallow mouthfuls until they empty the bowl. They also have a sweet tooth because they are omnivores and need to be able to tell when fruits and vegetables ripen.

FELINE FOOD FOIBLES

Cats are true carnivores ("animal eaters") and require a large amount of meat protein to provide the proper balance of nutrients. Think of the archetypical cat mouse meal, which contains just the right balance of meat, fiber (hair), and vitamins and minerals (bones and mouse stomach contents).

While cats and dogs require the same essential ten amino acids (components of proteins) in their diets, Sheba needs an eleventh amino acid called taurine. Dogs can make taurine from other nutrients that are eaten, but cats don't have this ability. That's why a vegetarian diet will kill a cat, and eating a food designed for dogs can prompt feline heart disease or make them go blind.

Cat ancestors hunted bite-size prey such as mice and birds. Single-serving meals created a cat preference to eat a mouthful at a time, with no leftovers to worry about. Cats also prefer foods at "prey body temperature," so refrigerated leftovers can be offputting unless warmed up before reserving. Cats hunt and (hopefully) eat three or four times a day, so modern cats also tend to nibble a bit, then return to the bowl throughout the day. Small cats with tiny tummies may not be able to eat everything they need in one sitting. Cats don't seem to get nearly as competitive over food as dogs do, perhaps because they are more likely to eat alone and because it takes less food to satisfy that one-meal mentality. Since cats developed to eat animals, they don't have a typical sweet tooth. Instead, cats detect a sort of "meaty-sweet" flavor found in animal protein.

COMFORT ZONE

Dogs can be humanely kept away from indoor, off-limit areas with a citronella collar, which emits a burst of strong scent when Rex gets too close. Spray Barrier (available from www.premier.com) consists of a citronella collar that first emits a warning tone, then a harmless, scented spray when the dog continues to approach a transmitter dish. The dish plugs into a home electric outlet and can be set to keep dogs out of a two- to ten-foot radius.

HUNGER STRIKES

Pets lose their appetite from a variety of causes, and you can narrow potential reasons by using the P.E.T. test. When you share your house with both cats and dogs and one of them snubs the bowl, chances are the problem stems from the other pet's presence.

Your dog may empty the bowl before Sheba gets a chance to eat, or make the cat afraid to venture into the kitchen for dinner. Dominant cats also throw their weight around food resources and may bully even big dogs to keep the goodies for themselves—or just to show they can. The emotional stress of dealing with a strange pet often kills the dog or cat's appetite (see also chapters 8 and 13). Start with these helpful hints for cat-dog dinnertime troubles.

FOR BOTH

 Visit the veterinarian dentist to assess the problem. Up to eighty percent of all cats and dogs develop some form of dental disease by the time they reach two or three years old. Painful teeth and gums can make pets refuse to eat; in the meantime, offer soft foods she chews more easily.

 Warm the pet's food in the microwave for ten seconds to unlock the odor that will encourage reluctant dogs and cats to eat.

 Moisten dry kibble with warm water or no-salt broth to improve pet appetites.

> ### CALMING SIGNALS: DIET CHANGES
>
> Cats or dogs fed the same diet throughout their lives may have difficulty recognizing new food as edible. A sudden change in diet also can upset the digestion. A gradual transition from the old to the new food works best. Begin by mixing one-quarter of the new diet with three-quarters of the old for a week. The second week, mix the two diets 50/50. The third week, mix three-quarters of the new with one-quarter of the old until finally the pet eats one hundred percent of the new food.

FOR CATS

 Choose a very pungent, canned fishy food to spark the cat's interest.

 Offer special treats such as meat baby food or tuna to turn on the cat's motor. Avoid baby foods that contain onion, though, which can cause problems for cats.

FOR DOGS

 Use canned cat food as a top dressing over Rex's regular fare to get him started. Once he swallows a mouthful, his appetite often returns.

 Provide "people" foods to tempt the anorectic pet until he's willing to eat regular chow again. Boiled chicken or mashed banana often appeal to dogs to get them eating again.

COME AND GET IT!

When you share your home with both cats and dogs, you must manage meals to account for individual living circumstances and the very different needs and social interactions of the pets. If your cats and dogs eat only from their assigned bowls, count your blessings—you can skip reading this section. When you are feeding more than one dog or cat, see also Chapters 8 and 13. To keep the dog from eating from the cat's bowl, and vice versa, use the following suggestions. Not all will work for every circumstance, so please use those that are best for your furry crew.

FOR BOTH

 Give cats and dogs their own bowls to accommodate the different foods for each.

 Schedule two or three meals a day so your pets can anticipate the routine. Meal feeding is healthier for pets and allows you to better monitor who eats what and to make adjustments if necessary.

Assign each pet a specific place to eat. When you have one dog and one cat, feeding them at the same time on opposite sides of the kitchen works well. In that way, the food bowl and surrounding area becomes the "owned" property of the dog, for instance, so the cat may be more willing to respect the territorial claim.

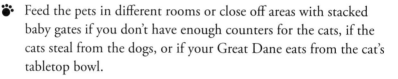 Feed the pets in different rooms or close off areas with stacked baby gates if you don't have enough counters for the cats, if the cats steal from the dogs, or if your Great Dane eats from the cat's tabletop bowl.

Stagger feeding times. Most pets eat all they want within ten to twenty minutes, so arranging times even ten minutes apart will help you supervise each meal and prevent pets from swiping food from each other.

Create a "boxed lunch" when the pets vary greatly in size to give the smallest a private dining area. Cut a tiny opening in a clear plastic storage container that's big enough for only the little guy to get through. Place the small pet's food bowl inside the box, to nibble at his leisure. The clear plastic also lets the pet see out and avoid being ambushed.

FOR CATS

Place Sheba's bowls out of reach of nosy dogs to reduce competition and keep all the critters happy. Felines prefer elevated spots such as countertops, cat trees, or the washing machine top and are less likely to graze from floor-level bowls when they can dine on high.

 Use a baby gate to segregate hallways or stairways to create separate feeding areas when you don't have enough rooms.

Make a food puzzle using a clear plastic container. Place the cat's dry food inside after cutting a half-dozen paw-size holes in the lid and sides for kitty to "fish" the food out. This keeps the cat occupied and prevents her from pestering the dog during mealtime; Rex can't reach her food inside the box, either.

FOR DOGS

 Time the glutton dog's meal so he finishes before the cat. Let Rex out into the fenced yard to "do his duty" while the cat has more time to finish her meal. Usually, ten to twenty minutes allows enough time for each meal.

 Put Rex's dinner in a commercial puzzle toy such as the Goody Ship, Buster Cube, or other treat dispenser if your teasing cat pesters the dog during meals or eats from his bowl.

Chapter 19
Pleased To Meet You

Most cats and dogs can get along famously, especially if properly socialized during puppyhood or kittenhood. But it will take longer to introduce them if either or both have never had positive experiences with the other species. Your rate of success also depends on the pet personalities involved. Some dog breeds tend to be more dangerous to small critters (including cats) simply because of their heritage. Terriers and sighthounds, for example, were bred to chase down prey, and the scurrying cat can trigger predatory aggression to chase, catch, or even kill. A great disparity in size also has inherent risk, even if the much bigger dog never intends harm. A Saint Bernard might sit on and squash a tiny kitten by accident, while a bruiser Maine Coon cat could injure a Chihuahua puppy during rough play.

Take care that your newest pet fits well with your existing family. Will your old, set-in-her-ways cat really appreciate a brash puppy? Are you getting the new kitten to keep Rex company, or are you just smitten and want Sheba for yourself? Be honest, and make sure you're doing this for all the right reasons. Dogs are such social creatures that they often welcome a new buddy even if it meows instead of barks. Cats tend to be quite reticent about strangers, though, and take longer to warm up so you'll need to be patient.

THE TEN COMMANDMENTS OF PET DYNAMICS

1. Introductions go much more smoothly when the resident pet already knows the rules of the house. At a minimum, they should understand "no." Dogs should be leash-trained.

2. Cats and dogs properly socialized as youngsters to each other will be most likely to accept new pets as friends. When the mother dog accepts cats or the mother cat accepts dogs as friends, their offspring learn more readily to accept the other species as "family."

3. Resident adult pets are more willing to accept babies because they're less of a challenge to the adult's social status. Kittens more readily integrate into a dog home, and resident adult cats feel less threatened by puppy-size newcomers.

4. All pets need space to claim as their own. If you don't have enough rooms to accommodate them, enrich the environment by adding vertical space for the cats and a safe, enclosed outdoor area for the dogs.

5. Newcomer cats must be familiar with the new environment before they are willing to meet resident dogs.

6. Choosing complementary pet personalities promotes better relationships. An outgoing cat can build confidence in your shy dog.

7. Choose complementary activity types. A playful cat as a partner with your lap-sitting pooch can work well because neither infringes on the other's preferred way of life. An energetic pup also helps get the overweight couch-potato cat off her furry tail, while the sedate cat may have a settling influence on the brash dynamo.

8. Introduce the new pet to one resident animal at a time. It's not fair to subject them to the whole "gang," and it's more difficult for you to supervise more than a pair.

9. *Always* pay more attention to the resident pet when he or she is within view. The resident pet will be much more willing to accept a newcomer as long as your affections aren't usurped.

10. Be patient. It may take days, weeks, or even months for the pets to accept each other and get along. Some pets may never become friends, and the best you can hope for is tolerance or avoidance.

STEP-BY-STEP INTRODUCTIONS

Introducing your cat and dog to each other may immediately result in love at first sight or, more commonly, will take time for the pair to accept each other. Follow the steps that follow when both the resident(s) and the new pet are confident, healthy animals that have been properly socialized as pups or kittens. Although dog-to-dog introductions are best begun on "neutral" territory, which often means the park or a neighbor's yard (see also Chapter 9), plunking a cat down in a carrier or on a leash in the middle of a park spells disaster on a grand scale! Therefore,

CALMING SIGNALS: A BARKING KITTY TOY

When Deborah Wood acquired a Papillon puppy, he was so small a baby gate couldn't keep him separated from Mews, her Persian. "Pogo pounced on Mews all the time," she said. "I attached a leash to the puppy for the better part of a year." The leash offered a handle so Wood could conveniently redirect Pogo's actions without having to chase him down. An unexpected bonus developed: Mews loved to play with the dragging leash—it turned Pogo into a safe, legal cat toy to follow around. "To this day, Pogo and Mews are buddies," Wood says. "I think in her mind, Mews associates Pogo with being fun!"

dog-to-cat introductions must take place in your home in a similar fashion to cat-to-cat introductions (see also Chapter 14), with accommodations made for the sensitivities of the dog and cat involved.

Watch your pets' body language to gauge their feelings. A tail-up greeting from the cat indicates a friendly approach, while a canine play-bow, an easygoing tail wag, perhaps a yawn or two, or rolling on his back says Rex means no harm. Delay the next step if you see the cat swish her tail or pin her ears flat to her head—that means she's fearful and may become aggressive. Dominant dogs may place a paw on the cat's back or signal aggression with raised hackles or a snarl.

Take care to curb the new baby pet's enthusiasm. Puppies and kittens may not understand the "keep back" signals of the older resident pet, so make sure the adults have enough room to get away to avoid a defensive snap. Containing clueless youngsters inside pet carriers or on leashes can be helpful. On the plus side, gregarious pups and juvenile cats don't discourage easily and often wear down curmudgeonly residents, as long as you run interference and ensure safety.

Adult-to-multiple-adult pet introductions take the longest time because each pair must meet individually and work out his or her own feelings about the interloper. Dogs tend to follow your lead, so make it clear you welcome the newcomer; your resident canine crew will be more accepting of the new cat.

It's vital that your resident "top dog" or "king cat" be fed first,

CALMING SIGNALS

When a sixteen-week old Devon Rex kitten came to live with Steve and Robin Dale of Chicago, Roxy had never seen dogs before. "But our dogs had been there, done that," says Steve, the host of Animal Planet Radio and a syndicated pet journalist. "Chaser and Lucy understand that you don't chase the kitten, and you act like you could care less. The more disinterested they are, the more interested the cat becomes and the safer the cat feels." They put Roxy at the top of the seven-foot cat tree to give her confidence as well as familiarity with a safe escape route. "It took about four days until she felt quite comfortable."

petted first, groomed first, and be given any other preferential treatment to ensure peace and harmony in the multipet household. Never show preferred attention to an animal lower in the hierarchy; that simply prompts confusion and may inspire the "king" to put the lower-ranking pet in his place. Old dogs or cats may need to have private feeding and resting times so they're not bothered by a more energetic newcomer.

The following techniques can help ease introductions. New dogs that meet resident cats won't always require the same steps as when introducing a new cat to resident dogs, but some tips apply to both scenarios. You live with your animals and know them best, so use your good judgment to create a workable program. In almost all cases, it's best to take extra time rather than rush through the techniques. Don't be afraid to start from scratch if one of the animals needs this help.

FOR BOTH

- Spay or neuter the newcomer *before* introductions. Fixed dogs and cats aren't as great a threat to the status quo.

- Use pheromone products to calm the pets and reduce the stress of introductions. The plug-in products Feliway for cats and D.A.P. for dogs diffuse in the air to benefit all the pets, or you can spray D.A.P. on a kerchief for a particular dog to wear.

- Add a few drops of Rescue Remedy to the drinking water of the pets.

- Sequester the new pet in a single room with all the necessary kitty or doggy accoutrements. If a new pet came with a favorite bed or toy, be sure to include those in his room so the old, familiar smells help keep him calm.

- Choose a room with a door that shuts completely, such as a second bedroom. Isolating the new pet tells your resident pet that only a small portion of the house has been invaded, not all the territory.

- Expect cats to posture or hiss and dogs to sniff, whine, growl, or bark whether they're new pets or current residents. Feel encouraged once the barking and hissing fade, especially if the canine "play-bows" at the door or the pair play patty-cake-paws under the door.

- Bring out something the new pet has scented, such as a plate of food where she just ate, and allow your resident dog or cat to smell it after the new pet has been in the room alone for a few days and the hisses or growls have faded.

- Dab vanilla extract—or your favorite perfume or cologne—at the base of the tail and on the back of the neck of both pets to make them smell alike. Sheba identifies friendly family members by their scent—and everyone smells alike when they like each other because of mutual grooming and cheek-rubbing behavior. Making the new dog smell like the cat goes a long way toward encouraging Sheba to accept him as a family member.

- Whenever possible, make initial meetings in an open room with lots of space and lots of cat second-story perches available. Sheba can then check out the dog from her cat tree, well beyond nose-sniffing range, and feel more comfortable.

- Keep first nose-to-nose meetings to only five or ten minutes, then give everyone a break and return the new pet to the safe room.

- When the dog and cat willingly nose sniff, the cat cheek-rubs the dog, and/or Rex play bows an invitation to a game, that's great! Allow play for a few minutes at a time, but interrupt before either pet becomes overexcited.

- Continue to offer planned meetings for another week, monitoring the dog until he can control himself and respects the cat even when off leash.

INTRODUCING THE NEW CAT TO THE RESIDENT DOG

- Put the dog in his yard out of sight while you bring the new cat into the house and leave her in her "isolation room." Problems are much less likely if a resident dog enters the house and finds the new kitty already there.

- Allow your new cat to wander around the rest of the house after the hissing fades and the paw pats increase. Don't force anything; simply open the isolation room door and let Sheba explore and "map" the location of all the good hiding places and high perches to feel safe. Make sure Rex stays outside in the yard.

- Let the resident dog check out the new cat smells in the "safe room" while Sheba explores one of the other rooms.

- Install a baby gate in the isolation room so the cat and dog can meet at their own speed and through the safety of the barrier. Pay attention to how each pet reacts before proceeding to the next step. Be on the lookout for confidence and interest, but if either pet shows shyness or aggression, give them more time (see also Chapter 17).

- Use a pet carrier to contain a *confident* new cat if you don't have access to the baby gate. If the cat is *shy* and the resident dog is small, place the dog in the carrier instead so the cat can approach while feeling safe. *Do not* place a frightened cat in a carrier and allow a pushy dog to sniff, or you'll further traumatize her and delay any acceptance of the resident dog.

- Prepare for whisker-to-whisker meetings once Sheba feels comfortable in the house and with the baby gate/carrier step. Avoid fanfare, put the dog on a leash, and then open the baby gate and watch what happens. Remember to confine this introduction to the new cat and only one of your dogs, not everybody at once.

- Keep the pets away from closely confined spaces during initial meetings. An open room with lots of space reduces tension.

- Feed both pets on opposite ends of a room during this initial meeting, to distract them and help them associate *food* with each other's presence.

- Engage the pets in play if they aren't interested in food. Whoever your dog feels closest to should interact with the cat so Rex sees that *you* accept the kitty and will be more willing to follow his beloved owner's example.

- Interrupt sniffing every now and then by calling the dog away or guiding him with the leash. Keep these initial meetings short— about five to ten minutes—so you don't wear out the pets.

- If they start to play, great! Allow play for a few minutes and then break up the games. End the session on a good note so they want more of each other.

- Continue to segregate the cat in her safe room whenever you cannot directly supervise the pair. Most cats can jump over the baby gate to regulate the interactions, or you can place a stepstool for Sheba—or raise the baby gate just enough for her to wiggle beneath.

- Offer more planned meetings for another week, monitoring the dog until he can control himself and respect the cat even when off leash.

INTRODUCING THE NEW DOG TO THE RESIDENT CAT

- Ask a friend to bring the new dog into the house out of sight of the resident cat so kitty won't associate you with the "scary" critter.

- Keep the isolation room door shut for at least the first week and longer if necessary. Resident cats become upset at the sight of a stranger but may be curious about the smell or sound.

- Isolate Rex while the resident cats are learning to accept the new smells and sounds of that dog behind the door. This way, the cats will feel less threatened.

- Schedule Rex's potty breaks to keep them from seeing each other too soon. Put Sheba in your bedroom during your dog's travels to and from the backyard.

- Offer Sheba the opportunity to check out the "safe room" while the dog is outside to become more familiar with the dog's smells. Don't force her into the room; just leave the door open and she'll explore at her leisure. Let it be the cat's idea.

- Replace the isolation room door with a baby gate so the pets can see each other and sniff or paw through the opening while they're safely separated. Your cat can control the interaction by jumping over or winding through the baby gate if she really feels the urge to check out Rex.

- If you don't have a baby gate and the dog is small enough, you can place Rex inside a crate or pet carrier for the cat to approach it in a safe, controlled way. Watch both pets' reactions closely and delay taking the next step until you are satisfied they feel comfortable.

Put Rex on a leash before removing the baby gate so he and the cat can finally meet. Remember, these initial introductions should be between the new pet and only *one* of your resident animals, not everybody at once.

 Keep Rex under leash control but give him some wiggle room; a tight leash can make him feel tense.

 Muzzle Rex to ensure the cat's safety (see also Chapter 5).

 Make initial meetings as pleasant as possible. If your cat feels proprietary toward you, engage her in a fishing pole game while another family member handles Rex so the cat associates the dog with good things for her. You can also give each animal a plate of food on opposite ends of a room to distract them and reward the fact that they ignore each other.

 Segregate the new pet alone in his "safe room" whenever you are not able to directly supervise, until you are satisfied that the cat and dog get along well and both have "safe places" they can retreat to when necessary.

CUTTING THE CHASE

Some dogs can't resist chasing the cat, but Sheba doesn't appreciate being turned into a windup toy for the dog's amusement. Teaching Rex to refrain from the chase not only enforces good manners, but also becomes a safety issue. You can train better doggy manners by placing a *confident cat* in a protective carrier, then giving the dog treats for behaving calmly. Ask the dog to sit, heel, stay, or perform other obedience commands, and offer the *best* treats (a bonanza of a whole handful!) for moving away from the cat. Be aware, though, that such a situation can be highly traumatic for shy cats even if you give treats to Sheba as well. A better technique for most cats uses classic conditioning. Just as Pavlov conditioned dogs to salivate when they heard a bell, you can teach your dog to respond to the cat's presence in an acceptable manner. You'll need a leash, treats, the cat and dog, and lots of patience.

- Ensure the cat's safety by keeping your dog under leash control. Prevent *any* chase from taking place because the activity feels so good to your dog he'll gladly ignore or give up any other type of reward. Even if the cat instigates the session (some cats tease dogs unmercifully), don't allow any chase or tag games until after the dog has learned proper manners.

- Have plenty of smelly, tasty treats handy ready to reinforce your dog at the drop of a hat—or the presence of a cat.

- Give the dog a treat every time (and I mean *every* time) the cat makes an appearance. Offer this reward whether he acts calm, excited, looks at the cat, barks, or anything else. The equation should be: CAT'S PRESENCE = DOG TREAT. Use the leash only to keep him a safe distance from the kitty, not to force his attention or behavior into what you want him to do. Let his brain process the equation on its own time. Some dogs "get it" right away; others take longer. Within a few sessions, nearly every dog will start to look to you for a treat each time the cat appears. Rather than lunging and chasing instinctively, you've conditioned a new response: to expect a reward.

- Reinforce this behavior for at least a week or two. Brush up with more training sessions as needed—for some dogs, that might be every month. Make sure the dog stays leashed and the pets separated when not supervised until you are confident the new canine response has become ingrained.

PART FIVE

COMMON MULTIPET
FRUSTRATIONS

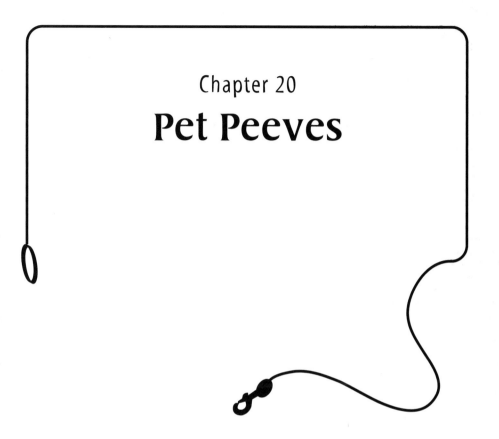

Chapter 20
Pet Peeves

Whether you have multiple cats, a pack of dogs, or each species, chances are you will experience one or more of these top complaints of pet owners. It's hard enough to train proper petiquette to a single cat or dog, but sharing your house with many animals complicates how to deal with these issues. Companion critters can tempt clueless pets into causing trouble. Cats and dogs don't behave badly to get your goat, though; understanding what prompts these behaviors is the first step toward finding a solution. What follows is an alphabetical list to guide you through the common pet incidents that annoy and destroy. The key is to make the objectionable behavior less appealing and to give the miscreant a better "legal" alternative.

CHEWING

Dogs chew to explore their world, manipulate objects, relieve boredom, and because it feels good; and they always target your most prized possessions as chew toys because they smell like you. Puppies and kittens test their world the same way human infants do—everything goes into the mouth. While cats usually outgrow the teething stage, adult dogs retain the chew habit. Oddly enough, some felines fixate on paper; nibbling kitties show a talent for creating confetti works of art from cardboard boxes.

Chewing not only damages property when pets target illegal objects, but it can break teeth and result in dangerous swallowed objects or deadly electrocution should Rex or Sheba gnaw the computer wire. Don't blame the pet for doing what comes naturally. Instead, prevent problems by reducing opportunities to make mistakes.

- Pet proof the house by picking up tempting objects and confining the chewer to a "safe" zone when you can't supervise her activity. A product such as Bitter Apple applied to forbidden electrical cords helps train dogs to leave dangerous items alone. If your pets like the taste of Bitter Apple, use mentholated Vicks Vapo-Rub to "paint" baseboards or apply to a cloth that's draped over forbidden targets to keep pets at bay.

- Offer dogs commercial rubber chew objects instead of old slippers, chew hooves, or nylon or real bones, which can break teeth. Make legal chew objects more attractive by soaking some of the dog's regular food into a mush, mashing it into a puzzle toy, and freezing it for summer treats.

- Discourage your dog from chewing forbidden objects by telling him "no" and offering to trade for a legal chew toy. The smallest flavored rawhide chews work well for gnawing cats, too. Soak one in warm water or broth and zap in the microwave for ten seconds to soften the leather and make it more pungent to cat cravings.

Don't chase dogs when they grab and chew forbidden items. These games reward the behavior—and you'll never catch him anyway. Instead, grit your teeth, close your eyes, and say nothing. Just walk away and ignore him. Have a legal object ready to swap once he drops your wallet.

 Provide a variety of eight to ten toys to help you figure out which ones really float the pet's boat. Rotate three or four at a time to keep them fresh and new to the pet.

 Reward chewing the *right* toy by secretly tossing a treat to land next to the pet. This should teach the cat or dog that when she chews the right toy, treats sometimes fall from the sky.

 Talk with your veterinarian about finding a weight-loss diet that makes your dog feel more full. Dogs placed on a weight-loss diet may chew illegal targets while searching for more food.

 Trap or otherwise remove rodents or insects that drive your pet buggy. If your pets chew a wall or baseboard, consider there may be critters running around inside the walls that prompt the behavior.

 Block access to the window and view of any animals that trespass on your dog's territory. Keep windows closed and move furniture to block access.

 Use an antibark trainer or a motion-detector booby trap if the behavior includes territorial displays such as barking. These keep the pet a legal distance from the window or other target (see also "Yapping Maniacs" in this chapter).

CLAWING

Nothing looks more appealing than a fluffy, cuddly kitten—until the claws come out. Clawing is hardwired into the feline brain and is a *natural, instinctive* behavior that can't be stopped. Claws are the equivalent of human fingernails and toenails and are composed of hard, nonliving protein (cuticle) that grows from the nerve and blood-rich quick. Feline claws arise from the last joint of each toe and extend and retract courtesy of two small "hinged" bones that rest nearly on top of each other. When relaxed, claws sheath inside a skin fold so the paws look soft and smooth. Flexing the tendon straightens the folded bones and pushes claws forward and down, spreading paws to almost twice their former width.

Clawing feels good and provides great aerobic exercise to stretch the shoulder and foreleg muscles. Cats don't wear down their claws walking about and playing the way dogs do. Clawing objects keeps nails healthy by helping to shed the old layer and expose the sharp, new growth. More importantly, scent pads in kitty paws leave invisible smell-cues of ownership. The visible marks also serve as messages to warn away other cats from prime feline real estate. Cats also claw to soothe upset feelings and increase clawing during times of stress—placing a scratch post in areas the cat urine-sprays can help by relieving angst with scratching instead.

If Sheba can't reach something she really wants, such as a toy the other cat has swiped, she may claw the post as a displacement behavior instead of expressing aggression toward the other feline. Other times, she'll use clawing to express positive emotions by running to scratch the post when you return for the day or when she knows the food bowl will be filled. A cat introduced into a new home may turn into a clawing maniac until she becomes more comfortable. Cats also use their claws to protect themselves from threats and use scratching as a displacement behavior.

CLIPPING CLAWS

Felines are great at bluffing and often "pull their punches" by bopping the nosy dog or other cat with claws withheld. But claws endanger dogs with more prominent eyes, such as pugs and Pekingese. Even before you train your cats to scratch appropriately, you can protect your furniture and other pets with a feline pedicure. When your cat relaxes on your lap or snoozes on the sofa, gently pet her and pick up a paw. Squeeze gently between your thumb and fingers to express the sharp nail tips and snip off the sharp, white hooked end with your own nail clippers or a pair designed for pets. Avoid the pink "quick" at the base of the toe, which contains the blood supply and will bleed if nicked.

No rule says you must trim every claw at one sitting. Clip only as many as Kitty will allow, stop before she struggles, then offer her a favorite treat or toy. Clip only two or three nails a night, offering bribes along the way; all four paws will be done in a week or so.

DECLAW SURGERY

Declaw surgery amputates the last joint of each toe to remove the claw and nail bed from which it grows. Declaw surgery has no health benefits to the cat and serves only as a convenience for owners. Surveys estimate twenty-five percent of cats in North America are declawed, but the procedure is condemned and even illegal in many other countries. Professional cat fanciers feel so strongly about this that pedigreed cats are not allowed to appear in cat shows if they have been declawed.

Surgery does eliminate potential claw damage to your belongings, and some declawed cats never have problems from the surgery. But a percentage of declawed cats become biters and/or develop litter box aversions due to painful paws, creating a host of new behavior issues that impact you and your multipet household. Declawing should not be considered routine, and

---

COMFORT ZONE: SOFT PAWS

Despite all best efforts, some hardcase cats are slow or stubborn and have problems following claw rules. Vinyl nail covers, called Soft Paws, reduce the potential for scratch damage in these cases. Soft Paws (www.softpaws.com) are also great for protecting the dog eyes from an upset cat's claws and can be a good option during initial introductions of new animals. Soft Paws Nail Caps for dogs are also available to protect wooden floors and other surfaces from doggy toenail scratches. The vinyl caps glue over the top of each nail and come in a variety of fashion colors. They are available from pet supply stores and some veterinary offices. You can learn to apply them yourself.

done only after exhausting all other options. Veterinary surveys estimate that as many as fifty percent of owners that had a cat declawed wouldn't otherwise have kept the cat.

Kittens recover more quickly than adult cats. Without claws for protection, declawed felines should be kept inside for their safety. The most recent (and humane) surgical techniques employ lasers, resulting in less pain and bleeding during recovery. Talk with your veterinarian and other cat owners before deciding to declaw.

TEACHING CLAW ETIQUETTE

Most cats can be trained to use appropriate scratching objects so they can keep their claws. When you introduce a young kitten into an adult cat home, the baby learns more quickly by observing the other felines' good behavior, which makes training easier.

- Provide several scratch objects. Spread them over the entire house to accommodate all the cats' territory and so one feline can't "guard" and own all the objects.

- Place scratch objects in high traffic areas or near important cat territory such as lookouts, food stations, and your bedroom (if you share a pillow). Clawing marks territory, so scratch objects must be located correctly for the cat to use them.

- Accommodate all the cats' exercise and stretching needs. Make sure the scratch object is long or tall enough for Sheba's full stretch and stable enough to withstand an all-out assault. Kittens outgrow small posts and need an upgrade once they're mature. If the post tips over onto the cat, you'll have an awful time convincing Sheba to try it again.

- Observe your cats' habits to figure out what type of scratch facilities they like best. The scratch surface, size, and shape of the post play key roles in motivating cat scratching. Some prefer wood, sisal, or carpet surfaces and want vertical or horizontal surfaces—a variety works best in multicat households.

- Spike new scratch objects with catnip to promote feline allegiance. Play-oriented cats can be lured to try out the post by dragging a feather or other toy across the surface so they sink in claws. Don't be afraid to demonstrate claw technique to Sheba, either. Cats learn by mimicking behavior, so the demonstration by you (or another feline) can help because it also marks the post with your scent, making it an even more attractive object for the cats to claim as their own.

- Place the new "legal" scratch object directly in front of the clawed sofa or on top of the clawed carpet. Cats return to the scene of the crime to refresh the marks/scent, so once the cat begins to use the legal object, you can slowly move it (a foot at a time) to a more convenient location that's still within the cat's territorial ideal.

- Use interruption, not physical punishment, to stop the behavior. Slap a newspaper against your thigh, clap hands, or shake an empty soda can full of pennies to stop Sheba in mid-claw. A long-distance squirt gun aimed at a furry tail can startle some cats out of the behavior. Once kitty stops, direct claws to the legal target with the feather toy and praise her when she does the right thing.

- Stay silent, with little to no movement while you are interrupting. Doing so out of sight is even more effective but hard to do. A remote control "booby trap" can be helpful. Try hooking up an alarm, hair dryer, Water Pik, or tape recording to a remote switch; place it in the area where the cat misbehaves. Watch for illegal activity and trigger the interruption when the cat enters the forbidden area.

- Make illegal targets unattractive to the cats with Sticky Paws so they'll leave them alone even when you're not around. There are several good claw-deterrents available, but not all work for every cat; experiment until one works for you.

- Try an innovative new training product called the ssscat aerosol to train cats to scat when a motion detector, triggered by their presence, sets it off. You don't have to be there for it to work.

- Use Feliway on forbidden objects to keep cats from scratching on top of this pheromone product.

- Apply strong scents such as citrus deodorants, Vicks, or No Scratch from pet product stores directly to forbidden objects or on fabric draped over the problem area.

* Put cinnamon on dark upholstery or baby powder on light fabric to prompt a poof of scented dust into the cat's face when she assaults with feline claws. Both the dust and the scent help to remind cats of their manners even when you aren't around to supervise.

* Tape bubble wrap to an illegal target to interrupt kitty scratching with a *pop!* when her claws hit it. Remember, booby traps aren't permanent but offer interim teaching aids to transition Sheba to a legal target. Once she uses the right scratching object, you can remove the bubble wrap or other decorator's eyesores.

DIGGING

Dogs, especially terrier breeds, can't resist the lure to kick up dirt. Terriers were bred to "go to ground," and if not allowed an outlet, they may dig through your sofa or carpet. Dogs dig up plants, tunnel beneath fences, or dig out of boredom. Hot dogs instinctively scoop out holes to rest their tummies against the cool soil. In the winter, dirt offers great insulation and a warm hole in which to rest. Other dogs may dig after critters in the ground. While canine company can reduce boredom and sometimes reduce digging problems, watching a doggy friend tunneling also can inspire the whole pack to join the fun.

Cats also enjoy recreational digging, but more typically scoop out and cover up a toilet spot. They particularly relish fine, soft textures, which means the soil in the indoor potted palm or freshly planted garden may receive unwanted attention. They'll also dig in these areas if their litter box situation doesn't please them. Understanding why dogs and cats dig can help you figure out ways to stem the excavation.

COMFORT ZONE

Remote communication can interrupt and stop/remind Rex not to dig up the roses. The Spray Commander Citronella Remote Trainer has a 300-yard range and uses scent and a tone to communicate with your dog. The system includes an adjustable nylon collar, spray device, remote control, aerosol refill, two 6-volt batteries, an instruction/training manual, a training video, and a carrying case; it costs about $180 at most pet product stores or online at www.premier.com.

FELINE EXCAVATIONS

 Keep litter boxes clean; otherwise cats will seek alternate places to go. Some cats won't want to share a bathroom, so provide one litter box for each cat, plus one (see also Chapter 11).

 Place Sticky Paws for Plants on indoor plants to keep them safe from pets. You can also turn plastic carpet runners nub-side up and set the potted plant in the middle so cats avoid walking on the nubs to reach the soil.

 Keep your own cats inside to prevent them from using your garden as a bathroom. Dissuade strays by scattering orange or lemon rinds in the flower beds (they hate the smell of citrus) or by planting rue—a natural cat repellent used by the ancient Egyptians.

 Use sprinklers fitted with motion detectors, such as the Scarecrow, to keep them out of your garden.

 Place chicken wire an inch below the topsoil or scatter cut up rose trimmings, holly, or other prickly mulch to keep cats' (and most dogs') sensitive paw pads from digging into the soil. Avoid cocoa mulch, which can be highly toxic to pets if ingested.

DIGGIDY DOGS

 Prevent weather-related digging by paying attention to how the seasons impact your dog. Bring dogs inside during temperature extremes or provide plenty of shade with lots of available water during the summer and a warm shelter out of the wind and wet when temperatures drop.

 See Chapter 7 for tips on boredom. Dogs that dig out of boredom need more one-on-one attention from the humans they love. Spayed and neutered dogs have much less incentive to escape a fenced yard in search of company.

 Interrupt your dogs' digging habit by first telling them to stop. Use an air horn, hand clap, or a short, emphatic "No!" Then praise when they stop and offer toys or treats to replace the forbidden activity.

Cover over the holes with canvas, chainlink fencing, bricks, or other impediments to discourage continued activity. Dog paw pads are pretty tough, though, and determined dogs simply dig around the obstacles. Booby-trapping by dumping some of the dogs' fresh feces into the holes will stop some dogs.

 Build a sandbox for the legal digging pleasure of hardcase dogs such as terriers. A shaded area about three feet wide, six feet long, and two feet deep will satisfy most dogs. Let them see you bury one or two toys (very shallowly), then encourage the dogs to dig them up by getting down on your hands and knees and demonstrating by pawing the sand with your hand.

JUMPING

Whether you have a leaping feline or an airborne dog, jumping can be quite a nuisance. Though we want our pets to be free to roam where they choose, there's nothing worse than muddy paw prints covering your new suit or finding cat hair in your linguini. Keeping your pets off forbidden objects—guests, the kitchen table, the Christmas tree—requires a lot of close attention so that they learn when and where to stay grounded. Below are tips for teaching Rex and Sheba the limitations on jumping, while providing healthy legal outlets for this animal instinct.

COUNTERTOP CRUISING

While some dogs such as Basenjis enjoy scaling heights, all cats naturally adore high places because they're safe lookouts and make a literal statement about the cat's place in the feline hierarchy. However, countertop cruising can be both a safety and a hygiene issue for owners and the cats. Nobody enjoys having a pet "graze" from the dinner table or skillet, and walking across a hot stovetop may cause serious burns.

Dealing with height-loving felines frustrates owners. Even when Sheba understands that a particular location (the mantel) is forbidden, she may avoid the place when you're present but plant her furry tail on high as soon as you leave the room. When you return and she sees you, she'll leap off even before you yell at her. A couple of things are going on. The cat that claims the highest position is the "top cat" in the scheme of feline hierarchy. Cats want to be able to see long distances and be out of reach of potential threats.

Second, cats practice a time-share mentality and schedule lounging time to avoid competition. When the "top cat" is not there to use the preferred perch, the cat feels within her rights to claim it. After all, *you* weren't using it! Then, when you catch her in the forbidden zone, she acknowledges you as the top cat and gets off, in deference to your social status. Multiple cats mean you'll constantly be chasing cats off second-story space because as soon as one vacates the real estate, another waits to take her place. When cats must share space with dogs, they'll be even more inclined to take the "high road" and avoid the ground-floor territory claimed by any canines. That can be a safety issue as well as a social statement for the cat. You will not win all these battles, but you can modify some of these irksome behaviors and encourage cats to stay off forbidden places with training techniques.

- Use an interruption, such as a loud "Off!" or clapped hands to get cats down. A long-distance squirt gun aimed at the backside may persuade some cats.

- Make it unattractive when you aren't around. Cover stovetops with aluminum foil. Many cats dislike walking on this surface.

- Set the ssscat aerosol motion detector in the offlimits area to keep Sheba at bay.

- Apply Sticky Paws to make other surfaces uncomfortable. Put the Sticky Paws on placemats set around on forbidden surfaces so you can easily position them but remove them when needed. You can also use clear plastic floormats, placed spike side up, on tabletops so cats will avoid the area.

- Offer your cats legal outlets that are higher and more attractive than the forbidden zones so they naturally choose the legal perches and leave your mantel alone. Cat trees are always a big hit.

- Choose your battles and perhaps allow cats to lounge on the television as long as they leave the kitchen island alone. Place a cat bed on a "legal" countertop or bookshelf to invite the cats' presence; they'll be less likely to trespass where not welcome

JUMPING JACK DOGS

His paws muddy slacks; her claws snag pantyhose. Being tackled by a dog is an unpleasant, dangerous surprise and rude behavior that should not be allowed in polite human-canine society. Dogs lick each other's faces as a greeting display, and a submissive dog aims attention at a dominant individual's eyes and mouth. Therefore, licking your face is a polite canine "Howdy," a way for him to acknowledge you are the boss, and to solicit attention.

Many owners consider jumping up to be cute during puppyhood, but lose their sense of humor as the Saint Bernard matures. This becomes a safety issue around children and elderly people who can be seriously injured by a jumping dog. Too, your circle of friends may include folks who (gasp!) dislike or are even frightened by dogs of any size.

Teach your dog a more appropriate way of greeting people. Once he realizes his behavior offends you, he'll strive to find another way to say hello.

- Use a dragline to prevent jumping up. Stepping on toes or kneeing Rex in his chest can be painful and prompts avoidance behaviors or even aggression. Fold your arms and look away to make your point that jumping up garners being ignored.

- Cross your arms and *lean* toward the dog. Use your body to block him and enter the space first, in the same way dogs control each other's movements by controlling space.

- Teach your dogs they only get attention when they sit on command (see also Chapter 4). Petting, playing, and happy talk in response to the jumping encourages it to continue.

GROUNDING LEAPING DOGS

1. Teach only one dog at a time. As you enter the front door, stand still and greet the dog with, "Rex, come," followed by, "Rex, sit."

2. Offer your hand for a sniff (very important to dogs in greetings) *only* after Rex sits. Stroke the dog's cheek or neck or feed him a treat, saying, "Goooood Rex," to reward the sit.

3. Step backward and turn away so the dog's feet miss if he insists on jumping up. That interrupts the canine "howdy" because a dog can't properly greet a person's back. To receive a greeting and treat, Rex must keep all four feet on the ground.

4. Say "Sit" again once the dog's feet hit the floor. Repeat the exercise.

5. Walk into the house and take a seat only after the proper sit and hand-sniff greeting has been exchanged. The dog will likely follow—have other family members waiting in the room to reinforce the good behavior with, "Good dog!"

6. Drill with your dog, until sitting during greeting prompts more attention for him than jumping up ever did. Enlist the aid of other family members, as well as friends, and practice the same drill until Rex learns to sit instead of jumping up whenever meeting a new person.

7. Drill with all the dogs together, once they've mastered individual sits when the doorbell rings. Note to owners: If a wet slurp across the mouth doesn't offend you, then kneel to doggy level to put yourself in range of his kiss so he doesn't have to break the rules and leap.

TALKING

When pet people think of noisy nuisances, most often barking dogs come to mind, but the reality is that this is a problem common to cats and dogs. Multiple pets not only increase the decibel level, it inevitably multiply headaches for you.

Understand your cats' and dogs' natural urge to communicate with their voices and give them a healthy outlet for this normal behavior. Here's some sound advice to help turn the volume down.

CAT-ERWAULING

Humans often overlook body language that makes up a great deal of cat communication, but feline yowls, growls, hisses, and purrs get our undivided attention—especially at 5:00 A.M. Not all cats are vocal. Persians and the beautiful blue Chartreux breeds, for instance, tend to be rather quiet while Siamese and Oriental-type breeds are especially talkative. One yodeler can get the whole furry crew caterwauling.

In multipet homes, troublemakers (the pestering of other pets) may prompt problem meowing. Cats introduced to other cats or dogs for the first time often meow more as a result. Felines use a wide range of vocalizations to communicate with other cats, but seem to reserve "meows" primarily for talking to their people. Meows are demands: let me out, let me in, pet me, play with me, feed me! As the cats become more passionate and insistent, meows grow more strident and lower-pitched.

Giving in to meow demands tells Sheba that pestering works to get her way. Any response, such as putting the pillow over your head, yelling at her, or pushing her off the bed still gives her the attention she craves. The only way to extinguish this behavior is to *totally ignore* the cat. That means you *don't* get up to feed her; you *don't* indulge in toe-tag games; you *don't* yell at her, spray her with water, or give any attention at all. That's hard to do when she's paw-

VET ALERT!

For some reason cats tend to become more vocal when suffering from hypertension (high blood pressure), which can be a result of kidney or heart disease. Excessive meowing also may be a sign of deafness in aging cats. When Sheba can't hear her own voice any longer, she tends to meow louder and longer. Check with your veterinarian about excessive meowing in any cat.

patting your nose or shaking the windows with yowls. It can take weeks to months to get rid of this behavior once established, but with patience, it can be done.

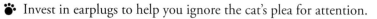 Invest in earplugs to help you ignore the cat's plea for attention.

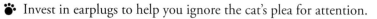 Cats that are a nighttime nuisance should be shut out of the bedroom. They may continue to pester from the other side of the door and may even scratch or otherwise cause damage. Choose a "safe room" on the other side of the house that's stocked with lots of toys, a litter box, a scratch object, and food to confine noisy cats out of earshot.

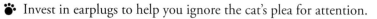 Separate and confine other cats or dogs that instigate the meowing. When the dog stays in his crate for the night, he can't chase and tease the cat, and vice versa.

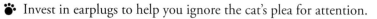 Offer a treat ball or other irresistible toy that keeps the cat's brain (and mouth) occupied so she won't meow.

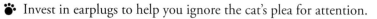 Close the windows so your cats can't hear or see outside strays. Anything that attracts roaming cats to visit during the night should be discouraged. For example, avoid leaving out food on the porch, and clean up brush piles that make attractive critter hiding places.

YAPPING MANIACS

Barking is a normal part of canine communication that rankles owners and their neighbors when dogs aren't taught proper limits. In multipet homes, troublemakers (other dogs or cats teasing the barker) may prompt problem barking, so play pet detective to figure out exactly what—or who—triggers the behavior. Dogs introduced to cats for the first time often feel intrigued, puzzled, and frustrated by their new housemates and bark more. Be creative and set up a video to see what pets do when you're gone so you can figure out the best solution.

Dogs bark during play, defense, when greeting, and when garnering attention. Think of barking as a canine fire alarm that alerts the dog's family to anything unusual. The arrival of friend or foe, a scary scent from visiting wildlife, or the sight of you wearing a hat may prompt barks. Dogs also bark to get their own way. When Rex barks at the mail carrier each day, the mail carrier leaves—this rewards him for barking. Smart dogs remember success and repeat the behavior again and again. Another dog barking or even a siren wailing can prompt the whole crew to erupt into a joyful barkfest. When you yell at the yodelers, they'll assume you're joining the chorus and bark even louder. Other times, Rex barks to get attention. Even if a scolding follows, Rex thinks, "Mom pays attention to me when I bark." You've rewarded his behavior.

You will never eliminate barking because dogs remain determined to warn and protect loved ones. However, you can teach dogs to respect barking limits. Save your sanity and your relationship with neighbors by offering alternatives to barking.

 Refer to Chapter 7 to give the bored dog something to occupy his mind and mouth. Nuisance barking often stems from boredom, with dogs "talking to themselves" when they have nothing interesting to do.

 Use a spoonful of peanut butter on the roof of the mouth to quiet barkers. The peanut butter dries the mouths enough that barking becomes less appealing. Timing is key, though. Only give the peanut butter when the dog is quiet, because offering it while he barks rewards the barking so he'll do it again.

 Engage the dog in games of hide-and-seek. Often dogs forgo barking when they are able to hunt for treats hidden around the house or yard. Work engages the dog's brain and helps keep him quiet.

 Block scary sounds such as sirens and thunder, which inspire barking and howling. White noise machines are available, or create white noise by tuning the radio to static on a normal volume.

 If they instigate Rex's barking, separate the other teasing pets when you are not there to supervise. A cat confined to "her" room can't tease the dog from the top of the refrigerator; once dogs become used to the feline interloper, the "cat alert" bark tends to fade away.

 Place a baby gate (single or stacked) between the animals to allow them to see each other and commune through the bars. Dogs that bark at the cat or pup behind a closed door often quiet down when they can see inside the room.

 Enlist the aid of an accomplice and "stage" arrivals at the front door (see also "Protecting Property" in Chapter 5). Ask people to arrive at the back door instead, since many dogs seem to go nuts only at the front entrance.

 Prevent audience-craving dogs from barking by thanking them for alerting you. Give them a two- to three-bark limit, then say, "Quiet." Praise and treat the dog that shushes—and make sure the other loudmouths see this so they'll compete to be the first to quiet.

 Turn your back and leave if the dogs keep barking. Since most dogs crave your company, they'll learn to be quiet if they want you to stay.

 Figure out places and times that prompt barks, such as the front door or a window when the school bus arrives. Try to wait with Rex in these places to watch for the bark-trigger, and preempt the barking by encouraging your dog to race with you to the kitchen for a special treat. This helps teach Rex that the triggers for barking should instead prompt him to run to find you for a reward.

 Find other enjoyable pastimes to occupy the dogs' minds during prime barking periods. Try moving dinnertime or a regular game of fetch to coincide with prime bark times.

 Install a pet door. Dogs often learn to bark when they want a bathroom break; owners reward the behavior by opening the door. A pet door will cut down on pester barking and reduce your doorman duties.

 Use an antibark collar. Researchers at Cornell University in New York found them to be twice as effective as electric shock collars. The Gentle Spray Anti-Bark Collar squirts scent that stops the barking. Some of these collars have remote activators so you can control when to spritz the scent.

 Try a tone collar, which employs a built-in microphone that emits a loud, short tone to startle and stop the barking. Make sure the antibark is adjusted properly or else it will punish the wrong dog if a pet friend barks (or meows) from across the street.

🐾 Employ ultrasonic trainers, which produce an aversive sound only dogs can hear and may work with or without collars or as handheld units the owner controls.

BARK MANNERS 101

The best way to stop nuisance barking and to teach a "shush" command is to first train your pooch to "speak" on cue. Barking self-rewards the dog because he *likes* to bark. Perhaps a squirrel cursed at him or maybe a dangerous vandal (or mail carrier) skulks around your property. You'll find it much easier to teach "shush" when the barking was your idea. Just remember to check if he had a good reason to bark. Train one dog at a time.

1. Identify a noise, such as the doorbell or phone, that reliably prompts a bark.

2. Choose an irresistible treat the dog *only* gets during training. Pieces of cheese, liverwurst, or even cat treats work well, but keep them small. The treats aren't to fill up his tummy, but give him a taste to whet his learning appetite.

3. Get an accomplice to stand outside the door and ring the bell on your cue. She should listen for you to loudly say, "Speak!" wait two beats (count "one Mississippi, two Mississippi"), and then ring the bell if the dog didn't bark.

COMFORT ZONE

Different breeds are more vocal than others, and not all barks are created equal. Beagles are born barking, Alaskan Malamutes howl, and a tiny terrier's shrill yaps can shatter glass. Some products work better than others with each barking dog, and you may need to experiment to find the best addition for your canine tool kit.

🐾 Puzzle toys come in differnet sizes, suited to both small- and big-mouth dogs.

🐾 Give out pig's ears and rawhide chews, available from pet product and grocery stores. For smaller dogs you may need to saok them first in water and zap in the microwave for a few seconds to soften and unlock the odor.

🐾 Look for a wide range of commercial bark trainers from pet product stores and online venues.

4. Say, "Yes!" the instant the dog barks. Give Rex one tiny treat, even if he barks before the doorbell rings.

5. Wait a few seconds and repeat the exercise. Say loudly, "Speak" (so your friend hears through the door and rings the bell). As the doorbell prompts the dog to bark, once again say, "Yes!" and reward him with another treat.

6. Keep doing this until all the treats are gone. You'll know your boy "gets it" and begins to know what *speak* means when he barks on command before the doorbell rings.

7. Train "shush" once your dog knows the *speak* command. Go through the previous steps, saying, "Speak." When he barks, praise the bark and then say, "Shush." As you say, "Shush," let him sniff the treat.

8. Allow him to sniff the treat. Say, "Yes," and release the treat. It's impossible for a dog to sniff, eat, and bark at the same time Repeat until he understands that *shush* means quiet, while *speak* means permission to bark.

9. Use other pets to make sure the hard-case dog gets the message. Just because he learns the words doesn't necessarily mean he'll always shush right away. When the dog continues to bark following the *shush* command, give him a time-out in the yard or a small room and make sure he knows he blew it by letting him hear you praise and give treats to the other pets in the home.

PART SIX

APPENDIXES

APPENDIX A: EXPERT SOURCES

Bonnie Beaver, DVM, MS, is president of the AVMA, executive director of the American College of Veterinary Behaviorists, and a behaviorist and professor in the department of small animal medicine and surgery at the College of Veterinary Medicine, Texas A&M University.

Margaret H. Bonham is the author of many dog books, an expert in Northern breeds, and owner of eighteen sled dogs and one cat.

Sharon L. Crowell-Davis, DVM, is a veterinarian and a behaviorist at the University of Georgia Veterinary Teaching Hospital.

Steve Dale is a syndicated newspaper pet columnist, radio host of WGW-AM Chicago's *Pet Central* and *Animal Planet Radio,* and owner of two dogs and a cat.

Ian Dunbar, Ph.D., MRCVS, is a veterinarian, animal behaviorist, dog trainer, and author of many dog training books. He is the creator of the Sirius Puppy Training Series and a founder of the Association of Pet Dog Trainers. He is currently director of the Center for Applied Animal Behavior in Berkeley, CA.

Bruce D. Elsey, DVM, is a veterinarian, owner of the All Cat Clinic in Englewood, Colorado, and creator of Precious Cat and Cat Attract cat litter.

Deborah Jones, Ph.D., is a dog trainer and assistant professor of psychology at Kent State University's Stark Campus.

Gary Landsberg, BSc, DVM, Diplomate ACVB, is a veterinary behaviorist and companion animal practitioner at the Doncaster Animal Clinic in Thornhill, Ontario.

Marie-Laure Loubiere, DVM, is a veterinarian involved in pheromone research and marketing with CEVA Santé Animale in France.

Andrew U. Luescher, DVM, Ph.D., Diplomate ACVB, is an associate professor of animal behavior at Purdue University.

Pat Miller, CPDT, CDBC, is a certified pet dog trainer, behavior consultant, and owner of Peaceable Paws Dog and Puppy Training and past president of the Association of Pet Dog Trainers.

Patricia McConnell, Ph.D., is a certified applied animal behaviorist, owner of Dog's Best Friend Ltd., and an adjunct assistant professor of zoology at the University of Wisconsin-Madison.

Daniel Mills, BVSc, Ph.D., is a professor and recognized specialist in veterinarian behavioral medicine, animal behavior, cognition, and welfare at the University of Lincoln, United Kingdom.

Karen L. Overall, M.A., DVM, Ph.D, is ABS certified applied animal behaviorist, author, and research associate at the Center for Neurobiology and Behavior, Psychiatry Department at Penn Med, PA.

Patrick Pageat, DVM, Ph.D., is a behaviorist diplomate of the French National Veterinary Schools, and research and development director of Pherosynthese in France.

Patricia Pryor, DVM, Diplomate, ACVB, is an assistant professor in the Department of Veterinary Clinical Services at Washington State University.

Kersti Seksel, BVSc, MRCVS, FACUSc, MACVSc (Animal Behavior), is a veterinarian and behaviorist practicing at Seaforth Veterinary Hospital in Sydney, Australia.

Deborah Wood is a dog trainer, dog book author, and pet columnist for *The Oregonian*.

APPENDIX B: ANIMAL BEHAVIOR CONSULTANTS AND TRAINERS

There are several behavior and training associations with professionals available who specialize in pet training and/or behavior problems. Behaviors such as aggression can be difficult to unlearn and require professional help teaching cats and dogs how to react in new, more positive ways.

The American College of Veterinary Behaviorists
Veterinarians with a special interest and additional study in the field of animal behavior. As veterinarians, they are also able to diagnose concurrent health conditions and prescribe drug therapies that may be helpful. Contact: Dr. Bonnie V. Beaver, ACVB Executive Director, Department of Small Animal Medicine and Surgery, Texas A&M University, College Station, TX. 77843-4474, or http://www.veterinarybehaviorists.org. Find a listing of members at http://www.dacvb.org/Diplomates.htm.

The Animal Behavior Society
This organization certifies qualified individuals as applied or associate applied animal behaviorists. Contact: Stephen

Zawistowski, Ph.D., Chair, Board of Professional Certification ASPCA, 424 E. 92nd St., New York, N.Y. 10128. Phone: 212-876-7700 ext. 4401, Fax: 212-860-3435, or e-mail stevez@aspca. org. See also http://www.animalbehavior.org/Applied/CAAB_directory.html.

The Association of Pet Dog Trainers

With 5,000 members worldwide, this organization certifies dog trainers as certified pet dog trainer (CPDT) and offers an annual educational conference. Many members are qualified to help you with canine aggression or other dog behavior problems, as well as training. For more information and a list of member trainers, see http://www.apdt.com.

Canine Good Citizen

The American Kennel Club's program, which began in 1989, is a certification program that promotes responsible pet ownership for owners and basic good manners for dogs. Go to: http://www.akc.org/love/cgc/program.cfm.

The International Association of Animal Behavior Consultants, Inc

This is a professional organization that accredits and qualifies members as certified animal behavior consultants (CABC) and addresses behavior issues of cats, dogs, and other companion animals. Go to: http://www.iaabc.org.

APPENDIX C: ACTIVITIES FOR PETS

Pet training, exhibition, or sports activities offer wonderful opportunities for owners and pets to enjoy each other, celebrate your bond, and develop communication skills. Dogs and cats that are encouraged to use their brains get into less trouble at home and have fewer behavior problems; too, they learn better ways to deal with other animals in a positive way. There are many more venues for dogs than cats. This list isn't inclusive by any means, but will get you started.

For Dogs:

- 🐾 Agility Association of Canada (www.aac.ca)

- 🐾 United States Dog Agility Association (www.usdaa.com)

- 🐾 North American Flyball Association (www.flyball.org)

- 🐾 National Capital Air Champions (flying disc) (www.discdog.com)

- 🐾 World Canine Freestyle Organization (dog dancing) (www.worldcaninefreestyle.org)

- 🐾 American Mixed Breed Obedience Registration (www.amborusa.org)

- 🐾 American Kennel Club (www.akc.org)

- 🐾 United Kennel Club, Inc. (www.ukcdogs.com)

For Cats:

- 🐾 International Cat Agility Tournaments (www.catagility.org)

- 🐾 The Cat Fanciers Association (www.cfainc.org)

- 🐾 The International cat Association (www.tica.org)

APPENDIX D: RECOMMENDED READING

An Introduction to Dog Agility
(Barrons)
Margaret Bonham

Click Here for a Well-Trained Dog
(Howln Moon)
Deb Jones

Complete Care for Your Aging Dog
(New American Library)

Amy D. Shojai

Complete Care for Your Aging Cat
(New American Library)
Amy D. Shojai

Complete Kitten Care
(New American Library)
Amy D. Shojai

Dog Behavior: An Owner's Guide to a Happy, Healthy Pet
(Howell Book House)
Ian Dunbar

Feeling Outnumbered? How to Manage and
Enjoy Your Multi-Dog Household
(Dog's Best Friend, Ltd)
Karen B. Johnson, Ph.D., and Patricia B. McConnell, Ph.D.

Getting Started: Clicker Training for Cats
(Sunshine Books)
Karen Pryor

Handbook of Behavior Problems of the Dog and Cat (Saunders)
G. Landsberg, BSc, DVM, Dip ACVB, W. Hunthausen, BA,
DVM, and L. Ackerman, DVM, DACVD, MBA, MPA

Help for Your Shy Dog: Turning Your
Terrified Dog into a Terrific Pet
(Howell Book House)
Deborah Wood

House Cat: How to Keep Your Indoor Cat Safe and Sound
(Howell Book House)
Christine Church

Quick Clicks: 40 Fast and Fun Behaviors to Train with a Clicker

(Legacy-By-Mail, Inc.)
Mandy Book and Cheryl S. Smith

The Domestic Cat: The Biology of Its Behaviour
(Cambridge University Press)
Edited by Dennis C. Turner and Patrick Bateson

The Other End of the Leash
(Ballantine Books)
Patricia McConnell

*The Rosetta Bone: The Key to Communication
Between Humans and Canines*
(Howell Dog Book of Distinction)
Cheryl S. Smith

The Simple Guide to Getting Active with Your Dog
(TFH Publications)
Margaret Bonham

ABOUT THE AUTHOR

Amy D. Shojai is a nationally known authority on pet care and behavior. She is the author of 19 nonfiction pet books and over 400 articles and columns. Her award-winning column appears online at www.catchchow.com and she is section leader for the Holistic and Behavior/Care portions of the CompuServe Cats Forum and Dogs Forum. In addition, she hosts "Your Pet's Well-Being with Amy Shojai" at ivillage.com.

Ms. Shojai is founder and President Emeritus of the Cat Writers' Association, a member of the Dog Writers Association of America, the Association of Pet Dog Trainers and a member of the International Association of Animal Behavior Consultants. Her work has been honored with over two-dozen writing awards from these and many other pet organizations, including the Texas Veterinary Medical Association.

She appears regularly on national radio and television in connection with her pet writing and has been featured on ABC, NBC, CBS, CNN, and in *USA Weekend*, *The New York Times*, *Washington Post*, *Reader's Digest*, *Woman's Day*, *Family Circle*, *Woman's World*, and many other leading newspapers and magazines. She frequently speaks to groups on a variety of pet-related issues, lectures at conferences such as Tufts Animal Expo and Chicago PetFood Forum, and conducts training and behavior demonstrations around the country. Ms. Shojai has lived in many multipet households over the years. She and her husband live in north Texas. More information about Ms. Shojai's work is available at her web site at www.shojai.com.

INDEX